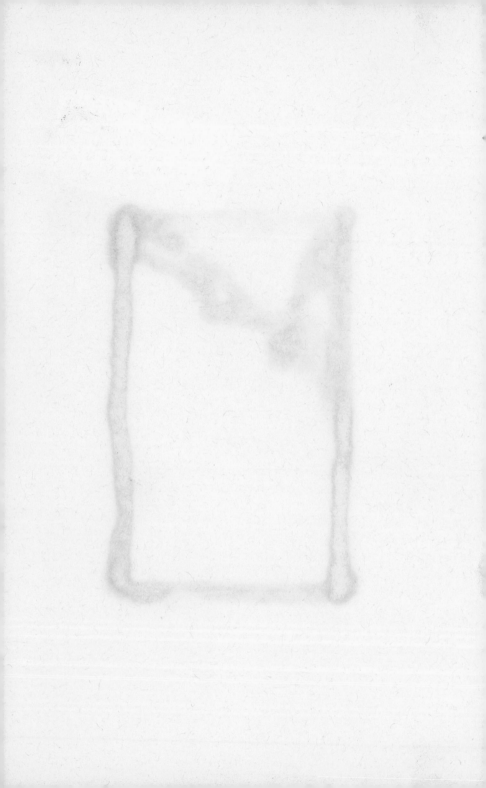

Kennikat Press
National University Publications
Interdisciplinary Urban Series

General Editor
Raymond A. Mohl
Florida Atlantic University

THE PARADOX OF
PROGRESSIVE EDUCATION

The Gary Plan and Urban Schooling

RONALD D. COHEN

and

RAYMOND A. MOHL

National University Publications
KENNIKAT PRESS // 1979
Port Washington, N. Y. // London

Manufactured in the United States of America

Published by
Kennikat Press Corp.
Port Washington, N. Y. / London

Library of Congress Cataloging in Publication Data

Cohen, Ronald D 1940–
    The paradox of progressive education.

    (Interdisciplinary urban series) (National university publications)
    Bibliography: p.
    Includes index.
    1. Education—United States—History. 2. Platoon schools—United States—History. I. Mohl, Raymond A., joint author. II. Title.
LA227.1.C63   370'.973   79-352
ISBN 0-8046-9237-8

The seal reproduced on the first page
is the logo of *The Platoon School.*

CONTENTS

This book is dedicated to our children
Alysha and Joshua
and
Raymond and Nancy

ACKNOWLEDGMENTS

This book began with a series of discussions in the early 1970s between two historians who were independently researching different aspects of the Gary or platoon school plan. Our ideas evolved over several years and were elaborated in papers at professional meetings and in a number of published articles. For permission to use material first published in their pages, usually in very different form, we are grateful to the editors of *Urban Education, Paedagogica Historica, Elementary School Journal, Review Journal of Philosophy and Social Science, Journal of Urban History,* and *Societas: A Review of Social History.* Portions of this material have been presented, again in different form and with different emphases, before meetings of the American Historical Association, the Organization of American Historians, the American Studies Association, the American Educational Research Association, the Southern History of Education Society, and the Popular Culture Association. We are thankful for the opportunity of testing our ideas before colleagues with similar interests in the history of education, and we have learned much from these efforts.

This book could not have been completed without university support, the cooperation of many libraries and archives, and the assistance of numerous friends and colleagues. Research grants from both Indiana University Northwest and Florida Atlantic University provided essential support in the early stages of the research. We greatly appreciate the assistance of librarians and archivists at Indiana University Northwest, Florida Atlantic University, the Gary Public Library, the Lilly Library at Indiana University, the National Archives, the Library of Congress, the New York City Municipal Archives and Records Center, the New York City Municipal Reference Library, the New-York Historical Society, the New York Public Library, the University of Maine, Columbia University, Cornell University, the University of Iowa, the Archives of Labor History and Urban Affairs at Wayne State University, the Immigration History Research Center at the University of Minnesota, the Women's History Archive at Smith College, and the Rockefeller Foundation Archives. In Gary we were kindly permitted to examine records at the International Institute, the School Service Center, and the Gary Teachers' Union, AFT Local No. 4. Individual scholars who have generously given us the benefit of their criticism, advice, and encouragement include Arthur Zilversmit, David B. Tyack, Ronald K. Goodenow, Selma Berrol, John Bodnar, Joseph Stipanovich, Selwyn K. Troen, Walter Feinberg, Patricia A. Graham, James B. Lane, and Gerald Seelig. We owe a special debt to Stephen Schlossman, who co-authored chapter 3. At Florida Atlantic University Samuel A. Portnoy graciously helped with translations from the New York City Yiddish press, and John O'Sullivan and Jack Suberman helped to create an academic environment conducive to serious scholarship. We would like to thank William F. Wirt, Sherwood Wirt, Maxine Wood, and Elsa Ueland for sharing with us their memories of people and events. We would also like to thank our typists, Rosalie Zak, Thelma Spangler, and especially Cecilia Bibby, who prepared many drafts of this book with care and competence.

THE PARADOX OF
PROGRESSIVE EDUCATION

ABOUT THE AUTHORS

Ronald D. Cohen is Professor of History at Indiana University Northwest in Gary, Indiana. He is the author of numerous articles in various scholarly journals.

Raymond A. Mohl is Professor of History at Florida Atlantic University. He has served as Fulbright Professor at Tel Aviv University in Israel. He has distinguished himself through his many articles, organizational activities, and has been the recipient of many professional honors in urban history.

INTRODUCTION

In recent years the social history of American education, broadly conceived, has become one of the most exciting areas of historical research. The old "pots and pans" variety of social history has given way to a kind of historical sociology—a scholarly concern about such things as work and residence patterns, occupational and residential mobility, ethnicity, family and household, and the social institutions which shape the lives of people. Few institutions can tell us more about a society than its schools. In addition to their cognitive functions, schools have served as central agents for the socialization of children according to prevailing patterns of thought and behavior. Like the family, the public schools have transmitted norms and values across the generations. Moreover, the schools generally reflect the interests and values of those who possess economic and political power. Accordingly, society has placed special importance on the schools as guardians of public order and virtue.

Under the leadership of Horace Mann the first stirrings of the common school movement emerged in the 1830s. Since that time Americans have uniformly conceived of public schools as playing a crucial role in the shaping of society. Few institutions have received such widespread support, and few have been bolstered with such optimistic rhetoric. The publicly supported common school was looked upon as a cure-all for the problems of American society. It would train youth in the duties of citizenship and provide an educated citizenry, both deemed essential in a democracy. Moreover, supporters contended that schools fostered equality of opportunity, thereby eliminating social distinctions and guaranteeing an open and mobile and fluid society. At the same time schools disseminated middle class morality among immigrants and the poor in order to keep them orderly, make

3

them contented with their "station" in life, and prevent crime, pauperism, and other social evils. With the growth of industrial capitalism schools became essential in molding a responsible, cooperative work force. Thus, schools served different and possibly contradictory purposes.

These ambiguities are nowhere more evident than in the several different thrusts of American education during the Progressive Era. Some progressive educators emphasized the necessity to make the schools creative, democratic, and humane environments for learning about life in its totality. These reformist educators or "social progressives" fostered school programs to achieve such goals. They promoted child-centered educational activities and individualized programs based on the child's interests and in which children learned at their own pace. They also sought to prepare children for life by replicating in the schools the larger societal reality. Thus, the social progressives generally envisioned the schools as positive agents for social reform and human advancement, as instruments for the achievement of a more just, equitable, and democratic society.

Other educators sought primarily efficiency and economy in education. Drawing upon the school-as-factory analogy, they adhered to Frederick W. Taylor's "cult of efficiency" and introduced businesslike administrative reforms in the schools. They desired the regular production of socially efficient children for whom personal happiness was thought secondary to the performance of some socially desirable task or occupation. These "administrative progressives," to use David B. Tyack's term, advocated paternalism, promoted a professionalized bureaucracy in the schools, and sought centralization of schools on the corporate model.[1] Denying the promise of an egalitarian society, they introduced psychological and intelligence testing, divided students according to presumed ability, and created a differentiated curriculum which channeled some students into more advanced study and others into the labor market. For the administrative progressives many of the educational innovations of the period accentuated the manipulative role of the schools. Vocational training and industrial education, for instance, reflected adherence to the American work ethic; kindergartens, high schools, and adult education—programs which expanded rapidly during the Progressive Era—were used to extend the schools' hold and influence over the individual at both ends of the traditional grammar school curriculum. Administrative progressives generally possessed power to implement their goals, while social progressives were usually on the fringe of decision making. The administrative progressives, then, molded the schools into willing servants of the emerging corporate-technological state.

Thus, progressivism in education has represented either the ideal implementation of democratic values in the schools, or the height of paternalistic and bureaucratic control of children. It either freed school children to follow their own instincts and interests, or chained them to a predetermined course of learning and behavior over which they had no control. In short, progressive education had different and contradictory meanings to its various advocates. Schooling was confusing to the educators and to the educational consumers of the progressive period, and it remains paradoxical to modern educational historians. It is the purpose of this book to analyze the contradictions, tensions, and ambiguities of progressive education by examining the most famous and widely imitated progressive school program—the Gary plan or platoon school.

In the new industrial city of Gary, Indiana, founded on the southern shore of Lake Michigan in 1906 by the United States Steel Corporation, Superintendent of Schools William A. Wirt gradually built an innovative school system that captured national attention. Under the direction of Wirt, whose tenure at the helm of the city's schools extended from 1907 to his death in 1938, the Gary platoon system incorporated numerous school reforms advocated by educators with vastly differing philosophies. Many progressive educators, for instance, were attracted to the Gary plan because of its economical features. With a school population increasing rapidly as the new city grew, but with only a few small, overcrowded school buildings at first, Wirt found it necessary to get maximum use out of his school plant. Thus, he established a program which in its idealized form divided the students in each building into two schools or platoons, labeled X and Y. For part of the school day platoon X filled all the classrooms, where they studied traditional academic subjects. Meanwhile platoon Y broke up into smaller groups for a succession of specialized activities: these students utilized the athletic fields, gymnasiums, and swimming pools; they took instruction in art, music, dancing, or dramatics; they studied in school libraries or science laboratories; some went on field trips into the community; by turns they attended auditorium periods for group singing, movies, student theatricals, or special lectures by outside speakers. Later in the school day students from platoon Y attended the classrooms, while those in platoon X went to the specialized activities.

In Wirt's platoon schools careful attention to scheduling made it possible to use all school facilities throughout the day. (Indeed, the continuous activity extended into the evening, as well; at one point in the 1920s, fantastic as it may seem, the Gary schools served more adults in evening classes than children in regular daytime classes.) The same flexibility of scheduling made it possible for some children to take remedial work in areas of difficulty, to take additional work in areas of special interest, to advance to higher levels more quickly, to attend school on Saturdays, to attend school only part-time, or to attend school on a year-round basis.

The successful implementation of a "work-study-play" program, as Wirt preferred to call the Gary plan, depended upon a full range of facilities in addition to classrooms. Wirt contended, however, that these facilities were essential in any school and that, in any case, they cost less than the new school buildings that otherwise would be required to handle the same number of students. Thus, to the administrative progressives, the Gary plan was ideal—it was flexible, it was businesslike, and above all it seemed super-efficient.

But the Gary schools seemed progressive in other ways, too. Essentially, Wirt sought to make each school "a self-sustaining child community," by which he meant that the environment of the schools should match life in the adult world. As Wirt wrote in 1913, "We try to give the children not a playground, not a shop, not a study room, but a life."[2] The Gary schools, in other words, aimed at preparation—or socialization—of children for the social realities of the time. This basic objective underlay many of the specialized activities of the Gary schools. Industrial and manual training facilities—including a printing shop, an electrical shop, a carpentry shop, a paint shop, and several different metal-working shops (forge, foundry, sheet metal)—tried to provide realistic work experiences and develop a variety of skills. In the early years children learned by participating in real and practical work, much of it going toward upkeep of the schools. Thus, the carpentry shop turned out desks, tables, bookcases, and cabinets for the classrooms; the print shop handled all the schools' printing needs (including publication of Superintendent Wirt's many speeches and addresses on the Gary plan); painting, electrical, and plumbing needs of the schools were supplied by student workers under the guidance of teacher-artisans. Under supervision of the botany department children also worked on the school grounds, trimming lawns and caring for trees, shrubs, and gardens. Students in commercial courses (typing, bookkeeping, stenography) worked in the school office and ran a store and bank for other children. Girls in cooking classes helped prepare school lunches. Pupils in sewing classes made their own clothing. As John Dewey wrote in his book *Schools of Tomorrow*, the Gary schools sought to train children to make "the most intelligent use of their own capabilities and of their environment."[3]

With so many seeming advantages, William Wirt's Gary plan began to receive national notice by 1912. The decade of the teens was essentially one of publicity for the new school plan. Hundreds of articles on the Gary plan appeared in educational journals and in popular magazines. Thousands of visitors trooped through the Emerson and Froebel schools in Gary. Wirt gave speeches and made addresses at meetings across the nation, while simultaneously boosting the plan in magazine articles and in his correspondence with schoolmen. The plan received its greatest exposure in the middle of the decade, when Wirt was hired as a consultant to help implement his new creation in the New York City school system. As will be demonstrated in chapter 2, the effort resulted in failure and notoriety: the Gary plan received a black eye. But, surprisingly, the decade of the 1920s saw a resurgence of interest in the Gary plan on the national level, and a full elaboration of the system in the schools in Gary. The U.S. Office of Education, under the prodding of school expert Alice Barrows, promoted the Wirt system, now called the platoon school plan, and by the end of the decade more than two hundred cities had adopted the plan. In Gary Wirt cut back his national publicity work and concentrated on the expansion of the program in his own school system. Thus, in contrast to many analyses of progressive schooling in the 1920s, the Gary plan did not die; rather, it remained vital and flexible in Gary and it proliferated nationwide. The situation changed in the 1930s, when economic depression forced a cutback in school programs everywhere. National promotion of the plan ceased, but the platoon school survived, and many of its most important features became standard ingredients in school programs throughout the nation.

Clearly, the Gary plan and, more generally, progressive education, meant different things to different people. For the business-oriented administrative progressives, the public schools represented a means of sustaining the emerging corporate-technological state by promoting such values as conformity, social order, work, productivity, and consumerism. Like most schools throughout the nation, Wirt's Gary schools fostered such goals. Wirt simultaneously established a high standard of bureaucratic efficiency. As one writer, David Gibson, noted of the Gary plan in 1912, for the first time "scientific methods have been applied to education, scientific management to a school system, the education capacity doubled and the cost of education cut in two, all at the same time." Similarly focusing on the administrative aspects of the Gary system, educator Herbert Roberts claimed that Wirt had created "the perfect piece of school mechanism."[4] Obviously enchanted by the system's apparent efficiency, Gibson and Roberts said little about the nature of the learning in the Gary schools. But for others it was the learning environment that was so exciting about the Wirt system. To such advocates, the educational features of the Gary plan appeared to be truly democratic, or radical, or even revolutionary in their social implications. Traditional schools were little more than "adjuncts of capitalist shops and factories," Floyd Dell typically wrote in the radical publication *The Liberator* in 1918. The Gary plan was "revolutionary" because "it made the child and his needs the center of the whole process of education."[5] Thus, the Gary schools epitomized two separate and contradictory goals of progressive education—the drive toward efficiency, economy, and scientific management, on the one hand, and the urge to provide a natural and enriched schooling in which children learned by doing, on the other. The same sorts of confused and paradoxical images have been perpetuated by historians who have examined the Gary schools. Lawrence A. Cremin, for instance, one of the leading interpreters of progressive education, praised the Gary plan as an important "lever of social progress." In his book *The Transformation of the School: Progressivism in American Education, 1876–1957,* Cremin portrayed the Wirt system in terms reminiscent of the social progressives who promoted the schools as agents of opportunity, freedom, democracy, and individual development.[6] On the other hand, in *Education and the Cult of Efficiency* Raymond E. Callahan described the Gary plan as the epitome of the factory system in education. Wirt's prime interest was efficiency, Callahan argued, not social reform or a humanitarian gospel of democracy and individual freedom.[7] Writing in a similar vein, Christopher Lasch contended that in the Gary schools "the progressive ideal of spontaneity and creativity lost out to considerations of bureaucratic efficiency."[8] Whatever the reality, there has been little agreement on the forms and purposes of schooling during the Progressive Era and after.

The chapters which follow seek to unravel both the perceived contradictions and the real tensions in progressive education by examining various facets of the platoon school system in Gary and New York City. These contradictions and tensions developed because of ideological, political, economic, racial, and ethnic differences. Chapters 1 and 2, for example, deal with fundamental ideological and political disparities, not only between supporters and opponents of the Gary plan, but also among those who were its strongest advocates. Chapter 3 illustrates how the "child-saving" impulse was riddled with doubt and conflict during the Progressive Era. Personality clashes, as well as differences over means and ends, seriously divided those involved in the movement. Chapters 4 and 5 deal with entirely different levels of conflict—between Americans and immigrants and between blacks and whites—over the purposes and functions of the public schools. Chapter 6 illustrates the explosive nature of racial tensions during the seemingly placid decade of the 1920s. It also demonstrates, however, that beneath the surface disagreements continued over the nature and meaning of progressive schooling and between teachers and school administrations. The economic collapse of the Great Depression, as chapter 7 suggests, brought into sharp focus serious political and economic conflicts over the role of schools in society.

Historians have always disagreed about how to interpret American schooling. In recent years many revisionist studies have tended to emphasize the connection between public schools and the political-economic system. In the final chapter we have examined many of these new interpretations in order to put our own study into the context of the larger debate on the meaning of schooling in American society. Although we do not always agree with these revisionists, we have been heavily influenced by them and their conflict models in our own work.

1

WILLIAM WIRT, ALICE BARROWS,
AND THE PARADOX OF PROGRESSIVE SCHOOLING

Few school systems in the Progressive Era captured the enthusiasm and attention of educators more than that of the new steel city of Gary, Indiana. Under the direction of Superintendent of Schools William A. Wirt, the Gary platoon schools combined the full range of educational reforms advocated by progressives of many different stripes. Magnificent athletic facilities, numerous and varied auditorium programs, workshops, libraries, laboratories, field trips, cooperation with community agencies, use of the schools as social centers, application of psychological testing, development of student government, evening schools, summer schools, continuation schools, work in art, music, dancing, home economics, and industrial training—all these and more were adopted as a regular part of the Gary system. It was a system in which the curriculum was enriched with activities far beyond those found in traditional schools, in which children learned by doing, in which the school became a miniature of the larger society. At the same time flexible scheduling, rotation of students from class to class and from activity to activity, and the use of every room, facility, and piece of equipment constantly throughout the day raised a high standard of bureaucratic efficiency. The Gary schools, then, reflected two powerful but contradictory themes which ran through the progressive education movement—the drive for efficiency and the urge to provide a more natural, humanistic, and democratic schooling. As one writer put it in 1912, perhaps without recognizing the irony of his statement, the Gary plan was "the most efficient, the most democratic public school system in this country."[1]

The internal contradictions of progressive education are highlighted by examining the Gary schools refracted through the careers and conflicting ideologies of their two leading advocates—Superintendent Wirt and educational publicist and activist Alice P. Barrows. Wirt represented the administrative reform or efficiency impulse, while Barrows was in the social reform or democratic camp. Despite radically different political and social outlooks, they worked together in support of the Gary plan for over twenty years. By exploring their contrasting perceptions of schooling and its purposes, we are better able to understand the unresolved tensions and complexities of the Gary plan and the paradox of progressive education.

1

William A. Wirt was a country boy. He would always remain so at heart, although he spent the last thirty-one years of his life in the city. Born on January 21, 1874, near Markle, Indiana, he attended school in Markle and Bluffton, and graduated from DePauw University in Greencastle in 1898 with an M.A. in political science. Wirt took his first teaching job after graduation in Redkey, but within a year he became superintendent in Bluffton, where he remained until moving to Gary in 1907. During the Bluffton years he took summer courses at the University of Chicago; this was his first contact with the urban environment. He would later be remembered for his "startling innovations" in Bluffton, which were hardly revolutionary but which formed the basis for the later work-study-play program.[2]

Wirt's early ideas and achievements were spelled out in his report to the state superintendent of public instruction in 1906. It was his goal in Bluffton, he wrote, "to start with the existing school system and along with the logical and natural growth and rational reorganization of this system evolve a manual training, domestic science and art, nature study, school garden, physical culture and fine arts departments." While he could glibly assert, in the best progressive phraseology, that the new curriculum was designed "in order that our young men and women might be fitted for the world's work and rational living," his reasoning was far more complex. Wirt's prime concern was the growing meaninglessness of life, the shift from purposeful, energetic farm work to the dissipated life of the city.[3]

A strong anti-urban bias shaped Wirt's conception of the purposes of public education. Cities, he often argued, had "never been good places for rearing children." Wirt much preferred the familiar environment from which he himself had been spawned—the self-contained family farm which provided all that was needed in the way of character building, physical development, and vocational training. In the new urban age the old values and skills taught by parents in the home and on the farm, or imparted by tradesmen to apprentices, had been undermined by the changed patterns of life and work in the industrial city. The average city youth, Wirt claimed, spent more time in the street than in the school. Such children quickly learned "the ideals of the loafers and the outcasts of society in the streets, gambling dens, cheap dance halls, and amusement halls." The street, according to Wirt's standard convention speech, became "a real school working at maximum efficiency educating children in the wrong direction." Moreover, city children associated with people "who look upon work as an evil," and they grew up in "an atmosphere emphasizing the consumption of the commodities of life rather than their production."[4]

Given these new urban conditions, it became the duty of the public schools to assume functions formerly exercised by farm, home, and shop. With the assistance of other community agencies, the school could counter the unwholesome temptations of urban life and lessen the influence of the crime school of the street and alley. By re-creating "the environment of the old time home and shops," the school could maintain the old value system. Indeed, Wirt would always be obsessed with the distinction between real and false values, hard work and idleness, country and city—good versus evil—and he never lost sight of which side he served. Schools would have to supply the virtues of country life missing in the city because the traditional bastions of morality and control—family, church, work—had declined in importance.[5]

Production and *work* were Wirt's keys to creating healthy individuals and a healthy society. In addition to introducing a practical curriculum in Bluffton, he implemented a longer school day, night classes, and weekend and summer school sessions. He conceived the schools' role was "to so interest children in work, nature and art that they forget themselves and are wholly absorbed in the thing which silently but surely is transforming them into something higher and nobler than they were." He hoped to create schools in which "the play impulse is transformed into a work impulse so that real pleasure is experienced in work." School work, however, would not be divorced from the real world. Practical application of academic as well as manual skills was his prime goal, all designed to instill in students a work ethic.

> Every agency of the school has been directed to secure a complete realization on the part of the children that work is not a curse, but a great blessing; that it was given as an antidote for the poison introduced into the world by the appearance of evil. The ambition of the school is to permeate the minds of its pupils with the thought that only through their work can they become the individuals that it is possible for them to be; that the school does not complete their education, but that their life's work is the greater school.

Wirt was as quick to damn a lazy worker as he was a lazy capitalist who manipulated stocks and currency. Public schools, endowed with the mission of "the ennobling of daily and common work by making it beautiful," could solve "the great economic and social problems of our time."[6] Bluffton, hardly the urban jungle that Wirt so feared, nonetheless seemed to represent the decline of rural America and thus served as a laboratory for his ideas. But Bluffton was small—only about 1,000 students in all the schools—not the best testing ground for his panacea for the country's growing ills. The true test would have to come in a large, industrial city. Only there would the real battle be joined between the street and the school, natural man and artificial man, work and leisure, individualism and regimentation. Not one to avoid conflict—indeed, he welcomed meeting the devil on his home ground—Wirt eagerly awaited an opportunity to apply his ideas in a city. In so doing he was following the common pattern for school superintendents. As David Tyack has written:

> Although superintendents often sought to escape the drab routine of farm lives they knew as children, they also tended to accept the values they learned in their small communities and to glorify socialization in the countryside. Indeed, they often saw the city as a source and center of social problems. . . . Ironically, the further his ambition propelled him—to the big city—the further he travelled from the source of virtue, small-town America.[7]

Wirt's chance came in 1906.

Gary, Indiana, was the creation of the United States Steel Corporation. In 1905 U.S. Steel quietly began buying up land along the southern tip of Lake Michigan; within a year the corporation owned nine thousand acres and had begun building a city and the most modern steel plant in the world. Gary had no permanent buildings, few organizations, indeed almost nothing in 1906. But it did have a school board. Its three members held their first meeting in mid-September, when they hired one teacher to manage their city's 67 children of school age. The next month Wirt was hired as superintendent at a yearly salary of $2,500. He would start the following July. "I have never taken hold of any work with more enthusiasm than I shall take hold of the school proposition in your city," the new appointee wrote optimistically. "It is a field of work for which I know that I am especially fitted and in which I shall be right at home." Believing, incorrectly, that Gary would be a metropolis of 75,000–100,000 within a decade, Wirt seemingly realized the magnitude of the job he was to undertake. He wasted no time in formulating teacher-hiring practices, planning permanent buildings, and generally molding the schools to his specifications.[8]

Wirt was fortunate in being able to organize the schools without hindrance from tradition or powerful entrenched interests. "He certainly is not handicapped by the board," the local paper asserted in September, 1907. "They are with him in every effort that will mean good for Gary schools."[9] He took every advantage of this unique opportunity, although he was constantly frustrated by inadequate facilities, overcrowding, and general economic difficulties. Until his death in 1938 the school board essentially gave him a free hand—because they believed in what he was doing and shared his values and interests. They were all part of the WASP elite that controlled city affairs until the 1940s.

Gary's population grew rapidly, from about 17,000 in 1910, to 55,000 in 1920, to over 100,000 in 1930. Almost 50 percent of the population in 1910 was foreign born; this percentage dropped over the following decades, reaching only 19 percent in 1930. When the rate of foreign immigration declined in the 1920s, there was a rise in the migration of blacks from the South; about 9 percent of the population was black in 1920, and 17 percent in 1930. Gary attracted able-bodied workers, men and women, who were in the prime of their childbearing years. Thus, the number of children increased rapidly. By September, 1908, there were over 1,000 students. The number grew to 3,000 in 1911, 5,300 in 1914, and 9,000 in 1920. Within another decade it had doubled again, to over 19,000, after which it leveled off because of the depression. The school population was, naturally, quite heterogeneous; by the mid-1920s about 30 percent were the children of native-born whites, over 50 percent the children of foreign-born whites, and the remainder were of black ancestry. These figures did not include all children of school age, however. For example, in May, 1910, some 2,534 children were listed in the school census, but by the fall only 1,500 were enrolled in school. The gap between census and enrollment narrowed in the following years, as schooling became more acceptable to parents and child labor declined, but in 1915 there were still 1,000 more children listed on the census than were attending classes. Teachers, naturally, also multiplied. There were two in 1906, 112 in 1911, 200 in 1920, and 600 in 1930, after which the number declined to about 550 by the late 1930s.[10]

For the administrative progressives, efficiency meant bureaucracy. This was not a new concern among schoolmen in the twentieth century, but with the growing number of students and the diversified new curriculum, the necessity of having a functional division of administrative labor took on added importance. In Gary, as in every other city in the country, the number of school administrators increased with enrollment. By March, 1908, there were three special teachers, quasi-supervisors, one each for manual training, music, and drawing. Five years later there were two assistant superintendents, and department heads for language, mathematics, history, science, manual training, music, commercial work, and girls' and boys' physical education. By the mid-1920s the bureaucracy had grown to include additional supervisors for the auditorium, testing, kindergarten and primary grades, penmanship, and the continuation school; assistant superintendent positions, however, had been reduced to one. Within another decade there were still more supervisors, including one for child welfare, and a psychiatrist and psychologist, but the assistant superintendent position had been dropped. It is hard to conceive of a large school system without an expanding bureaucracy, but Gary's was kept to a minimum. "A surprisingly small amount of administrative machinery for so varied a system is required by the schools of Gary," Randolph Bourne wrote in 1915. Moreover, Wirt, who could never shake his small-town mentality, kept tight personal control over the system. He tried to combine the personal touch of the small-town superintendent with the demands of a large and complex urban school system, which he was able to do only through extreme dedication and hard work. After 1938, once he was gone, the system quickly unraveled.[11]

Wirt, of course, believed in efficiency. His contribution here, as Raymond Callahan has pointed out, was in the area of scheduling and curriculum, not bureaucratic apparatus. In Wirt's idealized Gary plan, the students in a school above the primary grades were divided into two platoons; while one group used academic classrooms, the other would be divided between the shops, nature study, auditorium, gymnasium, and outdoor recreational equipment. All the facilities would thus be in use all the time. "The limited resources of the School Town and the overwhelming size of the school obligation to be met led to a most careful investigation and study of school plant economy," Wirt reported to the town council in 1909. "The purpose of the school administration has been to secure not only an efficient school plant but the most economical and efficient plant."[12] In actual practice, the Gary schools never achieved the total efficiency Wirt sought. But he never wavered from this goal.

Wirt was obsessed with waste, of any sort. The public would naturally support the Gary plan, he argued, because "they believe that when the wasted time of the street is used for wholesome work and play, supplementing the study hours, the school will be more successful in developing culture and scholarship and also able to fit boys and girls for life." Time lost, whether on the street or in an unsuitable job after graduation, had to be eliminated. Both the individual and society would lose if maximum productivity was not achieved early and continued throughout life.

> Under the old system, children are turned out of school at the age of fourteen or fifteen without chart or compass to steer them through the reefs and shoals of industrial life. The result is that the average

public school graduate seldom settles upon a permanent vocation until after he has wasted several years at least trying his hand at successive occupations. It is now believed that a lot of this wasted effort and time may be eliminated by giving the child while at school an opportunity to learn the rudiments of not one, but many of the ordinary trades and occupations.[13]

And just as the child's life should not be frittered away on the street or in taking useless subjects in school, the school should not waste any opportunity to keep and hold the child as long as possible.

While Wirt's preoccupation with efficiency cannot be ignored, many of his contemporary defenders and also historians such as Lawrence Cremin have concentrated on praising the stimulating curriculum in the Gary schools: the extensive manual and vocational training facilities, the elaborate gymnasiums, the auditorium activities, the art, nature study, and music classes, and the many extracurricular activities. Here, we are told, was the heart of the Gary system, truly a Deweyan paradise. Indeed, John Dewey himself, relying on his daughter Evelyn's observations, was enthusiastic about the schools because they were realistically confronting the question, "What did the Gary children need to make them good citizens and happy and prosperous human beings?" Wirt, certainly, was concerned about the development and well-being of children as healthy, creative, happy individuals, as he consistently argued. But, more importantly, he emphasized social productivity over personal happiness. Thus, the schools' recreational and cultural facilities were designed to transform play into "work-play."[14]

Initially concerned about instilling a work ethic and suitable vocational skills in children, by the 1920s Wirt had also become interested in education for leisure. He admitted in 1926:

> I do not believe that I saw clearly the tremendous importance of definite training for leisure. I had had so little leisure myself and I was completely carried away with the desire to develop a love for work by making work a joy for the worker. . . . I was soon forced to recognize leisure time as pure leisure time separate and distinct from work, and that the tastes that will make leisure time valuable must be developed through a definite educational instruction program in the school.

Leisure time, just like work time, should not be wasted. Here, perhaps, was the height of Wirt's obsession with efficiency.[15]

Wirt believed all children and adults could profit from public schooling no matter what their background and current circumstances. Rich and poor, old and young, black and white, native-born and immigrants (especially immigrants)—all would be elevated by public education. At the same time, he rigidly adhered to the elitist view that only an intelligent few in society were qualified to be leaders, with the mass relegated to the status of followers. He was no egalitarian. If parents or teachers disagreed with him, they were obviously wrong.

> In my twenty-five years of experience I found some teachers were anxious to make school more interesting but not so with parents and taxpayers. . . . They said they did not send their children to school to waste valuable time playing and getting dirty in shops. Any way they did not want their boy to be a carpenter or a plumber. Mothers as a class were not very much interested in having their girls become good home makers but tremendously interested in having them become social butterflies.[16]

But plumbers and homemakers many would be—Wirt and the schools would see to that. In Gary he was the unchallenged master of the schools, a superintendent who could do no wrong and who tolerated no criticism or opposition. If this attitude eventually led to problems in the 1930s, it nonetheless kept him going for most of his life, even in the face of numerous defeats and mistakes. Moreover, he was solidly aligned with society's elite—its businessmen, church leaders, and prominent educators—against the masses whose grumbling and organizing was beginning to challenge their authority in the early decades of the century. Wirt wanted an educated populace, but educated to take orders cheerfully and positively; above all he desired order, voluntary or otherwise.

Order had to be imposed because it was unnatural in a city. "The cities probably offer superior professional, commercial, industrial, and social opportunities to the strong men and women who can avail themselves of these advantages," Wirt wrote in 1937. "But the cities also offer every form of opportunity for dissipation and vice, and these temptations cannot be resisted by the weak men and women, and the children," who were assuredly in the majority. Their only hope was the work-study-play school, which was part of the city, yet simultaneously separated from it. Ideally, it would be sort of an oasis, the school building protected from its hostile surroundings by a public park in front, athletic fields and playground in back, and gardens on the sides. As Wirt's thinking developed, he envisioned the city as becoming more and more impersonal as well as socially chaotic. Only the work-study-play school could counteract these tendencies, by serving as a refuge and training ground for all citizens. Yet at the same time the school worked closely with the city's myriad cultural, social, intellectual, economic, and religious institutions, for they were all part of the same urban environment, which could not be ignored:

The school should so change its program that the churches, playgrounds, libraries, etc., may have the children for the activities they can provide better than the schools. When all these municipal institutions cooperate and work together there will arise a new type of municipal institution that will make the city a fit place for the rearing of children and a fit place to live in after they have been reared.

The longer school day, from 8:15 to 4:15, included time for children to go to private music lessons, weekday religious instruction, or the Y.M.C.A. The school thus functioned more as a clearing house than a closed institution. Similarly, it provided night classes and cultural activities for adults. In this paradoxical situation, set apart from the city yet a vital, functioning aspect of it, the work-study-play school was designed to assist all in becoming useful, productive citizens, even while the urban technological environment remained hostile and corrupt.[17]

Wirt's faith that society's leaders could preserve order despite severe environmental, social, and economic problems reflected his elitist social and political views. Evident during his early years in Gary, they did not become glaringly noticeable until the 1930s. For example, take his attitude toward labor unions. In the abstract he welcomed unions as a support of, rather than a challenge to, the corporate power structure, a reasonable stand considering the conservatism of Samuel Gompers and the American Federation of Labor. In 1916, when the AFL was considering an investigation of the Gary schools because of the controversy over their adoption in New York City, Wirt put up no opposition. He wrote to Gompers that his interest in unions dated back to his days in Redkey, and that he had even joined the AFL for a time in Bluffton. Wirt publicly welcomed the organization of a teachers' union in Gary in 1914. In a letter to union organizer R. D. Chadwick, Wirt wrote:

> I am heartily in favor of organization of teachers and it is entirely immaterial to me whether they are federated with National organizations, or not. I believe that it is very desirable that teachers have an opportunity to discuss problems connected with their professional work in an environment where they may be entirely independent. Opinions crystallized as result of such free and independent discussion will be considered very valuable by me in the administration of the schools with which I am connected.[18]

But Wirt desired a professional organization that would advise and cooperate with the administration, not a labor union that would challenge it. Thus, after the Gary teachers affiliated with the AFL in 1915, he wrote candidly to a friend:

Neither the Federation of Teachers nor the Affiliation of said Federation with the American Federation of Labor have been objectionable to the management of the Gary Public Schools. I would not hesitate to oppose any Federation of Teachers or any Affiliation if they were inimical to the highest welfare of the public schools. I believe that we must expect employees in any institution to organize for their mutual welfare and that the managers of all institutions public as well as private will have to learn how to work with such organizations. However, I think the principle of teachers aligning themselves with one element in society is unfortunate. The teachers should recognize that the education of children is a very great responsibility and that they represent the State in molding the ideas of its future citizens. An affiliation with any one class of society for the selfish interest of the teachers as a group or of this one particular class of society is unfortunate and will eventually weaken the influence of teachers and labor representatives, for teachers will be charged with using their position of trust given them by all the people to mold the ideas of the future citizens of the State in favor of one class of the people. I have spoken to you frankly in this matter for your own information and in return I hope that you will not give out this statement for publication. I am engaged in a vital piece of educational promotion work the success of which I do not wish to endanger by unnecessary controversy. I do not wish, therefore, to become publicly involved in any of the controversies in the Chicago School System or with the American Federation of Labor.[19]

Teachers' organizations should be seen but not heard. The Gary Teachers Union, one of the original locals of the American Federation of Teachers in 1916, collapsed in the early 1920s. Reorganized in 1937, it quickly became one of Wirt's most aggressive critics, thus eventually fulfilling his initial apprehensions.

While Wirt was quick to suspect teachers' unions of selfish motives and goals, he was convinced that his actions were motivated by pure altruism. Was this possible? Hardly, for Wirt was solidly aligned with the business and professional classes of the community. Wirt and the schools were not, certainly, the tools of the United States Steel Corporation, as many at the time charged; but relations between the two were always cordial. Judge Elbert H. Gary, chairman of the board of U.S. Steel, believed Wirt to be one of the foremost educators of the day, and in 1916 gave him $10,000 to subsidize his work in promoting the Gary plan. The gift was not just an act of generosity. "I have been very much interested in the schools at Gary because of their practical effect upon the boys and girls of our workmen and consequently upon the workmen themselves," Gary wrote to William Randolph Hearst in 1917.[20] This was a sentiment with which Wirt could heartily agree. He was not Judge Gary's lackey, just one who shared his social and economic values.

Wirt was a capitalist at heart. He believed in the private ownership of property and capital, and in the use of such capital to earn a profit for himself. Soon after arriving in Gary Wirt became part owner of the new Victoria Hotel; later he was involved in real estate development (at Dune Acres, along the Lake Michigan shoreline east of Gary), served as president of Gary's National Bank of America (which folded during the depression), became a partner in a planning firm with city planner A. P. Melton and school architect William Ittner, owned a golf course in upstate New York run by his brother Chester in the 1920s and later in the decade a Nash automobile dealership with his oldest son. None of these ventures proved successful, and all were abandoned in time. A brilliant school administrator and publicist, Wirt was a flop as a capitalist. He never abandoned his faith in the capitalist system, however, a commitment which became blatant in the 1920s, but to him the system meant the world of the small entrepreneur; he seemingly never understood the world of corporate capitalism and high finance. While the Gary schools were essentially turning out workers for the city's mills and factories and consumers for their products, of which Wirt was quite aware, he continued to think in terms of nineteenth-century self-sufficient businessmen (farmers and small shopkeepers) and housewives. He preached the necessity for preserving independence in a society increasingly marked by dependency—on goods, jobs, international economic conditions, technology, governmental activities, and the like. Perhaps somewhat indicative of his economic principles was his effort in 1922 to install savings machines in the Gary schools. Students deposited coins and, in return, received savings stamps. The stamps could later be redeemed for cash or deposited in bank accounts at Wirt's National Bank of America. The students were taught personal thrift and simultaneously introduced to the world of banking, while Wirt would profit from the increased business.[21]

Wirt's attitudes toward schooling were no different in the 1930s from what they had been two decades before; he still emphasized educating the whole child, believing "if only sixty percent of our people, generation after generation, actually loved learning, loved industry and justice, the future of our civilization would be secure."[22] But now he was disturbed by dangerous trends in the country, particularly the desire of some to abandon the old-fashioned individualism—or at least what survived of it in theory if not in practice—in favor of collectivism. After Roosevelt's victory in 1932 he turned increasingly to publicizing his ideas about how to save the economy without governmental planning. His natural allies in this crusade were the nation's businessmen. Soon he became the darling of every right-wing cause in the country.

Wirt became obsessed with the idea that manipulating the dollar was the key to solving the country's economic problems. There was, he fervently believed, nothing fundamentally wrong with capitalism. He wrote articles and pamphlets, gave lectures, and even completed an unpublished book-length manuscript on the subject. At the same time he did not ignore the role of the schools. Now, in addition to creating happy, productive individuals, they had the added burden of teaching the truth about the economy. Once so informed, the people would naturally rise up and save capitalism. If the country went socialist, he argued, it was the schools' fault for not properly educating the people. They should not propagandize for any particular economic system, only teach the "truth." They should present the "essential facts" about the economy so that citizens could "think straight and support the President against the *extreme Left Wingers* on the one side who want to destroy private enterprise and the *extreme Right Wingers* on the other side who prefer universal destruction to surrendering their special privileges in the old economic order." It was his opinion that "there should not be any propaganda in the schools either for or against the old economic order. The old economic order should stand or fall on its own record. All that I am asking is that we find out what that record is and that we be INTELLECTUALLY HONEST." Wirt recognized the failings of "pure capitalism," but also believed that the cure was worse than the disease.

> It is not that we love private enterprise so much [he wrote], but that we love the collective-state enterprises that are offered as alternatives, less. All that I am asking is that we make up balance sheets for the several forms of social and economic orders that we can have, BEFORE WE MAKE OUR CHOICE. Then we will know what we are choosing.[23]

And he was certain what the outcome would be. In all this, like his ideological bedfellows, Wirt was never able to comprehend the reality of the emerging corporate-technological state.

Wirt always considered himself a moderate. As he wrote of himself in a publicity notice in 1934:

> He [Wirt] believes in social reform and the elimination of the abuses of capitalism. He is in favor of the elimination of child labor and sweatshops. He favors the minimum wage, the maximum hour and the old age pension policies. He favors the elimination of the gambler's control of business and industry. . . . But he does not think that it is necessary to burn the house down in order to get rid

of a few vermin. He wants to continue the American type of government and social order and make the desired changes without accepting the national economic planning which will place all persons under the dictatorship of politicians, and put public opinion in a "straight jacket."[24]

An unreconstructed old progressive, his faith in the individual prevented him from accepting increased government planning and control. And as attacks on his beloved system increased, he became more anxious and concerned. The public became aware of Wirt's fears in early 1934 when he testified before a House Committee that communists were infiltrating the New Deal. Until his death in 1938 no matter what he personally believed, he was a hero to those on the right, and a clown to those in the center and on the left.

2

Wirt believed that education could promote American capitalism and individualism, within the framework of the corporate-technological society; Alice Barrows saw more creative possibilities in the reform of the public schools. Eventually going far beyond Wirt, she conceived of the Gary plan as a radical school experiment which could help achieve real social reconstruction in the United States. As educator Arthur Moehlman wrote in 1942: "Alice Barrows caught the educational significance and philosophy behind the administrative facade of the balanced work-study-play elementary plan and read, we are afraid, much deeper philosophy into the scheme than Mr. Wirt really meant."[25] As teacher, educational reformer, and government school specialist, Alice Barrows devoted more than forty years to promoting change in the schools. Beginning as a moderate progressive in the social reform camp, Barrows moved toward political and cultural radicalism by the end of the Progressive Era. During the twenties her radicalism remained mostly dormant, as she immersed herself in educational work. But during the New Deal period, World War 2, and the era of the Cold War, she moved even further to the left and became politically active in areas outside of education. Yet, until they broke in 1934, Barrows and Wirt managed to work closely together in promoting the Gary school idea, despite very real social and political differences.

Unlike Wirt, Alice Barrows did not reject urban life. She was born in 1877 in Lowell, Massachusetts, where her father, Charles Dana Barrows, served as a Congregational minister. In 1881 Charles Barrows accepted the pulpit at the First Congregational Church in San Francisco and moved his family to California. Although Alice Barrows grew up in Lowell and San Francisco, her family spent a considerable amount of time in Portland, Maine, at the home of her uncle, Speaker of the U.S. House of Representatives Thomas B. Reed. A graduate of Vassar College in 1900, Alice Barrows taught English at the Packer Collegiate Institute in Brooklyn for two years and at the Ethical Culture School in Manhattan for another year. In 1904 she returned to Vassar as an instructor in English, but left in 1907 for graduate work at Columbia University's Teachers College, where she took courses with John Dewey. From 1908 to 1911 Barrows worked as a social investigator with the Russell Sage Foundation, collaborating with Mary Van Kleeck in extensive studies of working women in the millinery and garment trades in New York City. Her work with the Russell Sage Foundation, essentially interviewing women workers in their homes and shops, stimulated her respect for working people; but she also became outraged over the intolerable living and working conditions which prevailed in the city. A passage in her unpublished autobiography records her anger and indignation following the devastating fire at the Triangle Shirtwaist Factory, which she had investigated the day before: "From that day I ceased to be merely an investigator. I was consumed with anger and loathing for the cupidity which made such a holocaust possible. This was murder. Something had to be done to change such conditions." During these years Barrows became committed to urban reform. Unlike Wirt, she did not desire to turn back the clock to recapture some lost rural purity; rather, she accepted the modern American city on its own terms and sought social and institutional changes to make urban life more decent and more humane.[26]

In 1911, when her work with the Russell Sage Foundation ended, Barrows turned again to education. Buoyed with the reform optimism of the Progressive Era, she was also consumed with "anger against the straightjacket methods of the traditional school." She saw the revamping of the public schools as a means of social salvation for the children. "Something," she later wrote, "had to be done about hurrying up the application of Dewey's educational theories to the masses of children in public schools. . . . I was going to do what I could to change the public school system. Nothing less!"[27] For Alice Barrows, the schools had to be reorganized on a democratic basis to permit children to achieve as much as they were capable of achieving. She accepted the position of the progressive reformers that the schools should provide equality of opportunity and avenues of upward mobility.

Barrows concentrated her first efforts for urban school reform in the area of vocational education. In 1911 she became director of a vocational guidance survey sponsored by the Public Education Association of New York City (PEA), a private group which promoted progressive educational reforms and worked closely with the New York City Board of Education. In 1912 the PEA broadened the scope of the survey to include other aspects of vocational education besides guidance. Efficiency-minded educators promoted the vocational guidance movement; it seemed a rational means of directing children of working age into the job market. Barrows, however, believed that vocational guidance pushed children out of the schools and into "dead-end" jobs—jobs with little future and little prospect of promotion or advancement. As she put it in her vocational guidance report, "There are no jobs for children under sixteen which they ought to take." Vocational guidance, as practiced in most urban schools, provided cheap, unskilled labor for city business and industry. It simply contributed to the child labor problem. The only acceptable approach was one in which the schools provided a broad vocational training, a program in which children learned "the mechanical principles or elements which lie at the base of all industrial civilization." Rather than equipping children to operate specific factory machines, vocational education courses had to emphasize "the mechanical elements which are found in nearly all machines." Thus, children would be prepared for any number of jobs in a complex industrial society. This theme—that education should broadly, rather than narrowly, prepare for life—lay at the heart of Barrows's views about the humanistic and democratic function of the schools. But like John Dewey and William Wirt, she accepted technology as a given and viewed the school as a mediating institution between the individual and the technological society.[28]

Alice Barrows's work in vocational education had familiarized her with the innovative schools of Gary, Indiana, which had introduced an elaborate program of industrial training. Wirt's school plan had begun to attract national attention by 1912, when he delivered the keynote address at a vocational guidance convention in New York City. Barrows was especially enthusiastic about the vocational aspects of the Gary plan because Wirt opposed narrow and specialized job training. Rather, he asserted the importance of developing fundamental industrial skills which could be utilized in a variety of trades—the same kind of program Barrows advocated in her final report on the Vocational Education Survey in 1914.

Barrows learned more about the Gary schools from Elsa Ueland and Elizabeth Roemer, her two assistants on the Vocational Education Survey, who had taken teaching jobs in Gary in September, 1914. Intrigued by their enthusiasm for the Wirt plan, Barrows herself visited Gary in the fall of 1914. In her autobiography she recalled her first day in Gary's Emerson

School as "one of the most astonishing and exhilarating experiences of my life." The playgrounds, the workshops, the laboratories, the library, the gardens, the special-purpose rooms for art, music, cooking, sewing—all reaffirmed in her mind "the rigidity and waste of the traditional school." At this point she thought of Wirt as "an educational engineer who was showing that Dewey's philosophy could be put into practice on a large scale in the public schools." Obviously captivated by Wirt, Barrows believed him to be committed to the school as an agent of democracy, as an institution which would not restrain or manipulate children but "make possible all their latent powers." She saw little contradiction, during this period, between her educational idealism and that of William Wirt.[29]

In mid-1914 Wirt had been hired as an educational consultant by New York City's reform mayor John Purroy Mitchel to transform the city's schools along the lines of the Gary platoon system. Wirt commuted to New York one week each month for more than three years to supervise the transition, first in two experimental schools and later in a larger number. Barrows was enlisted as Wirt's secretary for the New York work. Her job, essentially, was to publicize the platoon plan and build broad public support for the new school reform. She brought to this task a tremendous amount of creative energy. Over the next few years, from 1914 to 1917, Barrows orchestrated a massive propaganda campaign on behalf of the Gary plan. She wrote pamphlets and articles, gave innumerable speeches, sponsored meetings, organized parents' groups, mobilized civic leaders and reformers, fought obstructionist school officials, and lobbied. Randolph Bourne, a close friend of Barrows and author of a laudatory book on the Gary schools in 1916, described her as "a great general" and her work as a "Napoleonic campaign." "I hope she gets some reward for her supernatural energy in this enterprise," he wrote in late 1915. "She has put in enough to stand any ordinary school-system on its head."[30]

Equally important, Barrows the propagandist was a loyal admirer of William Wirt and deeply committed to the Gary plan. To her, the plan meant "the biggest thing in democratic educational reconstruction in the country"—a real effort at "free" schooling in an era when urban schools had become rigidly bureaucratized. The Wirt schools represented not an elitist experiment, as many opponents charged, but an "achievement in democracy."[31] The new plan, Barrows contended in 1917, was "part of a nation-wide movement for democracy and progress in public education. It makes the school exist for the child, not the child for the school system. It humanizes instruction and permits the child, for the first time, to be treated naturally and as a human being. It develops the child's individuality. It educates all his faculties." Moreover, it provided all children with "the rich educational advantages—play, opportunities for creative hand work, drawing, music, science, etc.—which up to the present time, in spite of all our pride in public schools, only the children of the rich have enjoyed in private schools." The Gary schools had succeeded in eliminating the inequity between "the education of the few and that of the many."[32] Clearly, the efficiency of the platoon plan was less important to Barrows than the opportunities for creative and humanistic schooling. Barrows, in short, rejected the central position of the administrative progressives, and promoted the Gary plan during this period as a child-centered school reform.

Despite the efforts of Barrows, Wirt, and Mayor Mitchel over a four-year period, the plan to introduce platoon schools in New York City was a dismal failure. The innovation failed when the schools became embroiled in partisan city politics, and efficiency-minded reformers in the Mitchel administration were unable to convince the voters that the Gary plan was anything more than a device to save money at the expense of their children's education. Incredibly, tensions aroused by the Gary plan touched off two weeks of striking and rioting among thousands of the city's elementary school children just before the 1917 mayoralty election. The victory of Tammany's John F. Hylan marked the end of the platoon school experiment in New York City.

To Barrows, the Tammany election after years of propaganda work suggested a new line of approach. Most of her reform efforts had been organized from the top down rather than from the bottom up. Writers, intellectuals, and middle class reformer types could meet and talk and write all they wanted, but they would have little impact if the people in the streets and neighborhoods of the city were not reached. "A great reform" like the Gary schools, she wrote in 1917, had to be "founded upon the intelligent understanding of the masses of the people." As Barrows wrote to Wirt in 1918, "If I had to do it again I would chloroform the Board of Education and most of the supporters of the plan and get enough money in the beginning to educate the people themselves." Borrowing from the organizational techniques of anti-war socialists, Barrows spent six months after the election organizing neighborhood units of a new group she called the People's Educational Council. Like the anti-war People's Councils upon which they were modeled, these small, local groups organized parents by city blocks; the purpose—to stimulate concern for education among parents and "to gradually arouse in the mass of people a desire for what the Gary plan gives." This effort disintegrated for lack of funds by the middle of 1918, but Barrows's use of the socialist technique of community organizing suggests her movement toward the left.[33]

The Gary school campaign in New York City was merely a warmup for Alice Barrows. Committed to social change through the schools, she accepted a position in the City Schools Division of the U.S. Bureau of Education in 1918. She promptly launched a nationwide platoon school campaign, this time backed by the resources of the federal government. Her job—first as a specialist in "social and industrial relations in education" and later as an expert in school building problems—was one of making surveys of urban public schools and recommending desirable curricular and building changes. Over the course of the next decade, she made extensive surveys of the schools in Memphis, Tennessee; Lexington, Kentucky; Passaic, New Jersey; Mount Vernon, New York; Portland, Oregon; Wilmington, Delaware; Wheeling, West Virginia; Alexandria, Virginia; and numerous other cities. In each case her published report convincingly laid out the educational and financial advantages of the platoon system over traditional curricular and building arrangements. From her position in the Bureau of Education, Barrows became the most forceful and aggressive promoter of the platoon plan during the twenties. Field service reports to the City Schools Division of the Bureau of Education show that Barrows traveled more often and for longer periods of time than any other staff member. She made more surveys, published more reports, and gave more speeches, as well. During the Portland, Oregon survey, for instance, she gave fifty platoon school speeches in twenty-four days. During several summers she taught platoon school courses for teachers at the University of Oregon. She also promoted the platoon plan in articles for *School Life* (the Bureau of Education's official monthly journal) and in her correspondence with school officials around the nation.[34]

In 1922, under the auspices of the Bureau of Education, she organized the first of several annual conferences on the platoon school plan. These meetings led to the formation in 1925 of a new and independent professional organization with the unwieldy name of the National Association for the Study of the Platoon or Work-Study-Play School Organization. For more than half a decade, while holding down her full-time government job, she served as the new association's executive secretary and as founder, editor, and frequent contributor to its quarterly journal, *The Platoon School*—virtually a second full-time job.[35]

By the end of the 1920s Barrows's double-barreled activism had brought real and positive results. More than two hundred cities had adopted the platoon school system for some or all of their elementary schools by 1930. Detroit had 110 schools on the work-study-play plan in 1928, and Pittsburgh had 75. Other major cities which had implemented the plan included Philadelphia, Cleveland, Los Angeles, Hartford, Memphis, Portland, Kansas City, Dallas, Seattle, Cincinnati, Toledo, Akron, and Birmingham. The financial pressures imposed upon cities and school systems by the Great Depression highlighted the financial savings of platoon schools. And one writer in 1934 argued that the platoon school perfectly

embodied "the spirit of the new deal in education." Thus, despite the
setback in New York City, Alice Barrows and her "platooniacs" made
significant progress through the twenties and into the thirties in changing
the character of American education.[36]

As William Wirt's fiscal and political conservatism became more apparent in the twenties and thirties, Alice Barrows's social radicalism became
more pronounced. By 1920 she had moved beyond the moderate brand
of social progressivism which had characterized her work and thought
in the New York City years. The controversy she aroused during her
school survey in Passaic, New Jersey, for instance, reflected this move to
the left. In the fall of 1919 the Bureau of Education sent her to Passaic—
a textile city with a large proportion of immigrant workers—to make a
study of adult education needs. Typically, instead of beginning her work
by interviewing the superintendent of schools, she spent two weeks at the
offices of Robert W. Dunn, organizer of the Passaic local of the Amalga-
mated Textile Workers of America. Her purpose was to determine from
the workers themselves what kind of adult education programs they
wanted; in the process she uncovered and publicly condemned an extensive industrial espionage system designed by the textile industry to
suppress union activities. Industry representatives denounced her in the
newspapers as a "misguided zealot" who would "turn the schools of
Passaic into breeding places for Bolshevists." Passaic Mayor John H.
Maguire labeled her an undesirable "foreign influence." Barrows quickly
responded with the argument that the schools were agencies of "the
people" rather than tools of suppression run by the textile industry.
"Schools are not things apart from the community," she wrote in a letter
to the *Passaic Daily News.* "They are of it. The public school system of
America is brother to the other institutions of human liberty for which our
fathers fought—freedom of speech, press and assemblage." She attacked
the espionage system as part of the "reign of terror" during the Red Scare
and as destructive of a free and democratic school system. The Woolen
Council of Passaic, representing the textile interests, threatened to protest
her activities to the Bureau of Education; in return, Barrows threatened
to divulge "further facts that I have been holding in reserve for just such
an emergency." As Dunn noted in his diary in February, 1920, "She has
them all on the run."[37]

The Passaic incident clearly suggests that Barrows had moved considerably beyond Wirt in her conception of the proper function of the public
schools. While Wirt operated on the paternalistic assumption that he was
the sole possessor of wisdom regarding the direction of the schools in
Gary, Barrows had fastened on the need for what she called the "socialized
school." "The schools," she wrote, "belong to the people and should grow

and change in accordance with their needs. . . . The schools must become the people's clubs." She recognized that the Gary plan's efficiency and savings made it attractive to schoolmen. But, in all of her writing and speaking, she emphasized the educational advantages of the platoon system. For instance, in recommending the platoon plan in Lexington, Kentucky, she emphasized not its economic efficiency but the "richer and fuller educational opportunities for children." In her survey of Gloucester, Massachusetts, she urged the work-study-play plan as a means of developing "democratic education"—education which served individual needs and helped each child to reach his potential. Children taught in platoon schools, she contended, "will know how to live." Barrows continued to emphasize the creative and humanistic side of the Gary plan. After a visit to platoon schools in Cleveland in the mid-twenties, she reported enthusiastically:

> I liked the spirit of the children and the teachers in all the schools. It was free and natural, and yet there was no disorder or lack of discipline. I felt that these children were learning how to think, that their school was a community in which they were engaged in worthwhile activities that had meaning to them. The teachers seemed alert and interested in their work, interested in experimenting and trying new things.

Similarly, in a 1930 article in *The Platoon School,* Barrows summarized her educational thought in a phrase straight out of John Dewey: the essence of education was "to learn through experience rather than to be governed by the dictates of authority."[38]

Wirt's educational thinking, of course, had remained static and unchanging. The efficiency of his school system and the social productivity of its graduates continued to absorb his attention and energy. For Wirt, the Gary schools served elitist purposes—Americanizing immigrant children and adults, molding docile workers and citizens, manipulating students for the purposes of an orderly society. But for Barrows, the public schools— and especially the platoon schools—provided the chief hope for achieving an egalitarian society. By the thirties, when Barrows had moved even further to the left, she conceived of the platoon school as an instrument of progressive social change. The Gary plan, she firmly believed, was "not so much an educational, as a social, reorganization." Despite these fundamental differences, the two continued to work together during the twenties and early thirties. Barrows brought Wirt into several of her surveys as a consultant—notably in Memphis and Portland. Wirt was centrally involved in the affairs of the new platoon school organization, and regular subsidies out of Wirt's own pocket helped keep *The Platoon School* magazine alive well into the thirties. Moreover, Barrows continued her voluminous correspondence with Wirt throughout the period (although Wirt hardly ever answered). By the early thirties Wirt's political and educational thinking clearly contradicted her conception of democratic schooling in a democratic society. Yet even as late as 1932 they remained very close. Returning from a trip to Gary, Barrows wrote to Wirt in October, 1932: "You have been in my thoughts constantly since I left Gary. . . . You are so precious to all of us, you are so important to the world at this time. . . . You nourish our spirits with beauty and with ideas of great vigor and originality." In 1933, with the New Deal getting under way, Barrows even promoted Wirt's name as a candidate for U.S. Commissioner of Education. Barrows apparently tolerated Wirt's increasing eccentricities, for he was after all the architect of the platoon school system.[39]

The break came in 1934. It started innocently enough. In the fall of 1933 Wirt had been called to Washington as an educational consultant for the subsistence homesteads project. Barrows gave a dinner party in his honor at her home, inviting a number of lower-level New Dealers as well. The evidence becomes contradictory at this point. Barrows and her friends later noted that Wirt dominated the conversation for hours with his crackpot economic schemes. Wirt, however, publicly charged that the dinner guests discussed detailed plans to overthrow the Roosevelt administration, replacing it with a communist dictatorship. The New Deal, he asserted, was filled with these communist plotters. The right-wing press sensationalized these charges, making Wirt an instant hero of anti–New Deal forces. Democrats in Congress, meanwhile, created a "select committee" headed by Congressman Alfred A. Bulwinkle of North Carolina to investigate the allegations. Wirt was called to testify, but his charges before the decidedly unfriendly committee were contradicted by each of the other dinner guests, including Barrows. Without any corroborating testimony, Wirt's statements about "red" plotters in government seemed just another bit of reactionary propaganda. The Bulwinkle Committee, reporting no evidence of revolutionary infiltration in the government, found Wirt's charges unfounded and untrue. Hereafter Barrows had no contact with Wirt. Their twenty-year partnership in promoting school reform had come to an abrupt end.[40]

In the following years, as Wirt became the champion of the extreme right wing, Alice Barrows moved considerably further to the left. Maxine Wood, her close friend during these years, traces this politicization to the heady optimism of the early Roosevelt presidency. Another friend, Elsa Ueland, saw Barrows caught up in the fervent belief of New Dealers that the good society could be achieved through planning. It is also probable, as Edmund Wilson suggested in 1934, that Barrows had come to the conclusion that "a new deal in education is impossible without a new social-economic system."[41] Captivated by the reform spirit of New Deal Washington, she became involved in many political and ideological causes besides education. She vigorously opposed Congressman Martin Dies and the House Un-American Activities Committee, and she spoke out for civil liberties for radicals and civil rights for blacks. As a member of the executive committee of the Washington branch of the radical American League for Peace and Democracy, which sought to preserve the progressive gains of the New Deal, she attacked "all those enemies of true America"—"the war monger and the profiteer, . . . labor-baiting, labor-smashing Big Business, . . . and the absentee landlord who fattens on the misery of the share cropper." Described as a "premature anti-fascist," she supported Loyalist Spain and organized consumers' boycotts against Japan protesting the invasion of China.[42]

Barrows pursued these radical activities even more vigorously after her retirement from the Bureau of Education in 1942. During the forties she assumed leadership positions in a variety of alleged communist-front organizations: director of the Congress of American-Soviet Friendship (1942–43); public relations director of the National Federation of Constitutional Liberties (1943–44); public relations director of the Abraham Lincoln School in Chicago (1944–45); national director of the Arts, Sciences, and Professions Division of the Progressive Citizens of America (1946–48); a sponsor of the Cultural and Scientific Conference for World Peace (1949); and secretary of the Marion Bachrach Defense Committee (1952). She actively supported Henry Wallace's presidential campaign in 1948, opposed the cold war policies of the Truman administration, and championed the civil liberties of communists and others arrested during the McCarthy hysteria of the late forties and early fifties.[43] Believing that "defense of the civil rights of American communists was the first line of defense of the liberties of all Americans," she filled her last years organizing meetings and demonstrations and writing letters to newspapers, congressmen, senators, and presidents in defense of civil liberties. If not a communist herself, many of her close friends and associates were members of the Communist Party, and she was a regular subscriber to the *Daily Worker*. In 1953 Barrows was called to testify before the Internal Security Subcommittee of the United States Senate. Asked if she was a communist, she invoked the Fifth Amendment and lectured the senators on the meaning of liberty, world peace, and human freedom and dignity.[44] Thus, by the time of her death in October, 1954, Alice Barrows had established a long record in behalf of radical social change in the United States.

Unlike William Wirt, who unswervingly promoted the schools as agents of the corporate-technological state, Alice Barrows worked to transform them into creative and humanistic institutions. Her social thought changed over time, as she moved from a child-centered progressivism toward a social reconstructionist position by the 1930s, but she never wavered in her conception of the school as an institution of social democracy. In her view, the widespread adoption of the platoon system made possible a good and just society. By loosening the mind-shackling grip of traditional schools, by encouraging thinking and creative play and enrichment activities, the Gary system became, in her mind, a positive force for social progress in the United States.

3

William Wirt and Alice Barrows represented the two principal strains of progressive education: he, the efficiency and control side, she, the human and reconstructionist side. They worked together, and yet apart. In accounting for this situation, for their ability to cooperate while seeking divergent goals, it is possible, on the simplest level, to assume that they were unaware of their differences, so blinded were they by the dazzling beauty and utility of the Gary plan. During the Progressive Era there were few clear-cut ideological lines separating the different reform camps, as the issues of social reform, efficiency, democracy, peace, and so forth overlapped; alliances formed, disintegrated, and re-formed time and again, depending on the specific circumstances and issues. It was possible for quite distinct types to agree on programs, while holding divergent ideologies. Only in the 1930s, with the emphasis more clearly on economic issues and political philosophies, did earlier antagonisms become evident, as the old progressives sorted themselves out on opposing sides of the New Deal.

Whether Wirt and Barrows recognized their earlier conflicting goals is less important, however, than understanding why they disagreed. One answer is that they had quite distinct roles and functions. That is, William Wirt was an administrator, better yet an educational entrepreneur, an organizer and manager who wielded power and controlled policy. He was part of a small elite group who believed that they knew best what was good for themselves and for the country. Moreover, they had the power to carry out their assumptions. Wirt and his fellow entrepreneurs believed in the sanctity of the individual, particularly themselves; they believed in the use of power for self-aggrandizement as well as for community welfare; they believed in personal financial gain as well as in social order, efficiency, and prosperity. They were surrounded by others with the same values and goals, and hardly challenged by those under them. From his boyhood in rural Indiana Wirt absorbed the values of initiative, individualism, work, and duty, which he carried with him all his life. And as school superintendent he was in a position to act out these values and have them reinforced.

Alice Barrows, on the other hand, was a thinker and activist, not an executive. From an urban background and extensive community action experience, she was used to suggesting policy, not making it. Her role was that of the gadfly, the publicist or critic who had the freedom to stand outside the offices of the great and powerful and encourage them to action; or to organize community interest groups demanding changes from the power structure. Like other women of her time, who were excluded from the seats of power, she was never able to give orders, to manipulate others (whether she wished to or not). She could only hope to persuade. By differentiating her background and role—as observer, intellectual, critic, and organizer—from that of Wirt—as executive or entrepreneur—we can gain some understanding of the contrast between their values and goals. He was used to working from the top down, she from the bottom up. While their politics were radically divergent, they yet managed to meet somewhere in the middle for twenty years, but the middle vanished after 1929 as the top and bottom grew further apart.

Both Wirt and Barrows believed that they had the best interest of society in mind in advocating the Gary plan. Like all progressives, they were supremely confident that they knew best what society needed to cure its ills and prepare for a brighter future. With hindsight, however, we are able to separate dream from reality, and thus should make judgments about whether they were right in their faith. It now seems clear, for example, that Wirt's belief in individualism, essentially a nineteenth-century liberalism, was sadly outdated in the corporate-technological world of the twentieth century. He seems to have recognized this, grudgingly, by promoting the schools as training grounds for factory workers and white collar bureaucrats, but in his economic theories he clung to a laissez-faire image of society. He wanted to believe in the integrity of the individual, yet established mass schools for the "educating" of citizens in a mass society. He was concerned about the welfare of children, their intellectual, social, and physical well-being, but he feared allowing them too much freedom because they were in a corrupt environment, the industrial city. Barrows, on the other hand, was more realistic in her appraisal of the emerging corporate society, with its power blocs and interest groups. She saw that people would have to organize to insure their welfare and a share of the power, but they could do this only if they were well educated, intellectually and socially. Both she and Wirt believed power should center in local institutions; otherwise, they fundamentally disagreed about what society was all about.

The clash between Wirt and Barrows was postponed until 1934, but disputes among and between politicians, reformers, and citizens over the form and meaning of public schooling had been going on for some time before this. The conflict in New York City over adopting the Gary plan in the years immediately preceding World War 1 brought these divergent views into sharp focus.

2

SCHOOLS, POLITICS, AND RIOTS
The Gary Plan in New York City

Schools cannot be isolated from the society within which they exist. They reflect societal patterns and mirror public perceptions of many kinds. During the Progressive Era American society was characterized by social, political, and economic upheaval. Heavy European immigration, internal migration, rapid urbanization and the consequent decline of small towns, intensified industrialization and the growth of monopoly capital—all these resulted in social turmoil, confusion, and conflict. Caught up in the midst of these changes, public schools became battlegrounds, both ideological and real, between elites and the powerless, traditionalists and progressives, parents and educators, machine politicians and reformers, and especially between reformers with differing sets of values.

An archetypal example of conflict over the direction of public school reform occurred in New York City. Between 1914 and 1917 reform Mayor John Purroy Mitchel sought to introduce the much-discussed Gary school plan. The ensuing struggle illustrates the ambiguities and contradictions of urban progressivism; for different reasons the Gary plan appealed both to radical social reformers and business-oriented structural or administrative reformers. More importantly, it also reveals how different groups and special interests used the schools and the issue of educational reform for their own purposes: politicians who brought the schools into the electoral arena; teachers and school administrators who sought to protect their status and influence in the school system; labor unions which viewed vocational training as a threat to their control over apprenticeship and access to trades, and which viewed the Gary plan generally as a scheme of corporate capitalism; reformers and propagandists who worked to forge new public perceptions of the schools and their purposes; radicals who believed schools could be instrumental in forging a new society; and conservatives who considered them a bulwark of the established order. The conflict, eventually boiling over into massive student strikes and riots, also suggests the role of parents and children, particularly in Jewish neighborhoods, in shaping the kinds of schools and education they wanted. The history of the Gary school campaign in New York City thus demonstrates the ways in which schools reflect conflicts and tensions in American society.

1

Elected as a fusion candidate in 1913, Mayor John Purroy Mitchel established a thoroughgoing reform administration in New York City. Dominated in previous decades by Tammany corruption and mismanagement, the metropolis under Mitchel's leadership became, in the words of one veteran contemporary observer, "the best governed city in the United States." Mitchel brought a progressive passion for businesslike efficiency to city government—a commitment to scientific management, however, which often outweighed the social needs of city residents. Mitchel made merit appointments to city departments, drove out corruption, streamlined municipal administration, clamped controls on city finances, sponsored important zoning legislation, fought for home rule, backed new subway construction, secured additional park sites and recreational facilities, and introduced administrative reforms in street cleaning, public utilities, fire protection, correctional facilities, public charities, and police protection. Mitchel's energetic municipal administration captured the imagination of reform-minded New Yorkers and of progressive politicians throughout the nation.[1] One of Mitchel's most ambitious programs involved reforms in the public schools.

For years the school system had imposed serious financial and administrative burdens on the city. By 1914, when Mitchel took office, the system had grown to tremendous size, provided a variety of specialized services, and absorbed the biggest chunk of the city's annual budget. Some 20,000 teachers handled almost 800,000 students in that year, while the Board of Education's budget totaled more than $44 million. The system was, as historian Sol Cohen has noted, "one of the marvels of the world of education." But expansion of the system had not kept pace with New York's population, swelled by the influx of new immigrants during the last decades of the nineteenth century and the early years of the twentieth. The city did not have enough schools, especially in rapidly growing sections in upper Manhattan, Brooklyn, and the Bronx. Existing schools were terribly over crowded, and close to 120,000 students attended double sessions or received only part-time schooling. The costs of new school buildings to accommodate these children and eliminate the "part-time evil" seemed prohibitive.[2]

Furthermore, some educators and progressive reformers faulted the system on educational grounds. Their primary complaint was that the curriculum failed to prepare the children for life and work. Progressive educators especially advocated the introduction of vocational and manual training in the curriculum, from the elementary grades through high school. Such additions were necessary, they argued, because about 50 percent of the city's children left school after the sixth grade, and only 10 percent graduated from high school. Thrown onto the labor market without any skills, these children were forced into low-wage jobs in factories and sweatshops. As an administration report noted, "The people were tired of seeing the children swarming all over the city the day after graduation looking for work and unfitted to do anything that could support them." Reform groups like the important Public Education Association of New York City—essentially an organization lobbying for progressive educational reforms—contended that the schools had failed such children, as well as the community at large.[3]

Administrative problems also beset the schools. Some critics focused on the bureaucratic nature of a system in which the Board of Estimate and Apportionment made appropriations, the Board of Education made policy decisions, and the superintendent of schools and his Board of Superintendents administered the schools. Moreover, the Board of Estimate increasingly sought to reduce the policy-making power of the Board of Education, creating serious conflict within the bureaucracy. The large size of the appointive Board of Education—forty-six in number during the Mitchel years—provided another bone of contention. Many thought the large board best represented divergent interests and permitted widespread community participation in school matters, but Mitchel believed a smaller school board would be more efficient (or perhaps more easily manipulated) and sought legislative approval for such a change. Efficiency-minded progressives—like Mitchel—viewed rising school costs with alarm, especially since these increases did not seem to be matched by greater productivity within the system. Attempts to move in that direction—in the form of larger classes, lower teacher salaries or, alternatively, a longer school year or a longer school day—met with strong opposition from teachers, adding to contention within the city's educational system.[4]

The most intense internal conflict pitted the Board of Estimate against the Board of Education; at stake lay the whole question of decision making and control over educational policy. Mitchel dominated the Board of Estimate, not only as mayor but in prior years when he served as president of the Board of Aldermen (which also gave him membership and three votes on the Board of Estimate). The Board of Education, headed from 1913 to 1916 by Tammany leader Thomas W. Churchill, fought to retain its authority over the schools—authority gradually slipping to the Board of Estimate because of its command of appropriations. In 1911 and 1912, when Mitchel headed the Board of Estimate's Committee on School Inquiry, the outlines of conflict clearly emerged.[5]

The Committee on School Inquiry hired the noted Harvard education professor Paul H. Hanus and several other outside educational experts to conduct a thorough examination of school affairs. Mitchel seemed primarily interested in probing budgetary matters, implying in his instructions to the investigators that there were irregularities in the methods used by the Board of Education to estimate annual financial needs. The Hanus inquiry lasted more than a year. The final report made to Mitchel's committee pointed to numerous defects in the city's schools—from teaching and curriculum to administration and supervision. Many of the committee's recommendations promised not only improved education but financial savings as well.[6] One section of the report, however, written by Ernest C. Moore of Yale University, was rejected by the Board of Estimate because it criticized the increased political control of the schools, suggesting that the Board of Education should make policy without interference from municipal government. The Board of Estimate then commissioned Frank J. Goodnow of Columbia University and Frederic C. Howe of the People's Institute to prepare a second report on this subject. As expected, Goodnow and Howe endorsed municipal control of the schools as a means of greater efficiency and further savings. Mitchel's role on the Committee on School Inquiry, then, revealed his determination to assert authority over the Board of Education, bring centralized and scientific management to the school system, and cut back on excessive expenditures for buildings and programs—policies he emphasized as mayor.[7]

But the Hanus report was also a typically progressive document. It not only demonstrated concern for efficiency, savings, and financial accountability, but sought as well to upgrade the quality and broaden the scope of schooling, bring the curriculum into the twentieth century, make education a preparation for life, and introduce important innovations such as cooperative education in the high schools and pre-vocational training in the elementary schools. At about the same time the Public Education Association (PEA) similarly urged reforms in the public schools, noting especially the need for a thorough program of industrial education. Mitchel's election as mayor in November, 1913 encouraged his progressive friends and supporters in the PEA to intensify their campaign to implement these school reforms.[8]

Thus, by the time he took office on January 1, 1914, Mayor Mitchel not only recognized the schools as one of his major problems, but he had acquired considerable knowledge and expertise about them. He resolved to bring efficiency to this branch of city administration, as well as to others, even if it meant asserting political control over the Board of Education. And he firmly believed that better education could be had for less money—a conclusion emphasized in the Hanus report. Cooperative programs with industry, pre-vocational training, and other progressive educational reforms could be introduced without extravagant expenditures. The school plan developed by Superintendent of Schools William A. Wirt in Gary, Indiana, seemed to promise fulfillment of both progressive goals.

Wirt's Gary system embodied both efficiency and curriculum enrichment. The lesson of Gary's platoon schools was not lost on efficiency-minded progressives. With some additional facilities, Wirt had apparently succeeded in squeezing twice as many students into the schools. Yet educational programs had been expanded. Here was the kind of productivity, accompanied by an enriched curriculum and potentially tremendous financial savings, which Mitchel sought for New York City. Although it had not mentioned the Gary plan, the report of the Committee on School Inquiry had urged changes in the New York schools designed to bring many of the same results. Wirt spoke at a teachers' conference in New York City in October, 1912, during the Hanus investigation, and the newspapers noted the advantages of his program. By 1912 specialists in vocational guidance had begun to advocate the Gary plan. And shortly after Mitchel's election Abraham Flexner of the Public Education Association began to promote the Gary system as well.[9]

The critical problems of overcrowded classrooms, part-time schooling, inadequate vocational training, an outdated curriculum, and excessive educational costs faced Mitchel as he assumed office in January, 1914. Within a month a progressive member of the Board of Education, Ira S. Wile, reminded Mitchel of serious shortcomings in industrial training in the city's schools and suggested that the Board of Education sponsor a vocational survey. For the job Wile recommended Alice Barrows, a former teacher and social worker who had studied with John Dewey at Columbia and had previously investigated vocational education for the PEA. Barrows provided the Mitchel administration with much of its early information on the Gary schools and proved a persistent and persuasive advocate of the new plan.[10] In March of 1914 several PEA and New York City school officials made separate trips to Gary, in each case describing the Wirt plan in glowing terms in their reports. By April one of the visitors, Principal William McAndrew of New York's Washington Irving High School, could write that "a number of the big men here are getting a Gary longing that is tremenjus [sic] ."[11] In June Mayor Mitchel, City Comptroller William A. Prendergast, Board of Education President Thomas W. Churchill, and other city officials traveled to the Midwest to examine personally the schools of Gary and discuss educational matters with Wirt. Favorably impressed, Mitchel soon hired Wirt as a part-time consultant to the Board of Estimate. Spending one week per month in New York City at an annual salary of $10,000—almost double his regular salary of $6,000 in Gary and equal to school Superintendent William H. Maxwell's full-time salary—Wirt was to supervise installation of the Gary plan in selected elementary schools on an experimental basis.[12] Mitchel was clearly optimistic that extension of the Gary system of platoon schools would end part-time schooling, improve industrial training, and provide better education—all at greatly reduced cost. The city administration, he later noted, was not prepared "to waste large amounts of public money on an inert educational administration"; adoption of the Gary plan would enable the city "to finance an infinitely richer and more practical education for its children."[13] For Mayor Mitchel and his supporters, the Gary school plan had become a panacea.

Within a month of beginning his New York work, Wirt had reorganized two elementary schools on the Gary plan. At P.S. 89 in Brooklyn, one of the most overcrowded schools in the city, modification of existing rooms and the addition of some specialized equipment helped establish the platoon system. Similar changes were made in another overcrowded school, P.S. 45 in the Bronx. Wirt contended that the Gary system was only partially complete in both schools, and that numerous additional facilities (gymnasium, playground, swimming pool, library, auditorium, workshops, and a long list of equipment) were necessary before a full test of the program could be made. Nevertheless, Mitchel and even the Board of Education remained optimistic about the larger possibilities of Wirt's innovations. In December, 1914, the Board of Education asked Wirt to draw up plans for a platoon program in eleven additional Bronx elementary schools.[14]

John Purroy Mitchel proved an impatient reformer. In the fall of 1915 he sought to expand the Gary system to all elementary schools throughout the city. In a letter of September 27 to school board President Churchill advocating the extension, Mitchel noted that the earlier demonstrations in Brooklyn and the Bronx had been successful. Considering the city's financial burdens, he wrote, "it is fortunate that we have available a method of utilizing the existing school facilities which will enable us to keep down expenses for new buildings and equipment, while actually improving the quality of education."[15] City Comptroller William A. Prendergast reiterated these points in an article in the *American Review of Reviews* entitled

"Why New York City Needs a New School Plan." The Gary system, Prendergast contended, was "the only plan that has presented a real germ of relief to New York City's difficult school problem, considered from the viewpoint of both education and finance."[16] Reinforcing its determination to promote Wirt's school reforms, the Board of Estimate, dominated by Mitchel and Prendergast, refused to increase the 1916 budget of the Board of Education above the appropriation of the previous year. The practical result of this decision was to prevent the construction of any new school buildings, making the Gary plan the only immediate and viable alternative to overcrowding in many parts of the city.[17]

Churchill viewed these efforts by the mayor and the Board of Estimate as improper meddling in the affairs of the Board of Education. Although he had originally praised Wirt's schools in Gary and endorsed the Gary experiment in New York, Churchill grew increasingly disenchanted. He felt Mitchel was pushing the Gary plan before it had been properly evaluated in the trial schools. He believed the administration's excessive concern with financial savings would undercut the quality of education in the schools. He was not convinced that the Gary plan meant better education at less cost. Moreover, he preferred another experimental plan for industrial training and duplicate organization being tried out in several schools—a plan devised by William L. Ettinger, an associate superintendent of schools in New York City, which required fewer changes in curriculum and less costly equipment.[18] Finally, Churchill objected to the way in which Mitchel and the Board of Estimate sought to usurp the school board's authority and dictate educational policy. In testimony before a legislative committee Churchill asserted that the Mitchel administration's proposed bill for a small Board of Education would destroy the board's independence and politicize the schools. He also went on record as opposing the mayor's power to appoint members of the Board of Education. Churchill lost these particular battles—he was replaced as president of the board in 1916 by the progressive Mitchel-supporter William G. Willcox, and the small board bill was passed in 1917—but the larger struggle over extension of the Gary schools continued.[19]

2

Mitchel's effort to whip the school board into line on the Gary issue was accompanied by a vigorous campaign to sell the Gary plan to New Yorkers. While Mitchel and Wirt were absorbed by the political and administrative problems accompanying the switch to the Gary plan, the task of promoting and propagandizing the school innovation was assumed almost single-handedly by Alice Barrows, a tireless activist for educational reform who served as Wirt's personal secretary in New York beginning early in 1915. Barrows was a natural and logical choice for the job. Her entire adult life had been spent in educational work. As director of the PEA's Vocational Educational Survey through 1914, she developed contacts in the Mitchel administration, on the Board of Education, and in the school bureaucracy. Moreover, she had numerous influential friends and acquaintances among radicals, reformers, intellectuals, educators, social workers, and journalists. She was dedicated to significant reform in public schooling, which she came to identify almost entirely with the Gary plan. At the same time this commitment was transformed into an intense loyalty to Wirt himself. And finally, she had unbounded energy and enthusiasm for her work. Interestingly, Barrows's salary of $200 a month came not from Wirt's $10,000 consultant fee, but from an additional $10,000 Wirt received annually from U.S. Steel's Elbert H. Gary to promote the Gary school plan.[20]

Essentially, Alice Barrows's job was that of full-time promoter and publicist. She conceived her task as one of overcoming bureaucratic and political opposition to the platoon plan, of selling school reform to New Yorkers. On taking the job early in 1915, she immediately began an ambitious program for shaping public attitudes. "I tried to reach different groups of people who would have influence in moulding public opinion," Barrows reported to Wirt in January, 1915. She took to lunch the three editors (Paul Kellogg, Graham Taylor, Jr., and Winthrop D. Lane) of the nation's leading social welfare journal, the *Survey,* successfully convincing them to run a number of positive articles on the Gary schools. A few days later she met with Herbert Croly and Walter Lippmann, editors of the new progressive magazine the *New Republic.* This meeting led to Randolph Bourne's series of favorable articles on the Gary schools, later expanded into a laudatory book. Both the *Survey* and the *New Republic* remained firm supporters of the plan over the next several years. Furthermore, Barrows set up meetings between Wirt and a number of influential New Yorkers: settlement leaders Lillian Wald, Florence Kelley, and Frances Perkins; several university people, including John and Evelyn Dewey and Charles and Mary Beard at Columbia; and leaders of such philanthropic groups as the Federation for Child Study and the National Child Labor Committee. These first efforts seemed productive; Barrows reported "some good seed has been sown and the main thing is for those of us who are on the spot to unobtrusively but persistently cultivate it."[21]

Alice Barrows was certainly persistent, but she was anything but unobtrusive. She promoted the Gary experiment in the most conspicuous ways possible. Arranging Wirt's appointment and speaking schedule for the time he spent in New York, she made sure he met the most prominent and influential people and spoke at the largest and most notable gatherings. Barrows herself spoke at innumerable meetings of parent, teacher, civic, neighborhood, religious, welfare, and labor groups. She accompanied prominent citizens and civic leaders on visits to schools converted to the platoon plan. She lined up a number of additional supporters for the Gary plan. Muckraking journalist Rheta Childe Dorr, for instance, conducted "a big crusade" for the Gary system in a regular column on education for the *New York Mail.* Agnes de Lima, social reform activist and executive secretary of the Women's Municipal League, wrote pamphlets on the Gary plan, contributed articles to neighborhood newspapers, challenged critics of the new school idea, and worked closely with Barrows. Howard Nudd, director of the PEA, bombarded the *New York Times* with letters and wrote several influential reports and articles, actively continuing the PEA's support of the Gary plan. Before long school reform became a matter of considerable interest in the city. Both New York University and Columbia University planned summer school courses on the Gary plan for teachers. And a seemingly unending stream of articles kept its main features before readers of scholarly journals, popular magazines, religious publications, and radical periodicals such as the *Masses* and the *Liberator.* [22]

Barrows promoted the Gary plan in other ways as well. She cultivated Mayor Mitchel and his aides. Mitchel's private secretary Paul Wilson was especially helpful, as was Wilson's wife Frances Perkins, later Franklin D. Roosevelt's secretary of labor. (Barrows and the Wilsons were close personal friends and lived in the same apartment building on Waverly Place in Greenwich Village.) Moreover, she established firm alliances with staff members of the Committee of Education of the Board of Estimate and Apportionment. She attended meetings of the Board of Estimate, the Board of Aldermen, and the Board of Education, challenged the way Wirt's recommendations were often distorted when actually implemented in the schools, and fought against administrative delays in extending the Gary plan. Realist that she was, Barrows recognized that school reorganization was being "continually hampered" by "opposition at the centre of the system." Using her contacts with the Mitchel administration, she sought, but not entirely successfully, to cut through this bureaucratic interference by influencing the school board's selection of district superintendents and principals, who were responsible for the success of the program. She also kept Wirt informed of her progress through long and regular letters filled with details of school matters and politics. [23]

Alice Barrows's enthusiasm was reflected in a variety of creative ideas for selling the Gary plan. Typically, she concocted an idea for a movie scenario. She described the plot in a 1915 letter to Wirt:

1. Incorrigible truant sitting in school with hands folded. Very glum. Everybody very glum. Teacher tense and stern.
2. Truant plays hookey, truant officer in pursuit, tongue hanging out with exhaustion. Appeals to parents, parents throw up hands, can't do anything with boy. Truant found and officer walks off with him, boy crying. 3. Truant back in school, very depressed. Same old teacher, same old drill. Everybody very depressed. 4. Truant runs away again. In his wandering stops to look at two or three boys working in a garden. Wants to play with them and wants to work with them. Discovers that they are in school—a Gary school. Great astonishment, but throws off jacket and starts to work. 5. Truant officer appears, tries to take boy away, boy shakes head, won't go back to old school, wants to go to school here. 6. Pictures of Gary school with truant happy and gleeful, with work, study and play.

This project never reached completion, but many other publicity techniques were successful, including a documentary movie of the platoon plan in P.S. 45. She was especially adept at orchestrating a campaign of written propaganda in newspapers, magazines, and pamphlets. Many pamphlets and leaflets were printed in Yiddish, German, and Italian to reach immigrant neighborhoods. These efforts became especially important as the Gary schools began to come under increasing public criticism. Like many promoters of radical causes, Barrows relished the idea of controversy, believing that the weak arguments of the opposition in favor of traditional school programs could easily be exposed and destroyed by debate on the speaker's platform and in the newspaper columns. As Randolph Bourne wrote in 1915, Barrows "seems to like explosions" and "believes in publicity, good or bad."[24]

While Barrows sought publicity for the Gary school plan, a handful of progressive educators within the school bureaucracy also promoted school reform. Predictably, Mitchel's 1916 appointee as school board president, William G. Willcox, publicly endorsed the Gary plan and its extension. The Gary system, he noted in an article in the *American City*, provided a "flexible and elastic" school program whose economical features made possible "richer educational advantages" for all children.[25] William McAndrew, now an associate superintendent of schools in Manhattan, became a strong spokesman for the Gary plan, helped drum up support through his contacts with newspapermen, and eventually was put in charge of all the "Garyized" schools in New York.[26] Impressed with Wirt's methods in Gary, Bronx District Superintendent Joseph L. Taylor supervised the Gary experiment in P.S. 45, urged expansion of the plan throughout his congested district, and promoted the new system in speeches, articles, and letters to his superiors.[27] The principals of the schools in which the plan was first tried, Alice E. B. Ritter of P.S. 89 and Angelo Patri of P.S. 45, were also enthusiastic supporters. Both spoke out for the Gary schools in local neighborhoods, at parent-teacher meetings, in reports to supervisors, and in letters to newspapers.[28] Apparently, teachers in the experimental schools favored the change as well; Ritter reported that in P.S. 89 all but six of forty-three teachers eagerly commended the Gary plan over the previous system.[29] John Martin, chairman of the school board's committee on vocational education, vigorously defended the vocational aspects of the plan against all critics. Martin warned, however, that excessive and unwarranted enthusiasm for the plan had its dangers, for unless city officials and educators prepared parents, teachers, and local communities for educational reform, "the volatile public which now applauds will be in full cry to run the system to death."[30]

There were many within the school system who sought such a result. Although replaced as school board president by Willcox in 1916, Thomas W. Churchill remained a member of the board and a vocal opponent of Mitchel's plan for full adoption of the Gary system. Superintendent of Schools William H. Maxwell considered Wirt an outsider, felt the Gary plan undermined traditional education by emphasizing "frills," and opposed the new system at every turn. Typically, after visiting P.S. 45 in 1915, Maxwell told the newspapers that "the only thing new was some children digging up a lot."[31] Associate Superintendent Ettinger, who later succeeded Maxwell, promoted his own less sweeping plan for duplicate school organization and vocational training while seeking to block full implementation of Wirt's program.[32] The Board of Superintendents, as the education editor of the *New York Globe* noted, had a "distinctly antagonistic attitude" toward the new plan and often protested the pro-Gary actions of the Board of Education.[33] Numerous principals also made known their opposition to change. Teachers came out against the plan because, among other things, it added an hour to the school day.[34] Adding to the controversy, Maxwell released a report by school statistician Burdette R. Buckingham purportedly showing that children in Gary schools failed to learn as rapidly as children in regular schools or in those which operated on the Ettinger plan.[35] With some notable exceptions, the weight of the educational bureaucracy was brought to bear against the Gary plan and Mayor Mitchel. As one teacher noted in a letter to Mitchel, "You had almost as well try to persuade the Hudson to find a new channel for itself on the other side of the Palisades" as change the bureaucratic nature of the school system.[36]

Hostility within educational circles was gradually transformed into more general, and occasionally political, opposition. Newspapers made the controversy over the schools daily reading matter. Influential journalists like Tristram Walker Metcalfe, who wrote a daily education column for the *New York Globe,* lost their original enthusiasm for the plan and became vocal propagandists for the opposition. Metcalfe believed that under the Mitchel administration the Gary plan was becoming "more and more, as each day passes, a device for reducing school costs and less and less a plan for enriching the educational opportunities for the children."[37] By the end of 1915 the public antagonism that some school reformers had feared became a reality. The opposition found its widest expression in local mothers' clubs organized as "anti-Gary leagues," a movement pushed by Tammany politicians, hostile schoolmen, and the *Globe*'s outspoken Metcalfe.[38] Using neighborhood meetings, public statements, and the newspaper columns, these anti-Gary groups attacked the educational reforms promised by the Gary plan. Both the Board of Education and the Board of Superintendents were bombarded with anti-Gary petitions from community and neighborhood groups such as the Mothers' Anti-Gary League of Flatbush, the East Side Neighborhood Association, and the Federation of Neighborhood Associations of the Bronx.[39] Despite a year of promotion and propaganda by Barrows and her associates, New Yorkers were still not ready for what they believed to be radical school reform.

The parental and community opposition to the Gary plan rested upon many complaints, both serious and frivolous. Some parents and organizations, for example, opposed Wirt's proposals for released-time religious instruction as an inappropriate or unconstitutional interference in church affairs.[40] Others conceived of vocational education as a method of forcing children into factory jobs. It was widely asserted that the steel trust and the Rockefeller interests stood behind the Gary plan. The fact that two of Mitchel's appointees to the Board of Education, Abraham Flexner and Raymond B. Fosdick, had been associated with the Rockefeller-financed General Education Board gave plausibility to the argument that the Gary schools were designed to stifle mobility and turn out "wage slaves" for American capitalism.[41] In addition, objections were raised about the departmental system in which elementary children moved from room to room for instruction in different subjects. One father claimed his daughter had been afflicted with the St. Vitus dance "because of the constant change of classes"; others complained of disorder and confusion in the corridors between classes.[42] Churchill added to the rhetoric on this point, contending in 1915 that "there would be no one to mother the little children" as in the traditional classroom. "A seat for every child" became the watchword of the anti-Gary forces.[43] Critics also asserted that the Gary schools were too noisy, that children played too much while traditional academic subjects were neglected, that classes were too large, that auditorium and play periods were improperly supervised, that workshops were inadequately equipped, that irregular lunch hours caused malnutrition, that swimming pools spread contagious diseases, and that the new educational "frills" were unnecessary and too costly. There was simply "too much freedom" in the Gary schools, one writer complained in the *Catholic World,* obviously "a dangerous thing for immature, inexperienced minds."[44] The Gary schools had become, one principal charged, "free-for-all circuses" in which children had "little opportunity to learn anything exact."[45] The very fact, one parent noted, that the Gary plan had "the support of every wild-eyed, long-haired, be-whiskered demagogue is enough to damn it without reservation."[46]

The intensified opposition to the platoon plan by the end of 1915 spurred Alice Barrows to greater efforts. She continued to plan Wirt's speaking schedule for the greatest effect and to lobby for the Gary schools among politicians, educators, journalists, editors, and leaders of religious, labor, and parent groups. Beginning in October, 1915, and running through March, 1916, she wrote a twice-weekly column in the *New York Tribune* entitled "What Is the Gary Plan?" which presented in straightforward fashion the advantages of the school reform and answered the arguments of its opponents.[47] She also began to recognize the importance of attending and speaking out at the public meetings of anti-Gary organizations to counter patent misrepresentation about the plan. Thus, she wrote Wirt on November 17, 1915:

> Whew! such a two weeks and a half. New York has gone mad on the subject of Gary, largely because of the agitation over the religious feature, and the opposition is using that feature to draw a red herring across the trail of the whole plan. Result,—Nudd and Agnes de Lima and Mrs. Dorr and Bourne and myself are having our hands full dashing about to cover meetings at which we are not supposed to speak, and speaking at meetings where we are supposed to speak. I'd give anything if I were ten people. . . . It's a great fight, but I wish I could be all over the acre at once.[48]

By early 1916 Barrows and her friends who favored democratic, rather than administrative, school reform had created their own organization of parents—the Gary School League.

Organized by a committee of one hundred women, the Gary School League stemmed from the realization of Barrows and other Gary school supporters that an effective campaign of publicity could not be carried out entirely through the newspapers and the other media. Nor was the backing of intellectuals, reformers, and civic leaders sufficient to win the Gary crusade. To be successful, democratic school reform and reorganization needed the support and active involvement of the parents who were most immediately involved. Tammany and other opponents of the Gary plan had accepted this elemental fact and had helped organize the anti-Gary mothers' leagues. Alice Barrows was not far behind in recognizing the need to broaden public participation in the Gary school campaign. For the next two years the Gary School League remained at the heart of Alice Barrows's aggressive effort to revitalize New York's schools. She served as its director, its chief money raiser, and its essential supplier of ideas, creativity, and energy.

Like the anti-Gary mothers' groups which it opposed, the Gary School League primarily disseminated educational propaganda. It attacked the problem of public ignorance and misinformation about the Gary platoon plan on many fronts at once. In May, 1916, the league began publishing in leaflet form a series of information bulletins explaining key features of the Gary plan. The group worked up several comprehensive graphic exhibits on the Gary schools that were put on display in settlement houses, public schools, and the league's midtown office. Along with other league leaders Barrows continued to speak at mass meetings, but she also set up a "school for speakers" so that pro-Gary parents could more effectively address small groups of people throughout the city. Foreign-language speakers were also sent into immigrant neighborhoods to promote the plan. In the Bronx the league organized committees in local school districts to take groups of parents to P.S. 45 "so that they can see what kind of a school they might have." Several paid field workers were employed to make personal visits to homes in districts where opposition ran strong. An organizer was hired in the Bronx to create pro-Gary mothers' leagues. Civic groups and social agencies, especially those at the neighborhood level, were enlisted for the campaign, and local groups of parents bombarded their aldermen with pro-Gary letters and petitions. The group also sought to combat misinformation among schoolmen, raising money to send ten doubting principals to Gary to get a first-hand look at Wirt's program.[49]

The Gary School League seems to have faltered during the summer and fall of 1916, but by 1917 it had been rejuvenated. The league reorganized in January, 1917, as an affiliate of the Public Education Association. Its staff was expanded, and Alice Barrows went on an aggressive fund-raising campaign. The organization now decided to focus almost entirely on reaching the public through a series of movies on the Gary plan. These films, which depicted the Gary schools in operation both in Gary and New York, were systematically shown in neighborhood theaters throughout the city. Each presentation was preceded by several weeks of intensive promotion by members of the league. Local organizations were contacted, posters placed in store windows, and leaflets and handbills distributed in factories, stores, and streets. Students brought home fliers urging parents to attend the showings. Numerous vacant stores were turned into temporary Gary School League offices, where literature was handed out and informational meetings held. News stories and paid ads were placed in local and metropolitan newspapers. And league workers began making streetcorner speeches. These preparations brought out thousands of interested and inquiring parents to each viewing of the Gary school films.[50]

As the November, 1917, municipal elections approached, and it became apparent that the Gary schools would be a major issue in the campaign, the Gary School League intensified its promotional efforts. The number of movie showings was increased, and a reported 110,000 people saw the pictures between June 1 and the election on November 7. During the same period about 200,000 people were reached by numerous paid and volunteer speakers at street meetings and indoor gatherings. During the week before the election, twenty-five speakers were in the streets every night. The league stepped up the distribution of leaflets and handbills, especially in subway stations crowded with working people. District headquarters were set up throughout the city to coordinate local efforts. The league also made a systematic effort to saturate the city's newspapers with information about the Gary schools, particularly widely read neighborhood papers like the *Bronx Home News,* the *Harlem Home News,* and the *Brooklyn Chat;* Barrows later reported an average of two news stories a day in the New York papers between September 17 and November 4. To generate further support for educational reform, the league sponsored formation of a subsidiary promotional group, the Parents' School League in Support of the Work-Study-Play Schools. This group, which had branches in the Bronx and in the Yorkville section of Manhattan (upper East Side), dispatched workers and speakers to counter anti-Gary propaganda. A Junior Gary League was formed among school children in the Bronx. All these efforts were coordinated with Mayor Mitchel's Fusion Campaign Committee, which set up its own Committee on Public Education to pump out additional information about Mitchel's school reforms. Barrows and other supporters of progressive educational change saw little distinction between working for the Gary schools and reelecting Mitchel. Thus, they had few qualms about permitting the Fusion campaign to fund the entire budget of the Gary School League during the six months prior to the election.[51]

Central to the Gary school effort in New York City, then, was the intensive propaganda campaign conceived and directed by Alice Barrows. Over three years she tirelessly worked to prepare the general public for school reform. The emergence of widespread and organized opposition to the Gary plan meant that the schools would inevitably be sucked into the whirlpool of partisan politics. And because of the opposition the Board of Education had moved much more slowly in extending the Gary plan between 1915 and 1917 than Mayor Mitchel wished. By the opening of school in September, 1917, the system had been implemented in only about thirty schools out of a total of more than 680.[52] The financial squeeze imposed by the Board of Estimate and the pro-Gary propaganda strengthened the opposition forces and made them more vocal. Schooling in New York City had become highly controversial. As Barrows later wrote, "Education was no longer a subject for ivory tower discussion. It was being discussed and fought over in the market place. In other words, it had become a matter of vital concern to hundreds of thousands of people."[53] Barrows, the propagandist, had done her work well—the Gary school campaign had sparked an acute public awareness of the schools. But neither Alice Barrows nor her colleagues in educational reform were prepared for what happened next.

3

Bringing educational policy into the political arena had its costs. The schools became open battlegrounds. Conflict between contending groups and political factions boiled over into unexpected violence. The municipal elections of November, 1917, provided the crucial test for the Mitchel educational program. They also supplied the backdrop for citywide outbreaks against the Gary plan.

In different ways each of the three major mayoral candidates brought the school issue into the campaign. Running again as the Fusion candidate, Mayor Mitchel stood on his record of reformed and efficient city government. The vocal strength of the anti-Gary forces led some in the Fusion campaign to downplay the school issue, but Mitchel stubbornly praised the Gary plan in speech after speech. The plan, he believed, was "the most valuable educational contribution of the last one hundred years." It broadened educational opportunities, democratized the schools, and eliminated the part-time evil. Like the city's educational reformers, he continued to argue that in the Gary schools children were "happier," academic work lost its "drudgery," and the educational program was richer, more free, more natural. Mitchel also focused on the system's efficiency and financial savings, although he emphasized that its educational features were more important. "This city," he stated in one speech, "can never afford to save money at the expense of its school children."[54] This last was a somewhat disingenuous position for Mitchel to take, given the ruthless way he had imposed the Gary plan on the schools. Indeed, the opposition found much to criticize in Mitchel's educational program.

Mitchel's strongest political opposition lay in Tammany Hall. Tammany politicos had early recognized the explosive political potential of the Gary school issue. As early as June, 1917, one observer noted that Tammany would make the schools "one of the turning points" in the fall election. But even before that it was obvious to many that Tammany was active in stirring up opposition among teachers and parents, and that the anti-Gary mothers' clubs and neighborhood associations had a strong Tammany odor about them. The Tammany candidate, Brooklyn Judge John F. Hylan, blasted the Mitchel school program and appealed to parents' fears and prejudices. Under the Mitchel administration, Hylan said, "the agents of special privilege have been controlling the schools." Behind the Gary schools, Hylan asserted again and again, stood the steel trust, the Rockefeller interests, and the "money power." The industrial and workshop training provided in the modified schools, Hylan contended, prepared children "only for the mill and the factory," turning them into "wage slaves" and "toilers for the trusts." The Gary schools ignored traditional academic subjects and stifled ambition and opportunity. It was a "makeshift" system which turned the schools into confusion. It was, Hylan argued in an appeal to ignorance, "a perpetual motion system which . . . exhausts the child, saps the vitality, enervates both body and brain, and leaves the little one unfit for either mental or physical activity." Moreover, the costs of implementing the Gary plan were exorbitant; rather than wasting school funds on frills and fads, the city should put a priority on new school buildings. Hylan promised to "banish this vicious Gary system" if elected.[55]

A more thoughtful line of criticism was provided by a third mayoral candidate, Morris Hillquit of the Socialist Party. Hillquit favored the Gary system, but contended that most of its best features had not been implemented in New York City. The problem lay in Mitchel's approach to municipal government. For Mitchel and his Fusion supporters, Hillquit charged, "the administration of a great community like New York is nothing but dry and cold-blooded business, the business of the business interests." Hillquit accused Mitchel of shortchanging the schools "in order to keep down the taxes of the possessing classes." The Gary plan, he contended, had been reduced "to a pure scheme for effecting economies in the education of the children by saving the cost of building schools and keeping down the salary list of teachers." Hillquit went on to propose an ambitious educational agenda for New York. The Socialist program included immediate construction of needed schools, reduction of class size by hiring more teachers, giving teachers a share of school governance, free medical and dental treatment in the schools, free food and clothing for needy students, free evening schools and public lectures, and the abolition of military training in the schools—all of this "regardless of the tender feelings of the tax payers."[56]

Hillquit rejected the Tammany approach of appealing to ignorance and fear. Some of his supporters, however, notably a group called the "Hillquit Non-Partisan Committee of One Thousand for the Children of New York and Their Schools," went beyond the Socialist candidate's stand. The group attacked Mitchel's "black school record," echoed Tammany on the links between the Gary plan and the Rockefeller interests, and hammered at the religious issue, for the released-time religious education feature of the Gary plan was offensive to many Socialists and Jews. Thus, there was some similarity between Tammany and Socialist attacks on the Mitchel school program. Both saw the schools as a central political issue. The essential difference, of course, was that the Socialists sought to use the schools "for the benefit of the masses" and for the building of a socialist society, while Tammany had a less grandiose purpose—the reacquisition of political power in the city. For Tammany, the problem with the schools was Mayor Mitchel, and the solution was to elect Hylan. The Socialists, however, blamed school problems on "the disease of capitalism." As the city's major Socialist newspaper, the *New York Call,* editorialized, the solution was "not to take the schools out of politics, but to take them out of the hands of the capitalists."[57]

From the time the schools opened in September, 1917, under an extended Gary plan until the November election, they remained at the center of political controversy. As one writer noted, the Gary plan had turned into "a grimy pawn in a very sordid game of politics."[58] Mitchel, Hylan, and Hillquit voiced their separate school policies at every opportunity. The newspapers were filled with the pros and cons of the Gary system. Both the Gary School League and the various anti-Gary organizations pumped out verbal and printed propaganda. Inflammatory streetcorner speechmaking by Socialists and Tammany workers heightened passions in the city's immigrant neighborhoods. Tammany, especially, sought to make political capital by misrepresenting the Gary plan and playing upon the confusion of voters. Socialists railed against the capitalist system and the schools which supported it. By the middle of October the school issue, which previously had pitted Hylan and Hillquit against Mitchel, aldermen against the city administration, and school officials and teachers against the school board, now brought mothers and elementary pupils into confrontation with teachers, principals, and police. The schools became battlefields, as the political conflict turned into demonstrations, student strikes, and school riots.

School violence began on the upper East Side on the evening of October 15, 1917. A crowd of about five hundred boys gathered around

P.S. 171 (Madison Avenue and 103rd Street), where the Gary plan had just been introduced. They stoned the building and broke school windows until dispersed by the police. The following morning the same group picketed the school. Older students from the nearby High School of Commerce, along with some parents, harangued the crowd of youthful protestors, which had swelled to over a thousand. Students who tried to attend were harrassed by the picketers, and some were beaten and "tumbled about," their schoolbooks seized and burned in a pile in the gutter. The strikers insisted that they would not return to school until the Gary plan had been abandoned. The students, a *New York World* reporter said, "howled and paraded, screamed and whistled and danced, cheered for Hillquit, and boohed [sic] the name of the Mayor until the arrival of the police." Assisted by teachers, the police broke up the disturbance, forcibly escorting some pupils into their classrooms. Other students dispersed to adjacent vacant lots and continued to barrage the school and police with stones, cans and bottles; another two hundred adjourned to nearby Central Park for a meeting, but were surrounded by policemen and truant officers and returned to school. Another large group of strikers made their way to P.S. 72, a girls' elementary school a few blocks away (Lexington Avenue and 105th Street), where they demonstrated again and shouted to the girls to join the anti-Gary strike. The police squashed this outbreak too, herding most of the demonstrators back to P.S. 171 in patrol wagons.[59]

But this was only the beginning. At noon, with students let out for lunch recess, the demonstrators repeated the activities of the morning. Disorders spread suddenly from P.S. 171 to P.S. 72 and to a third nearby school, P.S. 109 (99th Street and Second Avenue). Numerous speakers continued to harangue the pupils on the evils of the Gary system, militarism in the schools, and the Mitchel administration; a vote for Hillquit, one student orator asserted, was a vote against the Gary system. One girl on a soapbox at P.S. 72 attracted such a crowd that traffic ground to a stop on Lexington Avenue. Other gatherings were addressed by hysterical mothers, some high school and City College students, and a few men, presumed by the press to be socialist and IWW "agitators." The lunchtime streetcorner oratory had its impact. The *World* reporter described the results: "Little girls began marching around with Hillquit banners. Boys bombarded the schoolhouse with stones, smashing several windows. . . and the police swooped down upon the crowd for the second time." Blocking police efforts to quell the disturbances, groups of mothers ridiculed the police and interfered with the arrest of children. Nevertheless, fourteen children were arrested, nine of them under sixteen years of age; one of those arrested, identified as Sam Silverstein, was only eight. P.S. 171, where the agitation had centered all day, was closed down for the afternoon by school officials to reinforce police efforts. According to one report, more than three thousand elementary pupils from three schools had participated in the school strike at its most intense point. The same evening more than five thousand children marched through Harlem and Yorkville "shouting their disapproval of the Gary system."[60]

The newspapers uniformly blamed these first school outbreaks on Socialists and other "agitators." According to one report in the *New York Tribune,* neighborhood residents attributed the trouble to "an ardent street corner campaign" by Hillquit supporters. Other observers noted that the students had been "egged on by grown-ups." One boy, armed with a slingshot and arrested near P.S. 109, admitted to police that "a man had called him aside and urged him to 'start something' for Hillquit." The *New York Sun* observed that the political campaign had earlier generated "children's parades" for Hillquit on the East Side, implying that the school strikes had the same origin and the same purpose. Mothers interviewed by police, however, believed the disturbances to be the natural result of the new and unsettling Gary system—it "kept their children too long in school; it made them get up too early; it kept them so busy that they got home with ferocious appetites, which quite outstripped the family pocketbook." Some children claimed the longer school day interfered with their after-school jobs. The *New York Call* hinted that the disturbances were "an offshoot of the strikes that are taking place in some of the high schools against the introduction of military training." (A 1917 state law required an additional hour per day in the high schools for military training.) Later a teacher claimed that students from the high schools had "spread the spirit of opposition among the younger children."[61]

The school strikes continued on the upper East Side the following day, Wednesday, October 17. Although not as extensive as those of the previous day, the demonstrations involved several hundred students and mothers at the same three schools in Harlem and Yorkville, as well as at a fourth school, P.S. 37 (East 88th Street). Groups of strikers marched from school to school, shouted and sang, defied policemen and teachers, and mixed "leap-frog with indignation meetings." They carried Hillquit, Hylan, and anti-Mitchel banners and placards. P.S. 171, where 150 pupils stayed out of school, continued to be the storm center. But, "beyond a lively medley of harangue in several languages" and a police "scrimmage" with mothers at P.S. 109, these incidents remained relatively nonviolent.[62]

Newspaper accounts of the day's events continued to relate the school strikes to the political passions roused by the Gary plan. The *Sun* quoted William Willcox, president of the Board of Education, as saying that "some political agents have been busy in the affair." But the earlier allegations against Socialists began to give way to charges that Tammany had instigated the riots. Hillquit had endorsed the principles of the Gary plan (although not its application in New York), but Hylan had viciously attacked it for several months. The *Tribune* now laid the blame squarely at the doors of Tammany Hall. According to a reporter, "The outspoken criticism of the system voiced by Mr. Hylan . . . emboldened pupils and parents to participate in street demonstrations." A *Tribune* editorial was more direct: the school riots represented "Tammany's last desperate effort to fan the Gary school into a political issue. The strikes are unquestionably engineered by exactly the same troublehatchers who have been fighting the Gary idea with lies and class prejudice ever since the municipal campaign came within sight." "The whole affair smacks of Tammany," editorialized the *New York Times,* providing a taste of what "Tammanyization" would do to the city's schools. The *Sun* chimed in as well, contending that the riots resulted from Tammany's campaign to make public education "the football of politics."[63]

Tammany made headlines again the following day when new school riots broke out in the Bronx. "School Rioting New Tammany Political Trick," the *Sun* charged on page 1. Trouble began at P.S. 54 (Freeman Street and Intervale Avenue), where the Gary system had just been introduced and which had been the subject of a stone-throwing attack by three hundred boys the night before. As school opened on Thursday, several thousand children gathered outside the building and argued the merits of the Gary plan among themselves. The anti-Gary oratory apparently won out, for soon the strikers began stoning the school and then the police who came to disperse them. The crowd broke up and moved on to a nearby school, P.S. 50 (Bryant Avenue and 172nd Street), which had been operating on the Gary plan for two years with no problems. By this time the mob of student demonstrators had grown to more than five thousand. Encouraged by "grownups on the outskirts" and their own indigenous leadership, the boys and girls paraded in the streets, tore down Mitchel campaign posters, overturned garbage pails, wrote anti-Gary slogans on walls and sidewalks, smashed school windows, and chanted, "We won't go back till Gary gets out." Armed with stricks, stones, bricks, and bottles, they attacked the police who soon arrived in force. "Pitched battles" ensued, in which the children used garbage can covers as shields "to ward the blows of copper's sticks." And, as the *Sun* reported the incident, "good housewives from second stories jubilantly tossed milk bottles to aid their gladiators on the street." In some ways the school strike took on a holiday atmosphere, a mood captured by the *New York Call* reporter: "To the youngsters, the whole affair was a huge joke. They yelled and booed at the police, but as they ran they laughed with joy." Although the police seemed temporarily helpless, they eventually succeeded in breaking up the massive and unruly crowd. But smaller groups of strikers moved off in different directions, demonstrating and causing disturbances at four other schools—P.S. 6, P.S. 20, P.S. 44, and P.S. 55. Attendance at the six schools involved, and at some other Gary schools in the borough, was less than half the regular attendance. Many parents had kept their children home for protection, not for protest purposes.[64]

The same evening street demonstrations broke out in the Bronx again. Soapbox speakers attracted listeners on streetcorners throughout the borough. At one point about four thousand children and parents gathered for an open-air, anti-Gary meeting. Since no speaking or parade permits had been issued, the police tried to arrest the speakers and disband the large crowd. The demonstrators began stoning the police with such force that the officers, their few prisoners in tow, retreated to a nearby stationhouse, which was soon surrounded by the "hooting and yelling" crowd. Only when police reserves from other precincts arrived, accompanied by volunteers from the Home Defense League, was the angry anti-Gary mob quelled and dispersed. For a time some of the rioters regrouped at P.S. 54, where the day's disturbances had begun, again cheering speakers and stoning the school until arrival of the police. The seriousness and extent of the popular discontent and consequent violence in the Bronx had caught school officials and police by surprise. The school board ordered an investigation of the riots, instructed the Board of Truancy to catch the ringleaders, and warned of "sterner measures" to be taken against transgressors in the future. The police department announced a get-tough policy, but prepared for more trouble by posting a police guard at every school in the Bronx.[65]

The measures taken by school and police officials, however, did not halt the spread of school disturbances the following day, Friday, October 19. Trouble continued in the Bronx, where some five thousand rioting students went on strike at P.S. 42 (Claremont Parkway and Washington Avenue), paraded in the streets, stoned the building, and made things "extremely lively for a number of policemen." Police dispersed the crowd several times, arresting some students and mothers. Groups of striking boys and girls re-formed in nearby Crotona Park and marched to two other schools in the Bronx, P.S. 55 (Claremont Parkway and St. Paul's Place) and P.S. 53 (Findley and Teller Avenues), where less serious outbreaks occurred. Attendance was down as much as one-half at several other Gary schools in the borough. Disorders continued into the evening, as children rallied at streetcorner meetings all over the Bronx. Several children were arrested, including a nine-year-old boy charged with "conducting an open-air meeting" and a nine-year-old girl who assaulted a policeman.[66]

But while the school situation remained volatile in the Bronx, the most intense violence of the day occurred in the Brownsville and Williamsburg sections of Brooklyn, where rioting broke out for the first time. At P.S. 175 (Blake Avenue and Bristol Street), a crowd estimated at four to five thousand, including about five hundred mothers, broke windows, stoned the police, and forced the school to close down for the day. The aggressive mob of boys and girls also attacked a group of police reserves standing by in nearby Betsy Head Park. Reacting to charges of police brutality in previous skirmishes, Police Commissioner Arthur Woods had instructed his men to deal harshly with adult rioters but to treat children leniently. The student strikers did not show the same restraint, and four policemen were injured by bricks, stones, and bottles thrown from the street and from tenement rooftops. Next children viciously attacked an ambulance which arrived to take the injured men to a hospital; they slashed and hammered nails into its tires, ripped out its battery wires, and smashed its windshield. Police wagons received the same treatment. At the height of the disturbances about five hundred of the rioters marched to the Williamsburg Bridge Plaza, where they took possession of a statue of George Washington and used its pedestal for speechmaking.[67]

Other Brooklyn schools also experienced difficulties. At P.S. 50 in Williamsburg a crowd of elementary children smashed more than fifty windows and paraded with cardboard placards advocating "Down with the Gary system." At P.S. 72 older boys broke school windows and prevented younger pupils from entering the building. At P.S. 110 some rioting occurred and teachers were warned to stay away. At P.S. 125 big demonstrations convinced all but twelve students to stay out of school. Strikes and smaller riots also hit P.S. 165 and P.S. 174, both in Brooklyn. "The revolutionary spirit of the children," the *New York Call* asserted, "was remarkable." When sixteen Brooklyn schools were closed at midday, each protected by a special police detail, a semblance of order was restored in the borough.[68]

By week's end school and police officials seemed confident, at least publicly, that the school riots had run their course and that passions would cool during the weekend. These hopes quickly proved illusory. Over the weekend rumors of more trouble in Brooklyn and the Bronx swept the city, the *New York World* reported a plot against schools on the lower East Side, and several schools were stoned.[69] Charges and counter-charges covered the pages of the city's newspapers. Editorials blamed Tammany for turning the mayoral campaign into a "class war" by "capitalizing the ignorance of great alien populations in New York City." Mitchel supporters in the Fusion Committee and in the Gary School League also pointed to Tammany Hall. "The Tiger has ripped a few school doors open with his paw," charged John Collier, chairman of the Fusion campaign's Committee

on Public Education. In several speeches Mayor Mitchel blasted Judge
Hylan and Tammany chieftain Charles F. Murphy. Mitchel charged that
Tammany leaders, obviously desperate for votes, had "conceived the plan
of creating riots among the school children of New York, creating the
appearance of great popular uprising against the work, study and play
school plan." It was "a prostitution of the public school system," an act
of "public degradation" designed solely for "base political purposes."
Others continued to blame Socialist agitators, "IWW juveniles," or dis-
gruntled high school students. Meanwhile Hylan continued his attack on
Mitchel and the Gary plan in several speeches. Not surprisingly, renewed
disturbances marred the opening of the schools on Monday morning.[70]

In the Bronx students returned to their classrooms "as meek as lambs,"
and school officials reported 80 percent attendance at troubled schools.
But ten thousand truants in Brooklyn and about half that number in Manhattan kept principals, teachers, and police busy. Disturbances wracked at
least six elementary schools in the Brownsville section of Brooklyn (P.S.
174, P.S. 175, P.S. 32, P.S. 66, P.S. 84, and P.S. 167). Large numbers of
police stationed around the school buildings minimized property damage,
but the children nevertheless paraded with Hillquit and anti-Gary banners,
stopped those seeking to attend classes, and threw stones, potatoes, and
other vegetables "commandeered from pushcarts." Implementing a plan
contrived over the weekend, school officials sent batches of truant officers
to the schools involved, but when they began seizing boys and girls, numerous mothers, fathers, and older brothers came to the rescue. Several participants were arrested and several hundred children captured as truants.
School strikes also returned to Manhattan, this time on the lower East
Side, where about five thousand chanting and shouting pupils marched
and demonstrated in front of seven schools (P.S. 13, P.S. 25, P.S. 62,
P.S. 63, P.S. 79, P.S. 91, P.S. 97). Although none of these schools had
been converted to the Gary plan, the rumor that the new system was
about to be installed provided sufficient inducement to action. The strikers
carried anti-Gary posters, held streetcorner protest meetings, and stoned
the schools. Police broke up the demonstrators, who regrouped several
times for further protest. Reversing their earlier tactics of dispersing crowds
rather than making arrests, the police arrested sixty-five student rioters.
Yet the police still seemed generally ineffective, and one officer admitted
to a reporter that it was "impossible to arrest sufficient strikers to make
an impression on the rest."[71]

On Tuesday, October 23, the school disturbances tapered off considerably. About one thousand boys paraded outside P.S. 155 in Brooklyn
carrying anti-Gary and anti-Mitchel posters and banners, and a stone-
throwing incident occurred at P.S. 109, also in Brooklyn. At P.S. 37 on

the upper East Side, picketing students harrassed non-strikers and stole their schoolbooks. But with the exception of these fresh outbreaks, the school rioting seemed to have run its course and attendance was near normal in schools throughout the city.[72] By this time school officials had begun taking firm action against truants; several hundred students were expelled, suspended, or put on probation. Fines for violating compulsory attendance laws were levied against more than seven hundred parents in Children's Court. Pro-Gary forces sought to calm the fears of parents by intensifying their campaign to explain the Gary system and counter misrepresentations about it. The Board of Education began showing movies at schools throughout the city depicting the advantages of the Gary plan. The Gary School League, along with a new organization, the Parents' School League, stepped up its own movie propaganda, distributed literature, and held informational meetings for parents at parks, schools, and recreational centers. The Fusion campaign's Committee on Public Education sent out speakers, published pamphlets, and guided groups of clergymen, labor leaders, and parents through New York's two showcase Gary schools—P.S. 45 and P.S. 89. The indefatigable Alice Barrows followed Judge Hylan to political meetings, publicly challenging his statements on the Gary plan.[73] But although these efforts may have calmed public agitation after a week of strikes and riots, they came too late to save the Gary plan.

The school riots caused irreparable damage to Mitchel's candidacy and to the three-year effort to reorganize the New York City school system on the Gary plan. Stimulated by dissatisfaction within the school bureaucracy, inflammatory rhetoric of Tammany and the Socialists, and the critical journalism of reporters like the *Globe*'s Metcalfe, the Gary school controversy became a crucial element in the mayoral election. The school riots and the seeming ease with which they spread over the city's most populous boroughs demonstrated the extent of public disillusionment with the Mitchel school program. The Gary school controversy, combined with other grievances against Mitchel—his elitist personality and lifestyle, his strong support for military preparedness, his attack on Catholic charities—resulted in a Tammany landslide. Complete returns gave Hylan 297,282 votes to Mitchel's 149,307. Hillquit was a close third, with 142,178 votes—the largest vote ever for a citywide Socialist candidate. Republican candidate William S. Bennett, another critic of the Gary plan, received only 53,678 votes.[74] Thus, the administration which had introduced a wide range of administrative reforms in municipal government, which had promoted efficiency on the business and corporate model, went down to defeat. Shortly after taking office Mayor Hylan issued orders to dismantle the workshops and end the platoon school experiment. During

Hylan's two mayoral terms the city embarked on a massive school construction program with the aim of providing a seat for every child. Although surviving in a few schools into the 1920s, for all practical purposes the Gary plan had come to an ignominious end in New York City.[75]

4

Clearly, the Gary school riots in New York City had not been spontaneous. The pattern of each major school disturbance suggests planning, preparation, and organization. Virtually every school strike and riot had been preceded by evening meetings of local parent and neighborhood associations—meetings organized or dominated by anti-Gary speakers and politicians. These meetings were usually followed by smaller streetcorner gatherings, more speechmaking, and attacks on school buildings. Rumors about strikes, demonstrations, and violence circulated throughout the affected neighborhoods. Very often posters fastened to school doors announced the strike to arriving children. Adults and older children were present at each of the riots, often making speeches, distributing political literature, providing placards and banners, and advocating action. A Board of Education probe revealed evidence of adults moving "from one district to another encouraging the rioters at the height of the disturbances." After the initial outbreaks in Manhattan a city judge ordered an investigation of the role of adults in the school strikes, because, as the *New York Call* noted, "none of the boys brought before him seemed to know what they were striking about." "Like parrots," one observer remarked, the strikers "repeated the arguments of grown-up politicians opposed to the fusion administration." Investigation of the events by school and police officials seemed to confirm the politically inspired nature of the outbreaks. As a reporter for the *New York Tribune* put it, "Nothing in the Gary system as applied in New York would cause children to strike of their own initiative." Behind the parents and striking children, wrote Mary Graham Bonner in the *Outlook,* stood "the giant specter of Tammany Hall and the uncompromising pacifists."[76]

Tammany had the most to gain from the school riots. The strikes highlighted public disapproval of the cost-conscious Mitchel administration just prior to the mayoral election. As the newspapers suspected, Tammany had industriously mobilized anti-Gary forces. According to reports received in the Mitchel camp, Tammany worked vigorously in Italian and Jewish neighborhoods (most of the striking children were Jewish), sent ward leaders to visit the parents of school children, and even persuaded some teachers to explain the evils of the Gary plan in their classes. By

1917 many of the local anti-Gary organizations had been taken over by Tammany. Hylan men, including several Tammany members of the Board of Education, held leadership positions in several citywide groups: the Federated Parents' Association, the Parents' School Betterment League, the Federation of Neighborhood Associations, the Federated Bronx Neighborhood Association, and the Anti-Gary League. The *New York World* charged that Tammany had spent at least two years cultivating such organizations in preparation for the 1917 election. Advocates of the Gary system believed that former school board president Thomas Churchill, himself a Tammany leader, had a hand in the organized opposition. Churchill, however, denied these charges, blaming the strikes instead on the "unfathomable nature" of children.[77] Once the strikes began, Hylan encouraged the violence with inflammatory rhetoric. The school issue, as few failed to realize, presented Tammany with an obvious advantage in the political campaign.

For Tammany, the issues were used to regain power. As historians of bossism and political machines have noted, political office meant patronage and graft, contracts and franchises and payoffs. Thus, the school issue had broad implications for Tammany. Control of the schools could be translated into vast amounts of patronage. During past Tammany administrations, according to a critical writer in the *New York Call,* the bosses "appointed teachers who could scarcely write or read, so long as they were daughters of the faithful." The fact that so many teachers opposed the Gary plan and the Mitchel administration also suggests a strong Tammany influence within the school system. Mitchel had, of course, already incurred teacher enmity by working against salary increases, by requiring additional working hours, and by failing to consult teachers on his proposed innovations for the New York City schools. He recognized the danger of teacher opposition and in campaign speeches attacked teachers for "conducting a political campaign through the seduction of children of their schools to influence their parents against this administration." In turn, teachers formed a cadre of Tammany workers. Tammany, moreover, realized that expansion of the school system would require additional teachers, thus providing additional patronage for the machine.[78]

The Tammany machine saw other benefits in attacking the Mitchel school program. Generally, efficiency-minded and businesslike municipal administrations—such as that of Mayor Mitchel—sought to streamline government, reduce expenditures, and cut back taxes for property owners. By contrast, many boss-dominated political machines supported urban development and physical expansion, and they lavishly spent the taxpayers' dollars. Certain business interests—notably real estate, banking, construction, transportation, and utilities—looked with favor upon machine administrations which granted utility and transit franchises, bought and sold urban land, and awarded construction contracts. Graft, kickbacks, and payoffs became common in the conduct of municipal business, especially in the awarding of franchises and contracts. Mitchel's school program involved a reorganization of existing facilities, but Tammany wanted "a seat for every child." Obviously, such a proposal required a massive school building program. One astute writer in the *New York Call* saw the Tammany proposal for what it was: "It is only possible to make a political issue of the Gary schools because the economical use of buildings and facilities under the Wirt plan takes fat jobs out of the hands of contractors. Hence Tammany's position—Tammany being always pro-contraction." Thus, Tammany saw in the schools a perfect political issue. The elitism of the Mitchel administration and the alleged class nature of the Gary schools made the Tammany appeals popular in the immigrant and working class neighborhoods of the city. And the potential for new patronage, new real estate deals for school sites, and new contracts for school construction was not lost on the Tammany chieftains.[79]

While Tammany was out organizing the opposition, some Socialist leaders also stirred up local antagonism over the public schools, especially in the immigrant Jewish neighborhoods. In many ways the school strike conformed to an established pattern of Socialist agitation and street demonstrations in the city's Jewish working class districts. For the Jewish Socialists, there were three important issues involved in the Gary schools. First, many feared that the industrial education provided by the Gary schools would undermine the upward social and economic mobility of the children and force them into low-wage jobs in sweatshops, mills, and factories. Some anti-Mitchel labor leaders, notably Peter J. Brady, secretary of the Conference of Organized Labor on Industrial Education, in leaflets widely distributed in Jewish neighborhoods, linked the Gary plan with capitalist interests. Second, Jews and Socialists strongly resented the released-time religious education provision of the Gary plan, used primarily by the Catholic Church. Tammany workers added to the religious controversy, according to one Fusion leader, by "telling our Jewish voters that the Gary system forces the pupils in the school to learn the New Testament which our foreign Jews strongly resent." And finally, militarism became an issue among Socialist and pacifist Jews when in 1917 an extra hour had been added to the high school program for mandatory military training. These three issues became the heart of the Socialist attack on the Mitchel administration and the Gary plan.[80]

The recently dismissed Columbia University psychologist and anti-war advocate J. McKean Cattell organized the Hillquit Non-Partisan Committee, which led the drive against the added hour for military training and objected to the class character of industrial training in the Gary schools. Socialist propaganda had the effect of linking the issue of militarism in the high schools with the Gary plan in the elementary schools. Parents failed to distinguish between the two programs, since both required an additional hour of schooling, and thought the military training was part of the Gary plan. Many of the strikers in the high schools were Socialists, or came from Socialist families. They urged younger children to stay out of school as a protest against militarism and Mayor Mitchel, who strongly supported military training and the preparedness drive. One such student Socialist, George Cooperman, aged thirteen, who addressed a mass meeting of striking students at P.S. 165 in Brooklyn, was identified as the organizer of the Junior Young People's Socialist League. Thus, Socialist leaders, both adults and youths, fanned the protest against the Gary plan.[81]

The controversy over the Gary plan in New York uncovered an incredibly complex set of issues and vastly differing perceptions about the schools and their purposes. On the simplest level, the issues were political: who would be elected mayor and what kind of school policies would be followed. But, as cultural and value conflicts intensified, the school controversy became more confusing, more difficult to sort out. Political parties and factions with vastly different ideologies often shared similar positions pro or con, on the Gary plan and the public schools. Both radicals and reactionaries, as the *Jewish Daily Forward* pointed out, opposed the Gary system. At the same time, groups which united on other issues split over the Gary plan. An editorial in the *New York Call* in September, 1917, recognized the confusion: "Many of the teachers and principals of this city favor the system; many oppose it. But most do not understand it. Many of the most ardent advocates of the system are Socialist teachers and principals. Many of its bitterest opponents are Socialists. The fact of the matter is that there is as yet no consensus of opinion upon the question."[82] True enough. The issues were confusing and complex.

For Mayor Mitchel and his administrative progressive allies, the new school plan represented municipal efficiency at its peak, the application of the corporate model to the conduct of city affairs. Mitchel saw the Gary plan and his other school proposals, such as the small school board and lower teacher salaries, as necessary steps toward centralization and maximum productivity. They were technologically superior to the old system and facilitated elite decision making. The administrative progressives did not desire educational reform to promote social change. They believed innovations such as the Gary plan would make children into more efficient and productive adults in the emerging corporate-technological society, but they did not seek drastic changes in power relationships. This was William Wirt's position and it fit perfectly with John Purroy Mitchel's approach to government and to society. As his Socialist critics observed, Mitchel accepted corporate capitalism and he conceived of government and social institutions as bulwarks of order and stability.

The social progressives—Alice Barrows, Randolph Bourne, and their colleagues—shared the Mitchel administration's enthusiasm for the Gary plan, but for different reasons. Barrows and her friends recognized the technological efficiency of the new school plan, but for them the more efficient school had broader and more humanistic purposes—more freedom, more opportunity, more educational enrichment. It also meant less regimentation by the school system and less manipulation by the corporate power structure; children educated under the Gary plan would be better able to shape their own futures and deal with the realities of the corporate-technological state. Technology, in other words, was accepted as a given, but it was to be used for humanistic rather than impersonal business ends. Thus, Barrows and those who shared her convictions believed in educational reform as a means of achieving social change, of promoting what Barrows called "democratic social reconstruction" in the United States. Ironically, she at first accepted the Mitchel approach toward centralization to achieve her democratic goals, but gradually moved toward the necessity for local participation in and control over school matters.

By the end of the Gary school campaign, Barrows and the social progressives shared with the Jewish Socialists a belief in local neighborhood control. The Socialists, too, sought to create a humane society, and they recognized the importance of the schools in achieving this goal. But here the similarities between the Socialists and the social progressives end. Most of the Jewish Socialists did not believe the Gary plan as implemented in New York could achieve the good society. They viewed the new school plan, and especially its industrial training aspects, as a purely capitalist endeavor. They did not want their children slated for the assembly line or the war machine. To the Socialists and the immigrant Jews, the Gary plan represented capitalist manipulation and regimentation of children. Moreover, the Mitchel administration, they believed, sought to solidify class differences by denying equal opportunity in the schools. This conviction was also held by immigrant and working class parents, many of whom had accepted the traditional American rhetoric about the public school as the avenue of upward mobility. They did not like the politicians toying with the schools or using them to perpetuate social inequities.[83]

Hylan and his Tammany cohorts seemingly shared many of these same views. They rejected the centralization policies of the Mitchel administration. Tammany, after all, was built and functioned on neighborhood and local ward politics. The schools were considered neighborhood institutions.

Tammany originally supported the large school board because it more clearly reflected local interests and, not incidentally, could be more easily controlled and manipulated for political purposes. Unlike the Socialists and the social progressives, however, the Tammany Democrats did not seek any drastic changes or shifts in societal arrangements. Although their propaganda labeled the Gary plan a capitalist scheme, Tammany was, as a writer in the Yiddish magazine *Tsukunft (Future)* noted, "a capitalist party."[84] Tammany worked closely with and was supported by powerful capitalist interests in real estate, banking, construction, utilities, and so on; kickbacks and payoffs and graft helped to keep the machine well oiled and the bosses' pockets lined. Tammany did not seek any social or economic changes which would upset existing power arrangements. They simply saw in the Gary plan a popular issue with which to flay the Fusion administration, an issue which would put the machine back into power.

Thus, the Gary school plan in New York generated many contradictory responses. As one wit noted succinctly in 1917, "The Gary Plan needs only to be seen to be embraced, or, as the case may be, to be led out and shot at daybreak." Different groups perceived the Mitchel school reform in different ways. The issues were complex and confusing. Cultural values in a large and heterogeneous city like New York were varied and diverse, and there was no clear agreement on the meaning of schooling. In the absence of any consensus on the forms and purposes of education, it is not surprising that the public schools in Mayor Mitchel's New York became centers of controversy and even violence. While the results were not what Mitchel and the educational reformers intended, they were indicative, as a writer in *School and Society* noted in 1917, "of the interest which people take in their schools."[85]

Above all, the Gary school campaign demonstrates the important role parents and children can play in determining the kinds of schools they get. Most of the literature in the history of education portrays the educational consumers—the students and their parents—as passive recipients of schooling designed by professional educators, government officials, and business leaders. But the New York story reveals a different pattern. Parents and children, in a sense, took charge of their own educational futures. To be sure, political interests were busily shaping attitudes and instigating popular action. Nevertheless, it was the thousands of children who struck and rioted, and the hundreds of thousands of parents who rejected the Mitchel administration, who asserted their educational choices by their actions and their votes. The *Jewish Daily Forward* called the Gary school riots a "children's revolution," and in a certain sense the label fit.[86] Schools were important to the people of New York, important enough to battle over in the streets.

In Gary, where William Wirt was refining his platoon system, children and their schools were also of central importance. In the steel city, however, children and their parents were more passive than active participants, although not entirely so. Immigrants and blacks, for instance, often played a decisive role in determining the nature of schooling their children received. In the early years even Wirt, the architect of the Gary plan, recognized the limited ability of the schools to control children and was willing to share the burdens of child saving with other reformers.

3

WILLIS BROWN AND CHILD SAVING IN GARY

Trouble, oh yes we got/ Lots and lots a'/ Trouble, I'm thinkin' of
the/ Kids in the knickerbockers/ Shirt-tail young-ones/ Peekin in
the Pool Hall/ Winda after school,/ Look Folks!/ Right here in River/
City/ Trouble with a capital/ T and that rhymes with/ P and that
stands for/ Pool. Now I know/ All you folks are the/ Right kind a'
Parents./ I'm going to be/ Perfectly frank/ Would you like to know/
What kinda conver-/ Sation goes on while they're/ Loafin' around
that/ Hall? They're tryin' out/ Bevo, tryin' out/ Cubebs, tryin' out/
Tailor Mades like/ Cigarette Feends!/ and braaagin!/ All about how
they're gonna/ Cover up a tell-tale/Breath with Sen Sen. One fine
night/ They *leave* the/ Pool Hall, headin' fer the/ Dance at the
Arm'ry! Libertine men and/ Scarlet women! and/ RAG-TIME/
Shameless music that'll/ Grab your son and/ Your daughter with
the/ Arms of a Jungle/ Animal instinct/ MASS-steria!/ Friends, the
idle brain is the/ Devil's Playground. [*The Music Man,* act 1, scene 2]

Harold Hill was able to convince the good people of River City, Iowa, that
their children were on the verge of becoming irredeemable sinners, their
town on the brink of irreversible decay. Sex, tobacco, and idleness were
signs of a physical and spiritual corruption which had already infiltrated
the cities and was now, in 1912, seeping out to towns and villages in the
nation's heartland. A boys' band was Hill's response to River City's
juvenile troublemakers, and apparently it worked, even though comic
scenes throughout the play highlighted the dubious nature of the professor's scheme. Still, at the end Marian could confidently assert:

> Well, I should think there ought to be some of you who could for-
> get our everlasting Iowa stubborn chip-on-the-shoulder arrogance
> long enough to remember River City before Harold Hill arrived. Do
> you remember? Well, *do* you? Surely some of you ought to be grate-
> ful to him for what he's brought to River City and if so I should
> think you'd want to admit it.[1]

What Harold Hill brought to River City in the summer of 1912 was renewed confidence that mischievous and delinquent youth were not beyond redemption; that traditional values of decency and hard work were
still important; that dedication had its rewards; and that, above all, small
town America was not yet at the mercy of big city corruption and decay.
Such preoccupations, of course, were not limited to out-of-the-way places
like River City. "Child saving" was a central theme in progressive reform
endeavors, and many real Harold Hills became popular because they evoked
a pervasive fear that stability and progress were dependent on conditions
of child nurture in a period of rapid social change. Harold Hill and his
real-life counterparts shared with educators like William Wirt the conviction that they were in the vanguard of a vital and indispensable child-
centered search for order.[2]

Organized child saving began well before the Progressive Era. In the
early nineteenth century, reformers first began to establish special institutions for the nurture and rehabilitation of "problem" children. Public
schools, infant schools, reformatories, orphanages, industrial schools, and
children's aid societies all became popular before the Civil War in order to
cope with perceived family and communal disintegration.[3] By the end of
the century, however, these earlier efforts seemed increasingly inadequate.
In the aftermath of massive immigration, technological advance, and mush-
rooming cities, more strenuous and diversified campaigns appeared necessary to root out the causes of delinquency and degeneracy among youth,
to guarantee that even the children of "new" immigrants would mature
into law-abiding, God-fearing, cooperative, patriotic, hard-working adults.
Juvenile courts, probation, child guidance clinics, kindergartens, child
labor laws, visiting teachers and nurses, free lunch programs, truancy officers, boys' and girls' clubs, and so on, all emerged to obtain these results.[4]

Reform campaigns drew inspiration, theoretical formulations, and policy recommendations from the child-study movement, which began in the
antebellum period but reached maturity only in the progressive years.
Capped by the work of G. Stanley Hall, the movement attempted to lay
a scientific framework for programs to manipulate the instincts and emo-
tions of children into socially acceptable channels.[5] Hall and his disciples
stressed that both heredity and environment shaped the child. "Society is

slowly beginning to realize that Child Problems are the greatest problems
of our time," sociologist George B. Mangold wrote in 1910.

> This growing consciousness is a direct outgrowth of the increasing
> foresightedness of philanthropic workers and their continuous agita-
> tion in favor of preventive methods of social betterment. . . . It is
> slowly dawning upon the discerning philanthropist that the child
> is a bundle of miscellaneous propensities and is portentous of good
> or evil almost exactly in proportion to the training and opportuni-
> ties which he receives during the plastic period of his childhood.
> Therefore, the greater need of enthusiastic effort to mold the child
> into the symmetrically developed adult.[6]

Although some writers, influenced by Social Drawinism, eugenics, and
Lombrosian criminology, emphasized the paramount role of heredity in
child development, most commentators in the progressive period considered that view unnecessarily pessimistic. Mangold's evaluation was more
characteristic, precisely because it begged difficult theoretical issues and
placed a premium on action: "Attention to the environment of the child
both within and without the home is accordingly the *sine qua non* of the
solution of our child problems."[7]

Previous studies of juvenile reform in the Progressive Era have concentrated on major figures—Jacob A. Riis, Jane Addams, Ben B. Lindsey,
William R. George—to the neglect of dozens of others who, like Harold
Hill in *The Music Man,* attempted similar work on a smaller scale throughout the nation.[8] Gary, Indiana, temporarily harbored one of these ob-
scure reformers, Willis Brown, whose activities shed new light on the per-
sonalities, fears, and ideas of the more famous child savers. Moreover,
Brown's enthusiastic reception and work in Gary suggests the limitations
of the schools in controlling children during the city's early years.

Superintendent William Wirt believed fervently that schools should
carry the main burden of regulating children's lives, both to protect them
from the evils of urban life and to guarantee society's future prosperity
and stability. Nonetheless, during his first two decades in Gary he recognized that they were inadequate to the task of social control in the bur-
geoning industrial city. Wirt and his many friends among the city's elite
thus early sought additional means to monitor children's activities,
promoting such facilities as the YMCA, the institutional church, the public
library, the Boy Scouts, and settlement houses, all of which worked in
tandem with the schools to assure sustained vigilance. "The school does
not wish to monopolize the time of children but desires to serve as a
clearing-house for children's activities so that all child-welfare agencies

may be working simultaneously and efficiently, thus creating a child world within the city wherein all children may have a wholesome environment all of the day and every day," Wirt wrote as late as 1923.[9]

Truancy laws reinforced Gary's commitment to establishing better surveillance over potentially disruptive youth. Gary came under the jurisdiction of a 1901 state truancy law which provided for at least one officer per county. In October, 1908, the school board arranged to have the truant officer in town once a week; the following month the local district got its own officer. "The small *boy* who does not thirst for an education is going to get one whether he wants it or not," noted the *Gary Daily Tribune,* "for he will be under the eye of a truant officer at all times." School board member C. Oliver Holmes asserted the necessity for such an officer, for the city was plagued with "hundreds of truants that have not attended school a day since the term began." Moreover, he argued, the parents of truants took little interest in sending their children to school.[10] Though opinion divided on whether the child or parent was principally at fault, everyone seemed confident at first that truant officers would solve the problem by threatening to fine neglectful parents and commit truant youngsters to the state reformatory. This plan did not immediately work as well as anticipated, however; in July, 1910, truant officer W. P. Ray could still report 157 truants. Considering this number unacceptable, Wirt began searching for more effective methods to bolster the efficiency and comprehensiveness of the Gary school system.[11]

The arrival of Judge Willis Brown in Gary in September, 1910, provided an apparent solution to Wirt's problem. Like the founder of the Junior Republic movement, William R. George, and the world-renowned Denver juvenile judge, Ben B. Lindsey, Brown carried a reputation for being able to empathize and work well with troublesome adolescent boys. Though Brown's career had been checkered, he quickly gained support from Wirt, leading citizens, and numerous factory workers and their children. He was, everyone seemed to hope, Gary's Music Man.

Little is known about Brown before 1902. A native of Chicago and son of a north side minister, he became active in reform work around the turn of the century as editor of the American Anti-Cigaret League's magazine *Pluck,* "A Paper for Earnest Boys and Girls Who Wish to Become Useful Men and Women." At the same time he was director of an affiliated organization, the Christian Temple Boys' Club. Moral reform had long been tied to child-saving ventures, and Brown naturally embraced both the anti-liquor and anti-tobacco crusades. By 1902 he had established congenial relations with Lindsey, who also believed that the purchase of tobacco and liquor by children was the beginning of their moral ruin. Years later Lucy Page Gaston, a co-worker in the Anti-Cigaret League, testified that Brown, although "magnetic," had run up "bills of $600, paid himself $25 a week without authorization, and left with a grocer's bill in Evanston of $60 for the League to pay. I was almost a nervous wreck from the trouble he got the League into, and had to go to a sanitarium in Battle Creek." For the moment, though, Brown's earnestness was unquestioned and his reputation across the nation was excellent.[12]

Lindsey's support proved instrumental on several occasions. In Denver, Lindsey came to Brown's defense when the city's famous efficiency expert and school superintendent, Aaron Gove, tried to prevent Brown from speaking in behalf of the local Anti-Cigaret League. Gove claimed that he "'spotted' Brown at once, as a sort of fakir." Most tellingly, Lindsey supported Brown for a position with the juvenile court in Salt Lake City, Utah. As Lindsey reminisced in 1914:

> I received an invitation from Salt Lake people to discuss the Juvenile Court Legislation of the state during the Winter of 1905. Brown was there and immediately entered into the movement claiming to be a sort of representative of myself. He came back to Denver quite enthusiastic over the idea of getting a Court established there, and I gave him memoranda and drafts for a Juvenile Court Bill that I requested he see some reputable lawyer about before it was passed. Brown told me that he never read a law book, and I rather feared to trust the matter to him without legal advice from people on the ground. Instead of taking my advice, as I found out long afterwards, Brown patched up a bill, made up from the laws of Indiana, Colorado, and Illinois, got it through the legislature with a clause forbidding the payment of salary to the Judge—which he afterwards told me was done for the special purpose of getting himself appointed, since he said no lawyer would take it without a substantial salary.[13]

Though Lindsey cast doubt in this reminiscence on Brown's qualifications as a juvenile judge, it was somewhat hypocritical of him to do so. Lindsey had always insisted that a good heart, a capacity to love delinquents irrespective of their objectionable behavior, was the key to successful child saving. Moreover, his own conception of the juvenile court was so elastic and comprehensive that legal training was virtually superfluous to its social mission. Finally, Brown's patchwork juvenile court law for Salt Lake was not at all unusual. To borrow from Illinois, Colorado, and Indiana was to borrow from the mostly highly praised courts then in existence.[14]

Whatever his later views, Lindsey was most enthusiastic about Brown in 1905. "I want to assure you that I appreciate your good work. I want you to keep up the good work, and whenever I can help you you may count on me to do the best I can." Three days later Lindsey assured Brown that he was "delighted at the idea of your becoming the juvenile judge of Salt Lake and hope you will succeed." And in a public lecture the same year Lindsey observed of Brown: "I know of no man in the United States, who is any better judge of the best methods to bring out the good and suppress the evil in erring childhood. You will pardon me therefore if I say without hesitation that no one man in the city can be rendering a greater service to your people than he."[15]

Like Lindsey, Brown did not confine his energies to the juvenile court. In Salt Lake City he was responsible for establishing a Juvenile Betterment League, which combined the previous Anti-Cigaret Club and Boys' Betterment League in order to coordinate the city's child-saving effort. He also overcame the inertia of the local YMCA by convincing its sponsors to enlarge the boys' section and to sponsor frequent meetings between the youngsters and community leaders. Furthermore, Brown was instrumental in convincing several Protestant churches to adopt Social Gospel ideas. Under Brown's prodding Salt Lake Protestants actively pursued the ideal of the institutional church and recruited neglected children into club rooms, recreation programs, manual training exercises, and similar activities.[16] In short, Brown's efforts in Salt Lake were in the mainstream of progressive juvenile reform, though of course on a smaller scale than comparable programs in New York or Chicago. And like his idol Ben Lindsey, Brown was eclectic, inspirational, and capable of organizing people into a common reform crusade.

Despite Brown's popular crusade to provide "moral stamina and clean habits, clean cut Christian lives" for the city's boys, in early 1907 the Utah Supreme Court forced him to resign his judgeship.[17] In one of the most idiosyncratic decisions involving a juvenile court in the Progressive Era, the court rebuked Brown for failing to live up to the *spirit* of the court movement. The case in question involved thirteen-year-old Albert Mill, whom Brown had sent to the state reformatory for stealing a box of cigars. Mill's father challenged Brown's ruling, charging first, on technical grounds, that he had acted beyond his power and second, on due process grounds, that the juvenile court was unconstitutional. The Supreme Court dismissed the first set of charges and denied the second, but then affirmed, in what really amounted to an obiter dictum, that Brown had exceeded his authority by imposing sentence without first proving conclusively the elder Mill's inability to care for his son. Before the state could deprive a parent of legal guardianship, the court argued, specific charges had to be lodged against him. Because Brown had not obtained requisite proofs, Albert Mill was released—but only until his father was properly charged.

The Utah Supreme Court, however, did not stop there. In a remarkable personal attack on Brown, it alleged:

> To administer juvenile laws in accordance with their true spirit requires a man of broad mind, of almost infinite patience, and one who is the possessor of great faith in humanity and thoroughly imbued with that spirit. Those who come, and are intended to be brought, before the juvenile courts must be reached through love, not fear. . . . Their parents likewise must be met and dealt with in the same spirit. . . . The judge of any court, and especially a judge of a juvenile court, should, therefore, be willing at all times, not only to respect, but to maintain and preserve, the legal and natural rights of men and children alike. Respondent . . . either has not regard for, or is uninformed in respect to, the rules that the experience of past generations has evolved for the purpose of safeguarding the rights of all. . . . He seems to be a willing convert to the theory that he is better, if not wiser, than both law and rules of procedure, and that he may thus regard either or both at pleasure.

Coupled with a new juvenile court law in Utah requiring higher formal legal qualifications for judges, this pointed chastisement by the state's highest court finished Brown's career in Salt Lake.[18]

The decision of the Utah Supreme Court was anomalous at the time; its peremptory dismissal of Brown's methods, motives, ethics, and qualifications must therefore be placed in perspective. For one, the decision invoked mutually contradictory ideals. On the one hand, it spoke of the broadly humane qualities of love and compassion necessary to put into practice juvenile court goals. But on the other hand, it implied the need to respect traditional rules of procedure in juvenile court cases, rules which all leading court spokesmen condemned unequivocally as antithetical to the rehabilitative mission of the court. Second, more than its condemnation of Brown implied, the court vacillated on issues of civil liberty. The Utah judges refused, for example, to consider the elder Mill's complaint that his son had been denied specific due process safeguards such as right to trial by jury, to arraignment and plea, to suspension of sentence, to not being a witness against himself. The court's decision marked no new stand for the protection of civil liberties for juveniles. Instead, it represented an attack on one man whose faithful implementation of commonly held reformist goals threatened to bring the larger movement into disrepute. And third, very few judges in the Progressive

Era would have agreed that parents had constitutional rights which juvenile courts must scrupulously protect, or that parents had to be convicted formally of incompetency before their guardianship could be revoked. Indeed, most judges would have regarded this view as an unwarranted interference with the state's police powers, a refusal to recognize its equity jurisdiction, and an insidious attempt to undermine the court's mission by reinstating legal constraints. Brown's actions would very likely have been vindicated in nearly any other state; he was, in a sense, a victim of chance.

Soon after Brown's resignation Lindsey began attacking him in correspondence with other reformers. "Have been waiting to write you and tell you about the 'fake' I found Willis Brown to be," Lindsey wrote William George in 1907, "he is a crook pure and simple." Obviously, Lindsey held Brown responsible for the threat which the Utah Supreme Court decision posed momentarily to the juvenile court movement. Brown, Lindsey felt, caricatured the court by applying its goals too literally. Moreover, Brown's actions had revealed what most reformers generally downplayed, namely the potential for abuse inherent in the application of *parens patriae*—the assumption of parental authority by a court—to non-criminal youth. Lindsey was also perturbed that Brown had gone on the Chautauqua circuit in order to earn money and was telling Lindsey's best anecdotes. Brown even had the gall, Lindsey noted angrily, to claim to be the father of the juvenile court movement. "I can't let him cheapen & degrade a serious & sacred work by his buffoonery & plagiarism—do you think I can?" Lindsey queried George. These charges apparently became public knowledge, for Brown was forced to deny them. At any rate, he continued his campaign and tried to assuage Lindsey.[19]

In addition to his Chautauqua tour, Brown helped to establish a "boys' city" on Winona Lake in Indiana. This was an obvious imitation of William George's creation, the Junior Republic. Accompanied by a band composed of thirty youngsters (and still called Judge Brown), he addressed an overflow audience in Indianapolis on the need for a boys' city and urged the necessity of early intervention in order to rehabilitate youngsters before they appeared in juvenile court. The best way to stop delinquency at its source, Brown argued in imitation of George, was to group potential delinquents together during the summer months when school was out, and let them run their own mini-governments, businesses, and newspapers. After two years Boy City was moved from Winona Lake to Charlevoix, Michigan, where its reputation as a progressive summer camp continued to grow.[20]

Although an exciting summer activity, Boy City did not satisfy Brown's

sense of mission or his craving for a more established position. In Gary
he discovered a perfect location. A new city without entrenched leaders
to block his aspirations, or stodgy traditions to constrain his lofty imagination, Gary was rapidly developing the many social problems of larger
metropolises. Brown arrived in Gary in September, 1910, and presented
to the school board a vague but promising scheme for the prevention of
juvenile delinquency. Demonstrating his customary chutzpah, Brown
argued now not simply for a summer camp but for a year-long, permanent "separate school where moral instead of manual training can be
given. . . . The school would be a sort of reformatory and the transfer of
a child from the regular schools would be more for treatment than as a
punishment."[21]

Brown was well aware that there were diverse precedents for his ideas,
not only the Junior Republics but truant schools and student self-government organizations which were popular on the East Coast. He acknowledged
these precedents and used them to bolster support for his ventures in Gary.
Precedents notwithstanding, there was no denying the originality of
Brown's synthesis, especially his attempt to integrate the year-round
supplementary facility into the public school system. In so doing Brown
anticipated by several years the incisive critique of the juvenile court
movement by sociologist Thomas D. Eliot, whose book *The Juvenile
Court and the Community* (1914) called for the gradual disintegration
of juvenile courts and the assumption of their responsibility by the
schools.[22] As early as 1910 Brown suggested that juvenile courts be replaced by "a department of the schools for moral training." Viewing
delinquency as a "sickness of some kind," Brown proposed that "a clinic
be started [in the schools] and kept up by the local physicians to correct
the disease of children who are thought to be bad." Two years later
Brown enlarged upon his earlier ideas, calling for school-controlled
parental courts to replace traditional juvenile courts. Thus, Brown developed some original ideas regarding the role of the public schools in
combatting juvenile delinquency.[23]

Duly nicknamed "The King of Boys," Brown had his brashness re-
warded by Gary's adventuresome school board. Despite the assurances
of truant officer Ray in October, 1910, that truancy was already on the
decline because the "schools have been made so pleasant that the children enjoy the work," the board hired Brown, without salary, and placed
him in charge of a new Department of Civic and Moral Education.[24]
Brown's two-pronged program soon emerged. First, he established another "Boyville," a miniature children's government along the lines of
the George Junior Republic but integrated into the school system. Every
boy in the city between the ages of ten and eighteen was a citizen of

Boyville. Brown quickly formed two political parties ("Hike" and "Camp"),
followed by nominating conventions and citywide elections. Boyville
leaders soon began their own bank, newspaper, cooperative store, forty-
piece band, and assorted other institutions of a "miniature model city,"
all within the confines of the Gary schools. "In this utopian city there
will be no saloons, no cigarette stands, and no graft," editorialized the
Gary Daily Tribune. "Thus the boys in living up to the ideals of manhood,
may put their elders in an embarassing position." The child as redeemer
of corrupt adult institutions: this concept characterized the driving force
behind Willis Brown's child-saving crusade. By 1911 Boyville fever was
running high among the city's male youth, with Brown playing a discreet
but central role.[25]

Boyville was adequate to keep most boys on a straight and narrow path,
but what of children who committed criminal acts? For these children,
Brown developed a second program—a parental court and a parental farm.
The former would "provide probation before punishment to give delinquent children a chance to reform before branding them as criminals and
placing them in the state reformatories"; the latter would offer still another opportunity for "special instruction in morals" before an institutional
placement.[26] Brown did not disguise his desire to serve as the first parental
court judge and, as earlier in Utah, he took the initiative in seeking governmental support. After failing to obtain state legislation, he gained approval
from the Gary school board, but only after using scare tactics. The local
paper reported: "Investigations by Judge Brown within the past few weeks
have brought to light shocking conditions among some of the boys in the
city and the situation demands that a score or more boys either be committed to the state reformatories, or dealt with in a school set apart from
the public institutions where leaders of incorrigibles have secured re-
cruits." According to Brown, there was "a gang of perhaps twenty boys
. . . who appear to have an absolute disregard for the law. . . . Some of the
boys were found to be immoral, unclean and unfit to be among other
pupils."[27]

Superintendent Wirt and the school board enthusiastically supported
Brown. Quickly authorizing the purchase of property for a school farm,
Wirt emphasized that it "should not in any sense be used as an institution
for the punishing of boys. It should be solely an educational institution
for the education of the type of boy for which regular schools do not
supply the educational opportunity. In order to get into the separate
school it should not be necessary to be a bad boy."[28] Wirt's enthusiasm
for the parental farm is understandable in light of his own nostalgia for
rural life and the regenerative influence of manual labor. Equally important, though, was that the parental farm served Wirt's self-interest. As

superintendent of a nationally famous school system, Wirt was eager to blot out any possible marks against his pedagogical venture. Brown's scheme, he undoubtedly hoped, would quietly weed out boys least able to adjust to the Gary school system and thereby maintain its unblemished reputation. The parental school, in short, would both enhance the flexibility and hide the failures of the public schools.

The school board also appointed Brown head of the parental court. Arguing that they had the legal authority "to retain the custody of the child and transfer him to the parental school where special attention can be given to his moral development," the board vested Brown, as special judge, with power to hold hearings and "transfer delinquent children from the regular schools to the parental institution." Brown believed the parental court was the most humane method of reforming boys: "The child loses no self-respect and the truant or incorrigible child is on the same footing as far as school is concerned as the pupil in the ordinary school, with the exception that he is in a different school." Moreover, such removal would prevent contamination of "the clean, normal children when it is ascertained that any child has habits which are dangerous to the morals of other children." The farm would be "self-governing" and the boys paid for their labor, although charged for room and board—all designed to make the boys "self-respecting and self-supporting."[29]

With the basic machinery established, the *Gary Evening Post* announced that a new era in child saving had arrived. "By giving Judge Brown and the school authorities their support in this new school the parents of Gary can increase the efficiency of the Gary schools to an appreciable extent and they can save many of their own children from wrong doing, possibly from a life in the gutter. Get back of Judge Brown and it will be only a short time until the day of the truant child will be gone from Gary."[30] Notwithstanding his excellent local reputation, however, Brown continued to draw scorn from more prominent reformers, who still saw him as a fake and a threat to the juvenile court movement. "Our friend, Willis Brown, or his manager," Ben Lindsey informed William George in late 1910, "seems to have decided to swipe your George Junior Republic since I think Brown has 'swiped' everything that was 'swipeable.' . . . Dickey of Winona, Indiana, who first took up Brown and his Boy City, told me last summer that Brown was so dishonest that he had to get rid of him." To which George responded: "That man Brown is certainly our evil genius. . . . I think you and I would vote him the medal for consummate cheek. What fun you and I would have playing the game of Two Old Cat with Brown for the ball, wouldn't we?"[31]

Superintendent Wirt, however, was either not aware of, nor ready to lend credence to, such views. Even after receiving a letter from E. J. Buffington, president of the Gary Land Company, which alluded to Brown's controversial past, Wirt continued to defend him without reservation. Gary's delinquency problem would inevitably become more severe and beyond the control of the schools, Wirt admonished in 1911: "In many homes both the father and mother are drunkards. . . . The school can accomplish but little for the general education of the child. It is necessary to remove the child from this home environment before any headway can be made. This is one advantage of the separate school on a farm." The problem, though, went even deeper than that, deriving from Gary's unique status as a new industrial city without traditional moral constraints on aberrant behavior:

> First—In old established communities parents select the families with whom their children associate, and most homes have fences around their yards so that the children are confined and in a measure supervised by the mothers. In Gary the people are not acquainted with each other and very little effort is made to choose the playmates of the children, and since few homes have fences around their yards the children play promiscuously over the entire neighborhood. This gives a few bad boys and girls an exceptional opportunity to inoculate the other children in the neighborhood. Second—In a new community of this sort we have a very large percentage of delinquent children. People of this character are usually of a migratory disposition and move to new places. Also the close supervision of delinquent children in the City of Chicago is an inducement to their parents to move into the industrial outlying suburbs.

Finally, Wirt concluded, the county juvenile court, located in Crown Point, was simply too far away to serve Gary adequately.[32]

Wirt's confidence in Brown is easily explainable. Both agreed that to preserve social order in an era of rapid demographic and technological change, it was essential to instill school children of impoverished or irresponsible parents with traditional behavioral norms. Both emphasized the need to intervene in poor family situations to "prevent" delinquency. Both were ready to have the school system, if necessary, replace the home as principal socializer of youth. On only one substantive point did Wirt and Brown disagree. Whereas Wirt, in line with most juvenile court advocates, stressed the need to resocialize or reeducate parents of delinquent youth, Brown concentrated almost exclusively on the rehabilitation of children. His support for probation, or treatment of parents and children together in their natural home settings, was never more than lukewarm.[33]

Their attitudes were paternalistic. Just as doctors treated physical diseases, child reformers treated social diseases, such as delinquency. Neither could be self-cured. The patient might get worse or infect others. Both the diagnosis and the cure stemmed from the latest scientific findings and principles. Indeed, medical terminology was common among the child reformers of the period. For instance, as Lindsey commented to Wirt, "Brown is pretty well known to philanthropy as a notorious quack is known to medicine." Brown, in fact, believed a direct link existed between physical disease and delinquency, and he urged that all delinquents be given thorough physical examinations. "Many of the backward, truant and incorrigible children are sick," he stated. "I will not conduct an examination of any child sent to the Parental Court until I know the physical and mental condition of that child."[34]

By the fall of 1911 Brown was a well-established and respected figure in Gary. The parental court and parental farm were in operation; Boyville was channeling the extra time of students into socially acceptable activities; the first issue of the *Boyville News* appeared; and recent Boyville elections highlighted the civic functions which student self-government was designed to promote. "The idea of Boyville is to place boys on their honor then to trust them to play square," announced the newly elected juvenile mayor. "If a boy chose to break a law his own fellows make, then he knows unless he changes he will not care for laws when he is a man. Boyville is to teach boys square politics and how our cities and country is [sic] run."[35]

Though his responsibilities were many, Brown did not spend all his time in Gary. His personal ambition was always great. Imitating his one-time sponsor Ben Lindsey, he began again to lecture around the country on juvenile delinquency and juvenile courts. First in Pennsylvania, then in Louisville (where he was chairman of a committee of juvenile court judges to revise current laws), he attacked the operation of juvenile courts. He recommended their replacement by school-controlled institutions like his own in Gary, a plan by which "incorrigible children can first be given every advantage of public instruction . . . or, in extreme cases could be placed in one of the state institutions, but, instead of being sentenced, placed there under the guardianship of the head of the institution." Such a program, Brown asserted, did away with criminal procedure in juvenile delinquency cases. By early 1912 Brown had propounded his ideas in Buffalo (which established the nation's first so-called family court), Syracuse, Denver, Seattle, Los Angeles, San Francisco, and Portland. The *Gary Daily Tribune* proudly informed local residents: "All of the larger cities have been taking up the work earnestly and the Gary man has received many demands for outlines of his plan, which is becoming recognized as the most effective that has ever been worked out in the country." Brown's reputation for service to the community and the rest of the nation seemed solid indeed.[36]

What happened to Brown thereafter remains shrouded in mystery. Returning to Gary after his lecture tour, he left the city for good by the following summer. Though it is impossible to pinpoint the reasons for his departure, random pieces of evidence are suggestive. As earlier in his life, Brown's financial maneuverings appear to have been devious (in large measure, one may suspect, because he rarely demanded compensation for his services, even though he was not independently wealthy). The local paper claimed the Boyville Band "found itself heir to debts for instruments which were supposed to have been paid and several people were looking for rent and grocery bills." Understandably, "There were a number of angry parents who were pleased to see Brown depart." With his departure, the Boyville Bank reopened as the Emerson School Bank, and the band joined the YMCA.[37]

Brown's lack of personal integrity doubtless played a role, but his departure must also be understood in the context of the Gary school system. For one, his own parental school was clearly a flop, at least from Wirt's point of view. Rather than using the parental farm as originally planned, Brown had sent the great majority of delinquents to the state reformatory. Under his command the parental court became a vehicle for facilitating rather than preventing reformatory committals, while the parental farm fell into disuse.[38] (After his departure it temporarily became an agricultural school, then was sold in 1916.) Second, Wirt's effort to expand the school system's surveillance functions met with early success, and thus rendered some of Brown's program superfluous. In July, 1911, truant officer Ray optimistically reported that during the past year only eleven truants and delinquents from Gary had been arraigned in juvenile court, eight of whom had been sent to institutions. Ray attributed the low number to the "playground teachers [who] have done much to improve the cleanliness of the foreign children and to increase the interest of the parents, who are made to see the improvement in their children." "In the early days," Wirt wrote in September, 1911, "dozens of cases were found by the truant officers. Several arrests of parents were made and by dint of hard work, the foreigners were gradually brought to realize that they must keep their children in school. Last year the reports were satisfactory, truancy having decreased by a good percentage." The number barely increased the following year, with sixteen children sent to state institutions and another twenty sent home on probation (out of a total census of five thousand children). To Wirt and Ray, the problem was basically the lack of concern among foreign-born parents, who were now

being educated in the ways of their new country. Their view seriously contradicted Brown's emphasis on the corruptness of the child.[39] Finally,
Wirt and Brown may have had personal disagreements. Both, after all,
were egotistical men who craved national recognition. In 1912 they
were, in effect, competing to represent Gary's educational innovations to
the rest of the nation. Perhaps sensing a threat to his leadership, Wirt may
have attempted to undermine Brown's influence by withholding support
from his programs.

In any case, Brown's departure was little lamented. While the local newspaper observed that "Brown suddenly became disconnected with the school
organization and disappeared from the city," Wirt informed Ben Lindsey
that Brown had actually been dismissed. "We were taken in by Brown,
as many others have been," he wrote in 1914. "He moved here with his
family and as a citizen in the community attempted to start a great many
civic welfare enterprises. After a year and a half it became necessary to ask
him to leave the schools alone. He then moved away from the city and I
have not seen him during the past two years." A few months earlier, to
another inquiry, Wirt curtly responded that "I cannot recommend the
work that Willis Brown did in Gary."[40] Still, Wirt maintained some fond-
ness for Brown; at least his intentions were noble. Lindsey dismissed
Brown as "an ungrateful, irresponsible, unscrupulous kind of a creature,
exploiting philanthropy in a way that to my mind makes him much more
odious than the kind of crooked politician some of us have had to fight
in community struggles." Wirt was more charitable. To him, Brown was
less a conscious fraud than a man whose crusade to save children was un-
tempered by common sense or by a commitment to long-range planning.
"Brown impressed me as a man who would like to do a good work for
boys," Wirt reflected. "At first he created a great amount of enthusiasm
among the boys and the influential men and women in the community.
The matter had to run its course. I have always been inclined to feel rather
sorry for Brown, in that he does not seem to be able to confine his tremendous energy and enthusiasm to one definite sane proposition."[41] As
others would later hurl similar charges against Wirt, it was only fitting
that he recognized Brown as a kindred soul.

Meanwhile, what had become of Brown? He seems to have returned
for a time to Boy City in Charlevoix, where he increased his attack on
juvenile courts. In early 1915 he appeared in Salt Lake City promoting
his Boy City scheme. In December, back in his birthplace, Chicago, he
was arrested and jailed for allegedly selling worthless stock in the "Youth's
Welfare Film Company" to his boyhood friend L. A. Thompson, a railway
clerk. Brown maintained his innocence:

> Only a few days ago I went through Joliet prison with Gov. Dunne. I have visited many prisons, seeking to get an insight into prisoners' attitudes towards life. But no pseudo-term in jail could ever give a man the true perspective from the social outcast's viewpoint. Now I have it. I have been arrested. I have been denied a chance to speak with friends. I have been denied an opportunity to speak to Mayor Thompson, Chief Healey, or to use the telephone. I have felt the law's real grip.

This might have been the end of Brown, but it was not. In mid-1916 he appeared again, promoting a plan to establish a Boy City near Reno, Nevada. To the Nevada governor's inquiry, Wirt replied curtly, "I am not able to give you any information concerning Judge Willis Brown. It has been a number of years since I have seen him personally and his work in Gary was of such short duration and so long ago that I am not able to express myself definitely concerning his ability." By 1916 Brown had simply become a bad memory, the sooner forgotten the better. There is no further trace of him.[42]

What dare we conclude about Willis Brown, the man, and Willis Brown, the reformer? Was he simply a "crook," as Ben Lindsey saw him, an over-eager champion of popular causes, as William Wirt concluded, or a maligned man whose brashness and frank pursuit of fame offended better-known reformers to the point that they ignored his real accomplishments? With the limited evidence available, it is impossible to be sure. Clearly, Brown was nothing if not mischievous; that he provoked charges of financial impropriety and charlatanry so frequently seems more than fortuitous. Brown was also erratic, as Wirt claimed, unable to concentrate his attention on single ameliorative projects for very long. He was a publicist and a gadfly, not a practical man. Still, Brown also seems to have had a genuine, and rare, ability to relate to children in need or in trouble, and to inspire others to practical achievements like the creation of summer camps, boys' clubs, truant schools, parental courts, and so on. Moreover, there is no reason to accept solely at face value the harsh judgments made of him by more prominent reformers. Brown may well have scared Ben Lindsey and William George with their own distorted mirror images, for his actions, especially in Salt Lake City, highlighted dangers implicit in progressive child-saving ideology in general, and not simply his own personal liabilities.[43] If Brown erred in his application of the *parens patriae* doctrine, it was because he took the public statements of men like Lindsey and George too literally, not because he ignored them.

Brown's specific contribution in Gary was to provide temporary answers to perceived truancy and delinquency problems, giving Wirt time to mature his thinking and expand the complexity and scope of the schools' involvement in the lives of the city's citizens, children and adults alike. The superintendent did not arrive in Gary with his plan full-blown; rather, it gradually evolved, nourished by developments in the city and educational changes nationally, as well as by Wirt's own ideas. Indeed, not until the 1930s was the Gary plan fully matured. Some aspects of Boyville were later incorporated into the schools—the store, student government, the band, and other extracurricular activities—while others were dropped. Wirt's eclecticism allowed him to adopt what "worked" and reject what did not. Thus, Brown served his purpose.

Following Brown's departure, newer measures were introduced to check delinquency and truancy. For example, in 1915 the truant officer was renamed the attendance officer. "The attendance officer is no longer to be feared but is considered an advisor and an aid to the parents of school children," the *Gary Daily Tribune* commented. In addition, teachers were assigned districts of the city and asked to visit families to determine medical, social welfare, and other needs. Later in the year Wirt suggested the appointment of a woman attendance officer, a trained social worker, who would "go into the homes and teach the care of children and urge their attendance at school." A few years later a woman was appointed as the city's second attendance officer. In 1910, writing to Wirt, truant officer Ray had argued that "I have labored to create a sentiment favorable to the schools—have the people send their children to school through an *appreciation of its merits* rather than from a *fear of the law*—in this effort I have been most loyally supported by teachers." By the eve of World War 1 these techniques, aided by an expanding school curriculum and greater teacher participation, appear to have succeeded.[44] Not that Wirt would hereafter relax his efforts to extend the schools' reach into the community. Indeed, during the next decade day and night school enrollment mushroomed. Gary was not unique in this regard, certainly, but Wirt congratulated himself that success came because of the unique form and structure of his system. Perhaps so.

Nonetheless, Wirt was never satisfied. There was always more to do, more children to save, more immigrants to Americanize, more efforts to preserve small town structures and values in the urban jungle. His work was never done. Particularly challenging was the halting resistance of the city's recent immigrants, parents and children, to his programs and blandishments.

4

IMMIGRANTS AND THE GARY SCHOOLS

From Gary's establishment in 1906 its population was composed largely of immigrants and the children of immigrants. In 1910 some 49 percent of the city's residents were immigrants, while another 22 percent were native born with one or more foreign-born parents; over 70 percent were of foreign stock (see table 1—all tables will be found in the appendix). As late as 1930 over 45 percent of the city's population came from foreign stock. Naturally, the immigrant influx was also reflected in the Gary schools. In 1910 children of foreign parentage comprised 63.4 percent of the city's school population (see table 2). According to the report of the United States Immigration Commission in 1909, the nation's largest industrial cities had similarly high proportions of immigrant-stock children in their schools—71.5 percent in New York City, 67.3 percent in Chicago, and 63.5 percent in Boston.[1] The percentage of Gary's school children with foreign-born parents remained high over the next two decades—61.5 percent in 1920 and 50.7 percent in 1930 (see table 3). Thus, until the end of the 1930s the Gary public schools—like those of most other large industrial cities—confronted the challenge of molding the immigrants, both children and adults, into loyal and well-behaved American citizens, good capitalist consumers, and willing workers for the corporate-industrial state. The Americanization effort, William Wirt wrote in 1922, "is by far the most important phase of our work."[2]

Wirt was not alone in his concern for shaping the behavior and attitudes of the newcomers and their children. During the Progressive Era, World War 1, and after, the Americanization campaign became closely connected with public school programs throughout the nation. Fearful of the social consequences of mass immigration, most native-born Americans viewed the public school as a homogenizing agent, one which would break down immigrant cultures and traditions and secure adherence to more acceptable American habits, dispositions, beliefs, and values. Ellwood P. Cubberley, one of the nation's leading educators, articulated the goals of the Americanizers in 1909:

> Our task is to break up these groups or settlements, to assimilate and amalgamate these people as a part of our American race, and to implant in their children, so far as can be done, the Anglo-Saxon conception of righteousness, law and order, and popular government, and to awaken in them a reverence for our democratic institutions and for those things in our national life which we as a people hold to be of abiding worth.

For Cubberley and others, the schools were primarily responsible for the attainment of these objectives. The public schools became, as Boston Superintendent of Schools Frank V. Thompson wrote, "the chief instrument of Americanization."[3]

By the end of the nineteenth century, mass immigration posed special problems for public schools across the country. School construction programs lagged behind space requirements in the crowded immigrant districts of the nation's cities, forcing many school systems to adopt shortened or double sessions. The immigrant child presented difficulties from a teaching standpoint. Uprooted with parents from Europe or raised amid ethnic slums in the United States, these children had language problems and cultural patterns American children did not share. Moreover, immigrant parents were often illiterate or semiliterate, presenting the schools with additional educational tasks. Nor were all immigrants willing recipients of what the American public schools had to offer. Some ethnic groups, for economic, political, religious, or cultural reasons, rejected public education and resisted Americanization. As educational historian Raymond E. Callahan has noted, the heavy immigration from southern and eastern Europe after 1890 "constituted an educational problem unparalleled in human history."[4]

The immigrant influx and accompanying social problems stimulated numerous changes in American public education. By the early twentieth century kindergarten programs had been established in many large cities as a means of expanding the socialization function of the schools, especially in the immigrant slums. The kindergarten, editor Richard Watson Gilder asserted, was the "earliest opportunity to catch the little Russian, the little Italian, the little German, Pole, Syrian, and the rest and begin to make good American citizens of them."[5] Similarly, high school programs became widespread, extending the schools' influence beyond the traditional grammar school curriculum. To cope with demonstrated human and social needs, urban school systems established medical and health facilities and turned teachers into part-time social workers through visiting teacher programs. City schools became evening social and recreational centers, neighborhood institutions which served a multitude of community functions. Adults were drawn to the schools in increasing numbers for instruction in citizenship and English, for vocational courses, and for lectures, dramatics, sports, and other educational programs. The immigrant tide, then, was accompanied by a substantial expansion of school programs and activities.[6] In many ways the schools seemed innovative in dealing with the educational challenge posed by immigration.

But in other ways the schools seemed less innovative, for their purposes remained unchanged. As has been noted, in addition to their cognitive functions, schools have been designed to shape the behavioral development of children. As socializing agents seeking to produce loyal citizens and docile workers, schools manipulated behavior and values. Through testing and tracking, they sorted children into predetermined slots in the social and economic structure. As educational historian Joel Spring has recently noted, such socialization, or adaptation to the prevailing economic and social system, usually entailed "shaping a social character that would submit to the authority and goals of a capitalist society and would seek the security and order of a role within the bureaucratic enterprise."[7] For immigrant and native-born children alike, then, schools developed programs promoting conformity, cooperation, industriousness, thrift, temperance, cleanliness, patriotism, punctuality, self-discipline, self-reliance, respect for authority, and other values considered important in an orderly, industrial society. Under the direction of William Wirt the public schools of Gary reflected these educational practices and patterns during the Progressive Era and after.

To understand fully the relationship between immigrants and schools in Gary, it is necessary to examine the schooling process from at least two different perspectives. First, we need to know the values which shaped school policies and Americanization programs, and the ways in which these values were translated into actual practice in the Gary schools. Much of the recent writing in the history of American education has taken this line of inquiry.

But a full examination of immigrants in the Gary schools demands analysis from a second perspective—that of the educational consumers themselves. We need to know how the various immigrant groups in Gary responded to the public schools and the programs they offered. Were all ethnic groups, for instance, receptive to schooling in the same degree?

How much of a cultural defense were the parochial schools or the afternoon ethnic folk classes conducted in the immigrant communities? Did immigrant cultural traditions such as family values, religious fervor, or language maintenance affect the way ethnic groups responded to public schooling? Did immigrants with a tradition of communitarianism or radical politics reject public schools which taught capitalist values? How did the immigrants respond to the Americanization programs, and is it possible that the concept of "Americanization" meant different things to different immigrant groups? Since large percentages of immigrant children dropped out of school at, or even before, the legal age, we need to know more about immigrant perceptions of work. Perhaps some ethnic groups sought to achieve mobility and economic success through education, while others sought the same goals through work.

Historian Michael B. Katz has described education as "something the better part of the community did to the others to make them orderly, moral, and tractable."[8] Is this the only way of looking at immigrant education in Gary, or did immigrant parents exercise a degree of control and self-determination when it came to educational choices? Finally, given the large number of other immigrant institutions (family, churches, Sunday schools, Saturday schools, after-school schools, benevolent societies, musical and dramatic groups, political organizations, newspapers), have the public schools been as important for socialization and Americanization as we have been led to believe? To begin to answer these questions, we need to examine the immigrant experience in the context of the Gary schools. In the following sections, we attempt to explore the process of education in Gary from these two separate and very distinct perspectives.

1

William Wirt shared the assumptions of nativist America. He believed in the schools as Americanizers and as agents of social and cultural conformity. The old, traditional values Wirt hoped to restore and preserve in the city depended upon order, self-discipline, and obedience to authority. Thus, the Gary schools sought to shape and regulate behavior, turning children into workers and immigrants into Americans. The classrooms, the workshops, the playgrounds, the auditorium, the evening schools, the Saturday schools, the visiting teacher program—all played an integral part in the socialization-Americanization process. For the large number of immigrant children and adults who attended classes in Gary schools, education was preparation for life; it was, in short, indoctrination in American beliefs and capitalist values. Despite all the innovations of the platoon school system, Wirt had simply brought a new level of efficiency to the notion of the school as an instrument of socialization—socialization in the norms of a Protestant, rural America fast disappearing before the onslaught of industrialization, urbanization, and immigration.

Central to the Americanization process in the Gary schools was the effort to erase ethnic cultures—a task considered all the more urgent as southern and eastern European immigrants arrived in the steel city in growing numbers. Immigrant and second generation children made their first acquaintance with American life in the schools. What they found was not always pleasant. Their languages and cultures were often denigrated by an overwhelmingly WASP teaching force. They suffered daily indignities from native-born American students, who made fun of their speech and dress. Teachers arbitrarily Americanized their names. They were forced to conform to American values and patterns of behavior. In the auditorium period they were subjected to daily doses of patriotic and capitalistic propaganda; Assistant Superintendent Rossman labeled the auditorium "a real laboratory of Americanization and citizenship." Most of the programs and special activities in the schools—musical and dramatic programs, sports, student clubs, and so on—emphasized cooperation, conformity, unity, and patriotism. Under Wirt's leadership, then, the Gary schools consciously sought to undermine ethnic identification and promoted a rigorous Americanization.[9]

Despite the large number of immigrant children in the schools, no special provisions were made to ease their adjustment to the American way. The schools' handling of language difficulties, for example, suggested a rigorous and insensitive approach to Americanization. Immigrant children were forced to pick up English as they went along. In a 1914 speech in New York City, Wirt noted that of about 2,000 children in one Gary school, some 400 could not speak a word of English. The implications of such a situation, however, were ignored. There is no evidence that Wirt made any effort to hire teachers with ethnic backgrounds or with multiple language skills. Not until the mid-twenties did the school system establish even a single special English class for foreign-born children in the Froebel School.[10]

Despite language difficulties and cultural differences, immigrant children were expected to act like Americans from their first day at school. That the Gary schools imposed such demands in the classrooms and the workshops is also suggested by the comment of journalist Rheta Childe Dorr, who wrote in 1911 that Gary's immigrant students "look like American children, act like American children, and to all intents and purposes they are American children." E. A. Spaulding, principal of Gary's Emerson School for more than forty years, articulated a similar view: "We were just not aware that there were foreign children . . . and, in any case, one looked for them in vain after the first semester."[11]

As the comments of Spaulding and Dorr suggest, the Gary schools were Americanization factories. Indeed, as the *Gary Daily Tribune* insisted in a 1911 editorial, the foreign-born had to be "made over into real Americans," and only the schools could do the job. The city's nativist establishment—the newspapers, the business community, Protestant churchmen, municipal and school officials—accepted without hesitation or argument the idea that the schools' function was to turn immigrants into Americans. The Gary schools were often praised in the newspapers, in the businessmen's luncheons, and in the Protestant pulpit as great melting pots. But the only melting pot these people envisioned was one in which the newcomers were melted into Americans.[12]

The Froebel School, especially, was conceived of as an indispensable agency for immigrant assimilation, and rightly so. A K–12 school opened in 1912 and located in the center of Gary's immigrant neighborhoods on the city's shabby south side, Froebel predictably had an overwhelmingly immigrant and second generation student body. According to a 1916 school census, for instance, 87 percent of Froebel's students came from foreign stock. By comparison, the schools of the more fashionable, primarily American section on the city's north side had much smaller proportions of foreign students; the Jefferson School student population was 54 percent native born of native parents in 1916, while the Emerson School was 44 percent native-born American.[13]

Moreover, distinct ethnic variations existed among the three schools. Froebel's foreign-stock students in 1916 overwhelmingly came from eastern and southeastern Europe—54 percent from the Austro-Hungarian empire, 25 percent from the Russian empire, and 6 percent from Italy, but only 5 percent from Great Britain, Ireland, Canada, Germany, and the Scandinavian countries. In contrast, both Jefferson and Emerson had substantially smaller proportions of foreign-stock students from eastern and southeastern Europe, and much larger proportions from northern and western Europe (see table 4). Thus, not only was Froebel a heavily immigrant school, but most of its immigrant children came from Russia, Poland, Italy, and the Balkans—regions of Europe considered "culturally backward" by the nativists and the Americanizers.[14]

These attendance patterns continued to prevail over the next several years. A 1924 school census reported an incredibly small 1.6 percent native American white students at Froebel. Of the remainder, 21.8 percent were American-born blacks, and 76.6 percent came from foreign stock.

Again, by comparison, almost 62 percent of Emerson's students in 1924 were native-born Americans, while the percentage of foreign-stock students had been reduced to about 38 percent. At the Jefferson School 76 percent of the student body was native-born American, while the remaining 24 percent came from foreign stock. At the new Horace Mann School the proportions were similar: 71 percent native American and 29 percent foreign stock. (Jefferson had six black students in 1924, Emerson had only one, and Horace Mann had none.)[15]

School attendance patterns, then, reflected residential realities. Immigrant and second generation children attended schools in proximity to their neighborhoods. This meant that schools like Froebel and Pulaski, an elementary school where 96 percent of the children in 1924 came from foreign stock, enrolled the largest proportions of immigrant children. Naturally, the burdens of Americanization were also heaviest in these same schools.

Gary's nativist establishment expected schools such as Froebel to pursue Americanization as a matter of course. Froebel, the *Gary Daily Tribune* editorialized in 1911, would be "in a position to carry on a work of the greatest import to all who see in the Americanization of the foreign-born the cure for most of the ills that have come from the large immigration to American manufacturing centers in recent years." Years later, in 1939, Froebel's long-time principal C. S. Coons reflected on his school's contribution to "the great cause" of Americanization: "We believe we have solved it here at Froebel. Boys and girls of every nationality and racial background mix and mingle here in the classrooms, laboratories, in our musical organizations, on the athletic field. They are all alike to us and they are learning to live together as good Americans."[16]

Yet, the process of Americanization at Froebel was not as simple, or as easy, or as humane as Coons made it seem. The curriculum at Froebel reflected discrimination against immigrant children. As suggested by the survey of the Gary schools conducted by the General Education Board (GEB) in 1916, the sorting and channeling process began early in the elementary years. Students in the elementary grades at Froebel, for instance, received less reading instruction than those at Jefferson. In the fourth grade Froebel students received no instruction in history or geography, while fourth graders at both Emerson and Jefferson took work in both subjects. Froebel students were consistently channeled into manual training and industrial education. At Froebel children took manual training during the first four years of elementary school, while Jefferson students did not. In the eighth grade Froebel students spent 600 minutes per week in manual training and mechanical drawing classes, while Jefferson students spent only 165 and Emerson students none. At the high school level Froebel offered substantially fewer academic courses than Emerson, partially because Froebel had fewer high school students: in mathematics Emerson offered four years of instruction and Froebel three; in history Emerson offered three years of course work but Froebel only one; in science Emerson supplied four years of work and Froebel about two and one-half; in languages Emerson offered seven separate courses in Latin, German, and French, but Froebel had only two years of Latin and three years of German. Science teaching at Froebel, especially zoology, physics, and chemistry, was "distinctly inferior" to that at Emerson. Froebel students, the GEB's report revealed, were shortchanged academically. For most immigrant students at Froebel, Americanization meant a course of study emphasizing cooking, sewing, bookkeeping, and typing for girls and manual training and mechanical arts for boys.[17]

The manual training and shopwork at both Froebel and Emerson aimed at preparing students for trades and for industrial occupations. Emerson began with shopwork in cabinet making, painting, and printing; in 1912 three metal shops—forge, foundry, and machine—were added to the program, and in 1914, cabinet making and painting were discontinued. The metal shops clearly comprised the heart of the Emerson program. In 1916, when the GEB surveyed the Gary schools, the forge and foundry shops had the largest enrollments during the academic year (91 and 92, respectively, while printing enrolled 68 and machine shop 38). Also, substantially more students elected these metal shops for more than one thirteen-week term, and those enrolled averaged more shop hours per day than those in the other shops. Froebel had a somewhat more balanced program of industrial education, with shops in sheet metal, woodworking, shoemaking, plumbing, printing, and painting. Woodworking, shoemaking, and sheet metal were the most popular of the shops, enrolling about 60 percent of the students taking industrial work at Froebel in 1916. In addition, the auditorium period at Froebel was frequently used for programs on "the advantages and disadvantages of each of the school trades as an occupation." Both schools, then, had an extensive program of industrial shopwork. They differed in that Emerson had a wider range of courses in its regular academic curriculum. At Froebel the manual training of the elementary curriculum led directly to the industrial shops of the high school program.[18]

Wirt and his colleagues consistently denied that the shopwork in the Gary schools sought to prepare academically weak children for the steel mills and related local industry. Yet in reality the workshop programs were accomplishing that very goal. Even those who praised the shopwork as educationally sound and individually fulfilling provided unwitting evidence for Wirt's critics. For instance, Eva W. White, who participated in the GEB survey, recognized that the schools were socializing male children for industrial work. Shop activities, she wrote, were designed "to furnish growing boys with opportunities for the development of senses and muscles and concrete experience which will enable them to participate intelligently in a social order in which industry bulks large." Similarly, Abraham Flexner and Frank P. Bachman, authors of the summary volume of the GEB report, admitted that "the training received by some pupils in some of the shops proves of direct vocational value when they enter certain of the industries on which the prosperity of the city is based." As one observer noted in 1916, the Gary school system became "a feeder to the one and only industry at its doors."

School dropout statistics provide another kind of evidence. Sixty percent of the boys aged fourteen through eighteen who had dropped out of school in 1916 to take up jobs were working in manufacturing and industry. Similarly, almost 63 percent of the girls who had dropped out of school were engaged in domestic and personal service and in clerical occupations—the areas emphasized in the schools' household arts program for girls. The evidence seems to suggest, therefore, that the Gary schools, especially Emerson and Froebel, were preparing their students for the kind of work they might expect to obtain in the new industrial city. For the immigrant boys and girls in the schools, this sort of socialization for the workplace represented an important side of the Americanization process.[19]

If the immigrant and second generation children at Froebel and Emerson were shortchanged academically and shunted into shopwork and household arts, the results were predictable. The GEB, using a variety of educational measurements, found that Froebel students performed poorly in spelling, handwriting, oral reading, silent reading, and science. To a large degree, this poor academic performance can be attributed to the language difficulties of the immigrant children and to the nativist bias of the GEB tests. But it is also true that the less academic curriculum at Froebel tended to emphasize manual training, household arts, physical education, and auditorium—subjects hardly conducive to positive performance on tests measuring academic abilities and knowledge.[20]

The results of an inferior education were measurable in other ways, too. Froebel students had higher rates of retardation than other Gary schools; in 1916 56 percent of Froebel's elementary students were an average of one year behind their grade level, compared to 30 percent at Emerson and 23 percent at Jefferson. Many Froebel classes had substantial numbers of students as much as three and four years behind their grade level. At the same time only 10 percent of the Froebel children were ahead of their grade level, while 25 percent of the Emerson students and 35 percent of the Jefferson children were a grade level ahead.[21]

Moreover, Froebel students had highly irregular attendance patterns and tended to drop out of school earlier and in larger numbers than students at other Gary schools. Teachers, administrators, and truant officers complained about poor attendance at Froebel, and the newspapers periodically editorialized about truancy among the immigrant children. "The greatest cause for retardation," school supervisor Annie Klingensmith wrote to Wirt in 1917, "is the great irregularity in attendance." A good deal of the absence, Klingensmith reported, "is of the sort where the children are in and out, seldom long gone, and seldom long in at a time." She noted one Froebel class of 51 students which had an average attendance of from 25 to 35, the composition of the class "varying from day to day." "Any one of these 51 may appear tomorrow and be gone the next day." Even those who attended school, Klingensmith complained, did not always go to their classes. Instead, they often gathered in corridors and corners, and passing teachers got "a vague feeling that it was their lunch or play time instead of their recitation time." Similarly noting the "continually fluctuating" classes at Froebel, the GEB investigation confirmed what most schoolmen in Gary already knew—that the schools had little holding power in the immigrant communities.[22]

The statistics on high school attendance provide dramatic evidence of this lack of holding power. In September, 1918, for instance, Froebel had a total of 1,725 students, but only 125 of them, or about 7 percent, were enrolled in the high school grades. By comparison, Emerson had 1,295 students, with 452 of these, or about 35 percent, in high school. By September, 1920, Froebel enrolled a total of 2,400 children, with only 165 in high school grades. At the same time Emerson had 2,000 students, but 527 of them were in high school. High school attendance increased in Gary during the twenties and thirties, as it did throughout the nation. But even as late as 1937 high school attendance at Froebel was distinctly different from that at other K-12 schools in Gary. In September of that year Froebel had 2,000 students in the grades and 743 in high school. Emerson enrolled 1,281 in the grades but 1,025 in high school. The newer Horace Mann School had 1,138 children in the grades and 1,173 in high school. Thus, substantially fewer Froebel students went on to high school compared to children at Emerson or Horace Mann. Obviously, large numbers of immigrant children dropped out of school after the eighth grade, which generally corresponded with the age limit of fourteen—sixteen after state legislation in 1922—for compulsory education in the state of Indiana.[23]

Even the Froebel eighth graders who continued on to high school did not fare as well as their counterparts at other Gary schools. According to a Purdue University study published in 1941, only 57 percent of Froebel's entering ninth graders eventually graduated from high school, compared to 83 percent for Horace Mann. Interestingly, Emerson's high school completion rate of 56 percent did not even equal Froebel's. The same Purdue survey revealed that only 11 percent of Froebel's graduates continued their education beyond high school, compared to 21 percent for Emerson and 38 percent for Horace Mann. Thus, even Froebel's immigrant and second generation students who stayed in school beyond the eighth grade had a smaller chance of completing high school or of going on to higher education.[24]

The Froebel pattern clearly suggests that immigrant children were educationally shortchanged in Gary. Their educational difficulties, especially language and culture, were handled insensitively, and their teachers often treated them and their traditions with contempt. They had fewer academic opportunities, and the system pushed them into manual training and household arts at an early age. Not surprisingly, these students scored poorly in achievement tests, attended school irregularly, and dropped out of school at the legal age in large numbers. The Gary schools under William Wirt simply were not receptive to cultural differences. Rather, they systematically sought to socialize ethnic children according to standard American values and beliefs. Americanization, in short, formed the heart of the schools' mission in Gary.

The Americanization impulse also underlay another of Wirt's educational programs—the released-time plan for religious instruction, initiated in 1914 in cooperation with the city's Protestant churches. Wirt and other church school sponsors viewed the program as an additional means of promoting WASP morality and upholding basic American values and virtues in the face of the foreign influx. By 1919 virtually all the English-speaking white Protestant churches in Gary participated in the cooperative effort, now partly supported by steel company donations; more than three thousand students attended eight church schools for one hour a day during the auditorium or special activities period. Wirt believed that moralistic education would help achieve a unified and orderly society. With a curriculum emphasizing Bible study and "habits of obedience, truthfulness, loyalty, service, self-control and consideration," the religious schools reinforced the public school role as regulator of social behavior.[25]

This religious instruction was clearly viewed as another avenue of Americanization. For Gary's Protestant church leaders, becoming an American meant becoming a Protestant, and they sought to attract immigrant children to the church schools. Immigrant children in these

Protestant classes were encouraged to take Bibles and hymn books home, so that they could "tell the Bible stories to their parents at night and sing the songs to them." "As an agency for Americanization of the best sort," one religious advocate asserted, "nothing can equal the Church Schools of Gary." Yet these religious schools had only limited success among the immigrants, who generally resisted Protestantization and preferred their own separate system of Sunday schools, afternoon folk schools, and parochial schools. As two of the religious teachers noted, "Very few of the foreigners are contributing to the support of these schools for religious instruction." Clearly, however, Gary's Protestant educators in the public schools and in the churches conceived of the weekday religious schools as an additional means of promoting Americanization, cultural conformity, and a uniform Protestant morality.[26]

If the Gary schools sought to socialize and Americanize immigrant children, they worked for similar goals among adults through the evening school program. In 1908 the Gary school board established a night school for teaching English to foreigners. The *Gary Daily Tribune* expressed its support for this program to "make better citizens" and suggested that immigrants who attended would "vastly better their chances of earning a livelihood and add much to their standing among their countrymen." As in the regular day schools, "The teachers employed will speak the English language alone, this system being now considered the best for teaching languages." Attendance in the early years was quite small, and not many Gary immigrants took advantage of this opportunity "to become more thoroughly Americanized," as the *Daily Tribune* put it.[27]

Gradually, however, night school enrollment grew, especially as Wirt added new subjects and programs to the evening school curriculum. By the mid-teens Gary adults could choose from subjects ranging from standard academic courses to commercial and vocational classes, musical and auditorium activities, and physical training and athletics. Each Gary school became a sort of community social center, providing a wide range of programs and activities throughout the day and well into the evening. Rising enrollments accompanied the expanded curriculum, and by 1915 the night schools had as many students as the regular daytime schools. Heavy night school enrollments continued through the twenties, dropping off suddenly in the early thirties as the financial stringencies brought by the Great Depression forced the school board to cut back the night school curriculum (see table 5).[28]

From the beginning the English and citizenship classes were considered the foundation of the night school program. The schools cooperated with the U.S. Bureau of Naturalization and other agencies in preparing newcomers for naturalization. From World War 1 until well into the 1920s, heavy pressure was put on immigrants to attend the Gary night schools. School officials, local industries, newspapers, and groups such as the YMCA and the American Legion all urged immigrant attendance at night schools. Over the years courses multiplied not just in English but in American history and government. By 1927 some twenty-five such classes were conducted for the foreign-born in twelve separate educational centers. During the depression years the school board cut back its night school programs, partially because of financial difficulties, but also because the immigration restriction of the 1920s resulted in lessened demand in the 1930s. However, some English and citizenship classes were continued under WPA sponsorship during the New Deal period. Throughout, the goal of Americanization remained uppermost. Assistant Superintendent Rossman, for instance, noted in 1927 that "groups of foreigners from the night school English classes [were] taken to the auditorium frequently for programs on Americanization." Froebel Principal Coons asserted that "the Froebel evening school is the great melting pot of Gary," a place in which the immigrants learned "respect for American laws and institutions" and were "transformed into truly American citizens." As the *Gary Post-Tribune* noted in 1927, "the romance of Americanization" was being written in the Gary night schools.[29]

But, as might be suspected, the process of Americanization was not always "romantic" from the point of view of the immigrant. Rather, it generally reflected a harsh and unyielding demand that immigrants abandon old-country ways and quickly conform to those of the new land. The following incident suggests the pattern. In December, 1910, a delegation of Gary Poles, led by two Polish city councilmen, petitioned the school board for a class in the Polish language in the night schools. In commenting on the petition the *Daily Tribune* noted that "a department of Polish can be established in the night schools if a sufficiently large class is established to pay the expense of providing an instructor." A few weeks later the paper reported Wirt's decision on the Polish petition: "Tonight the Polish people of the south side will get what they asked for in the way of a night school except that English will be taught instead of Polish." And a few days later, apparently mystified, the *Daily Tribune* reported that the English class had been canceled because "no students appeared at the Polish night school."[30]

There was other evidence, as well, that Gary's immigrant communities resisted night school Americanization programs. A Cincinnati Americanizer, Estelle M. Sternberger, writing about Gary in 1919 during the peak of the Americanization crusade, noted that the foreign-born generally resented the schools' efforts "to crush out every spark of love and attachment . . . toward the land of [their] birth." Sternberger described one immigrant group which had traditionally been deeply divided on political grounds. However, when the local Americanization campaign was announced, they promptly forgot their differences and "combined their strength and expended every effort in a propaganda among their own numbers to discourage attendance at classes or activities fostered by any local Americanization agency." As a result, Sternberger wrote, "school authorities noticed an appreciable decrease in the attendance at the night-school classes."[31]

In other ways the schools generated feelings of humiliation and inferiority among immigrant adults. In 1931, for instance, the International Institute of Gary, an immigrant social service agency, received complaints from the immigrant community that teachers were discourteous, disrespectful, and contemptuous of immigrants in the Froebel night school. The teachers, according to the complaint, ridiculed the names of the foreign-born and called adult students by their last names, a form of address used in Europe only for servants and "inferiors." Many of the immigrant students, as a result, felt "greatly distressed and humiliated, and some have left the school for this reason." Later an International Institute social worker lamented the teachers' practice of Americanizing the names of school children, claiming that immigrant parents were "unable to counteract the sense of inferiority induced by incidents like these." Both the regular day schools and the adult night schools, then, promoted a rigorous and intolerant brand of Americanization designed to bring conformity to Gary's polyglot community.[32]

The Americanization role of the schools greatly intensified during World War 1 and in postwar years, when fears generated by the Red Scare and the steel strike of 1919 cast tremendous suspicion upon anything foreign or un-American. Patriotism was demanded throughout the school system, and Wirt threatened to fire "any teacher . . . not actively loyal in support of American interests." A music teacher, under criticism for allegedly teaching German music and songs, protested to Wirt that he taught primarily American songs (although he did admit to teaching the Austrian national anthem, but with the English words); the teacher noted in defense, however, that he had "given regular teaching in patriotism every day for two weeks and . . . succeeded in stirring up great enthusiasm." Responding to pressure from such diverse groups as the American Legion, the Lake County Committee on Educational War Propaganda, the Lake County Americanization League, and the Ku Klux Klan, the Gary schools, like others throughout the country, dropped the German language from the curriculum and emphasized Americanism and patriotic activities in the classroom. Secondary school students were mobilized into a statewide Patriotic Service League devoted to "the truest form of patriotism."[33]

The Gary schools reflected the new nativism and intolerance of the period. In cooperation with the U.S. Bureau of Naturalization, which sought to transform the public schools into propaganda machines, Wirt multiplied evening classes for adults in English, citizenship, and American history. The Gary public schools became, in the words of one observer, "the foremost agency in Americanization work" in the city. The 1917 report of the U.S. commissioner of naturalization typically asserted that "the spirit of alienage can not survive in the presence of the intense Americanizing force that is being built up in the public schoolhouses in these communities throughout the land." Wirt sympathized with these wartime Americanization activities and cooperated with the nativists during the conflict and the Red Scare which followed. By bowing to nativist demands, by transforming the schools into blatant propaganda agencies, and by writing and speaking in support of an intolerant patriotism, Wirt put the Gary schools squarely behind the intensive Americanization campaign of the war years and after.[34]

In a variety of ways, then, the Gary public schools under William Wirt served the functions of socialization and Americanization. Traditional middle class WASP values determined school programs and policies. The schools sought to shape the behavior of the students, wipe out ethnic backgrounds, turn immigrants into patriotic Americans, and socialize children for the workplace. As one perceptive early observer of the Gary schools noted in the *Nation* in 1916, "The aims of the school authorities were to keep the children busy during their waking hours and off the streets, to mold them into the American matrix, to smother and extinguish old-country traditions and prejudices, to make reasonably good citizens of them—and finally, to teach them, or the most of them, a trade more or less connected with steel making."[35]

2

None of the foregoing should be surprising, really, since the Gary schools were only doing what public schools in the United States have always done—what society has established schools to do. Indeed, the long-standing popular mythology of the public school as an agent of rationalism, humanitarianism, economic opportunity, and democracy has been challenged and undermined by the recent writings of such revisionist historians as Michael B. Katz, Colin Greer, Joel H. Spring, and David B. Tyack. Generally critical and condemnatory of the purposes and forms of American education, these revisionist writers found the public schools from the nineteenth century on to be characterized by bureaucracy, racism, paternalism, class bias, and social control. Schools served the capitalist system and the modern corporate-industrial state, they supported existing social and economic structures, they manipulated children and parents, and they propagated such values as order, conformity, and docility. The writings of these revisionist historians have stripped away much of the traditional mythology from the history of education. Clearly, the patterns of socialization and Americanization in the Gary public schools fit within the conceptual framework established by the revisionist writers on educational history.

But this is only part of the story. The revisionists have adequately detailed the role and function of the school in society, but the almost singleminded emphasis on what schools were doing to children has tended to create a new mythology of educational history. Neither the revisionist view nor the traditionalist position, in our opinion, is entirely satisfactory; neither goes beyond a functional view of the school as a social institution; neither accommodates the motivations and behavior of the educational consumers—the children and their parents; neither explains exactly what was happening in the Gary schools under Superintendent William Wirt.

The complete story of the relationship between immigrant children and public education in the city is much more complicated than either the traditionalists or the revisionists would have us believe. It is a mistake, for example, to believe that all immigrants responded to the public schools in exactly the same ways. As Colin Greer has noted, "There was a large-scale and persistent difference in the experience of different ethnic groups after they reached America."[36] Because of different backgrounds, traditions, cultures, and values, different ethnic groups reacted differently to the socialization and Americanization programs of the schools. Thus, the experiences of first and second generation immigrants in public schools were complex and varied, depending heavily on their particular ethnic and cultural background.

Immigrants in Gary were not always passive educational consumers. In the first place, there is considerable evidence that numbers of immigrant newcomers in Gary saw positive advantages in what the public schools had to offer. With some exceptions, Gary's immigrants, like those in most other cities, had been sucked into the American dream. To be sure, some immigrants—east European Jews, for instance—had left Europe because of religious persecution, others to avoid military service or because of conflicts revolving around politics or national loyalties. But for most of Gary's immigrants from southern and eastern Europe, it was the magnet of economic opportunity that drew them to the United States. One way up the occupational and economic ladder—for their children, if not for themselves—was through education. The rhetoric of opportunity in America said, get as much of it as possible. Indeed, according to historian Timothy L. Smith, many immigrant groups came to the United States with high levels of educational aspiration. For such newcomers, Smith has written, "education was the key to the good life, the gateway to health, wealth, and happiness."[37] The behavior of such immigrant families in pursuing schooling in the new land thus corresponded to cultural values which prized education and learning.

In Gary this pattern of strong support for public education was prevalent among such nationality groups as the English, Scotch, Swedes, Czechs, Romanians, Bulgarians, Serbians, and Jews. According to two Gary school surveys in the 1920s, a relatively large percentage of parents from these ethnic groups consistently sent their children to public schools, as opposed to those who sent children to parochial schools or permitted children to drop out of school to go to work. More than 70 percent of the children from these immigrant communities attended public schools in both 1922 and 1924. The 1922 survey, for instance, reported that 87.7 percent of the city's Jewish school-age children (age 4–19) attended Gary public schools. In the same year 81 percent of Romanian children were enrolled in the public schools. Public school attendance was similarly high among the other groups mentioned: English—74.1, Scotch—77.5, Swedes—74.7, Czechs—70.1, Bulgarians—72.7, Serbians—72.1. The 1924 school census demonstrated an even greater faith in public education, as public school attendance had increased among all these groups except Jews: English—84.4, Scotch—79.3, Swedes—80.1, Czechs—81.2, Bulgarians—82.6, Serbians—81.5, Romanians—81.5 (see table 6). For these groups, the power and pervasiveness of the American dream, of the idea of opportunity and economic success through education, apparently made acceptable the kind of socialization and Americanization that took place in the Gary schools. Interestingly, in both years the public school attendance rates were higher for these immigrant groups than for native-born American whites. At the same time relatively low public school attendance (under 60 percent) prevailed among Poles, Slovaks, Hungarians, Croatians, Lithuanians, Germans, and Irish.[38]

It would be helpful if such school attendance statistics existed for other years. However, neither the school board records nor the voluminous papers of William Wirt contain such materials. These school surveys of 1922 and 1924, then, remain the best evidence we have for determining the educational choices made by Gary's immigrant parents and their children during the 1920s. Statistics from other cities in the same period suggest that the school attendance patterns in Gary were not very different from the situation elsewhere. Recent scholarship in ethnic and immigration history has demonstrated that immigrant groups from Scandinavia and the British Isles, as well as east European Jews, Romanians, and Japanese, adhered to the positive value of public schooling in the United States. Children with these ethnic backgrounds scored better on I.Q. tests, were less likely to be retarded (behind their age-grade level), stayed in school longer, and generally had greater success in school and after than Irish, Polish, Italian, and Slavic children.[39]

But there is another aspect to this story, as well. Americanization was not necessarily a pejorative term or an alien concept. As a matter of fact, for many immigrants Americanization was a two-way street; the receiving society sought to erase ethnic differences and create homogeneity, but immigrants in large numbers sought to become part of the new culture. This is not to say that immigrants abandoned their heritage and traditions wholesale, but it is to suggest that strong ethnic identification and adoption of American patriotism and other values were not mutually exclusive characteristics. It was a standard practice at meetings of ethnic benevolent associations, for instance, to sing both the American national anthem and that of the old country, and to display the flags of both nations. These practices were not imposed by the Americanizers. Rather, they grew out of the conscious desires of the immigrants to identify with, to become part of, the new culture and the adopted nation. In addition, some immigrant groups brought to the United States many of the same values being promoted in the schools—individualism, work, thrift, self-discipline, obedience to the law, and so on. Thus, the schools were not undermining these aspects of immigrant culture, but reinforcing them. Under such circumstances, the schooling process for immigrant children might have been perceived by foreign-born parents to be both necessary and positive.[40]

Moreover, historians need to be conscious of the many possible meanings of the word "Americanization." It could mean being patriotic and speaking a common language, but for some it could also mean getting a good job, saving money, getting ahead, buying a house, going to school, adopting a middle class lifestyle, becoming a citizen, voting, becoming Protestant, accepting the dominant economic and political system, and a variety of other things. Clearly, immigrants could accept some of these kinds of things without losing ethnic consciousness or discarding the old culture. That Gary's native white establishment supported the public schools in providing a rigorous, culture-destroying brand of Americanization should not blind us to the fact that certain nationality groups such as Czechs, Romanians, Jews, Swedes, and others may have had entirely different perceptions of what Americanization meant. For these groups, the drive to achieve the American dream, especially for their children, did not lead to rejection of the public schools. Rather, it induced such immigrant parents to use the public schools for their own purposes, at least until the high school years.

Immigrant perceptions of work also had an important bearing on the pattern of ethnic schooling in Gary. While certain nationality groups conceived of education as the avenue to economic success and personal happiness, others sought the same goals through work. William Wirt and his fellow WASP educators in Gary believed that devotion to work needed to be inculcated among immigrant children. But, ironically, the schools really did not have to promote the work ethic, since most immigrants came with it. Work was the kind of behavioral value which was heavily emphasized in the immigrant family. For many of Gary's immigrants, economic survival and property acquisition, especially home ownership, were more important goals than completion of a high school education. In such immigrant families children of school age were often sent to work to contribute to the family income and to make home ownership possible.[41]

This pattern seems to have prevailed among Gary's largest immigrant groups—Poles, Greeks, Russians, Croatians, Lithuanians, Serbians, Slovaks, and Italians. Among the Greeks, for example, according to the 1922 school census, 33.3 percent of the school-age children did not attend any school and presumably were working to supplement family income. The percentage of school-age dropouts was relatively high for the other groups mentioned as well: Poles—30.5, Lithuanians—28.3, Russians—25, Croatians—24.5, Serbians—23.5, Italians—22.1, Slovaks—20.8. By comparison, the school-age dropout rate for native-born whites was 19.8 percent, for blacks it was 15.9 percent, and for Jews it was 11.3 percent (see table 6).[42]

The school dropout pattern among Gary's ethnic groups generally conforms to the national experience. Writing in 1912 of the new immigrants from southern and eastern Europe, immigration expert Peter Roberts asserted that "foreign-born parents generally expect their children to work. They send them out at a tender age to earn a living. . . . The sons of the new immigrants are not found in the higher walks of learning: they are workers as their fathers were." More recent research tends to support the generalizations of Roberts and other early observers. In a study of Greek immigrants in Chicago, for instance, George A. Kourvetaris noted that Greek immigrants in America had little educational success, especially in the first generation. "The Greek immigrant knew his limitations in education," Kourvetaris wrote, "and he tried to compensate for his lack of education by working hard." Italian parents in New York City "had little regard for schooling," according to historian Thomas Kessner. They rejected the American values taught in the schools, and they needed the earnings their children brought home. Similarly, recent scholarship suggests that Poles, Slovaks, Croatians, and other Slavic immigrants had little regard for education, especially the sort of education available in public schools, and routinely sent their children to work at the legal age.[43]

It would appear that in Gary, then, immigrant parents from certain nationality groups pulled their children out of school and sent them to work as soon as they reached the legal age for withdrawal. Until the early 1920s school attendance in Indiana was required until age fourteen, or about the eighth grade. In 1922 state legislation mandated school attendance to age sixteen; however, children could still leave school after age fourteen if they graduated from the eighth grade, obtained a work permit, and attended one of Gary's continuation schools. The school surveys of 1922 and 1924 clearly indicate that, although some parents apparently withdrew children illegally prior to age sixteen, the great bulk of children not attending school were age sixteen and above (see table 7).[44] High school attendance statistics, as well, support these observations about the withdrawal patterns of immigrant children in Gary. In 1914, for instance, when public school enrollment totaled 5,050, some 4,777 students were enrolled in kindergarten through eighth grade, but only 273 attended high school. Even by 1925, when public school enrollment surpassed 14,000 students, only about 1,800 of these attended Gary high schools.[45] And, throughout this period, as noted earlier, the largest number of high school students attended Emerson school, which had the smallest number of immigrant students. High school attendance increased substantially during the 1920s, as table 8 indicates, partially because of the 1922 law requiring school attendance until age sixteen. Rising high school enrollment continued into the 1930s, but it is likely that the state of the American economy and the lessened availability of jobs for school dropouts had something to do with it. Clearly, then, until the late 1920s and early 1930s, large numbers of immigrant children attended public grade schools in Gary, but relatively few went on through high school. Immigrants from southern and eastern Europe, especially, placed a high value on work as opposed to a high school education for their children.

Colin Greer has argued that public schools tended to force lower class children out into the labor market at an early age. In Gary, however, the school system tried to prolong adolescence and keep the children in school as long as possible.[46] The high school curriculum, especially, in which students were enabled to specialize in academic, business, or vocational programs, was central to William Wirt's goal of keeping children in school. In addition, through industrial arts, vocational training, extracurricular activities, athletics, counseling, special tutoring, flexible scheduling, continuation schools, Saturday schools, night schools, and summer schools, Wirt sought to lower the failure and dropout rates and retain the system's control over children. Nevertheless, the Gary high schools, especially those in immigrant neighborhoods, experienced high dropout rates. It is likely that the immigrant perception of work, the strong positive value placed upon it, and the need for additional family income, undermined the necessity for prolonged schooling in Polish, Greek, Slovak, Lithuanian, Italian, and other southern and eastern European immigrant families.

For many immigrant parents, rejection of the public schools, especially at the high school level, represented a financial choice. But for others—those who adopted the parochial school alternative for the elementary years—rejection of the public schools was a cultural choice. During the first three decades of the twentieth century, as the currents of nativism ran strong, some ethnic groups resisted the often intolerant Americanization encountered in the public schools. A study of immigrants on the Minnesota iron range, for example, suggests that Finnish and Slovenian radicals and Socialists opposed public education because it supported capitalistic values and undermined ethnic culture. Similarly, Slavic immigrants resisted American public schooling because of their hostility to the materialism of American life and their adherence to traditional ethnic culture and values. A recent study of immigrants and education contends that southern Italian immigrants rejected public schooling because it indoctrinated their children with "ideas antagonistic to the traditional codes of family life."[47] For such immigrants, many of whom had a communitarian as opposed to an individualistic tradition, the parochial school often served as an alternative to public education.

Ethnic and cultural background was an obvious factor in deciding between the public schools and parochial schools. In Gary, for instance, according to the 1924 school census, only 1.4 percent of Jewish children, 3.2 percent of Romanian children, 3.4 percent of Swedish children, 4 percent of Greek children, 5.7 percent of English children, 5.8 percent of Serbian children, and 6.3 percent of Italian children attended parochial elementary schools in the city (see table 6). By contrast, 32.8 percent of German children, 29.7 percent of Irish children, 24.1 percent of Croatian children, 23.1 percent of Lithuanian children, and 22.4 percent of Hungarian children attended parochial elementary schools. The Poles in Gary demonstrated the most extreme rejection of public education. According to the same 1924 school census, only 33.8 percent of Polish children between ages four and nineteen attended public schools, while 41.8 percent attended parochial schools; another 24.4 percent attended no schools and presumably had dropped out of school to work (see table 6).[48]

To a certain degree, the parochial school alternative was possible only when the nationality group was large enough to support its own church and school. Moreover, it was generally the immigrant Roman Catholic parishes that built parochial schools. In Gary by the 1920s ethnic churches with attached parochial elementary schools had been established by German Catholics, Irish Catholics, Polish Catholics, Lithuanian Catholics, Slovak Catholics, Croatian Catholics, and Hungarian Catholics. The Polish parochial school of St. Hedwig's parish was one of the largest of these ethnic parochial schools in Gary, consistently enrolling 600 to 1,000 students during the 1920s and 1930s. St. Hedwig's School had a typical curriculum. In addition to standard academic subjects, the school offered classes in Polish history, culture, and language. Polish nuns instructed classes in the Polish language as well as in English, directed dramatic performances in Polish, and taught prayers and catechism in Polish. The programs of the other Catholic parochial schools were much the same. In every case these parochial schools fostered ethnic identity, supported the language and culture of the immigrant group, bolstered cohesiveness in the ethnic family, and promoted positive attitudes, understanding, and knowledge of the old country among the children of the parish.[49] Interestingly, three other Catholic immigrant groups in Gary—Spaniards, Italians, and Mexicans—did not follow the parochial school pattern. All three groups had anti-clerical traditions in the old country and were courted by local Protestant missionary elements as possible converts.

All Gary's immigrant Catholic parishes were lay-founded and were generally autonomous churches closely reflecting the needs and aspirations of their members. They were not controlled by the Irish-dominated hierarchy of the Roman Catholic Church. Indeed, most of these parishes had been established, had hired their own priests, and had built their parochial schools long before the Catholic hierarchy knew of their existence. Thus, these parishes retained close control over their parochial schools and determined the nature of the schooling which went on inside the classroom. This lay control was not always the case in other places, especially in large cities such as Chicago, where the Roman Catholic hierarchy was more visible and more powerful. In Chicago, as historian James W. Sanders has recently demonstrated, the Catholic hierarchy under the leadership of Archbishop George Mundelein after 1916 sought to undermine ethnic separatism and promote the assimilation of the city's ethnic Catholics. Mundelein's goal was a citywide parochial school system with English as the only language of instruction. Indeed, Catholic parochial education became increasingly systematized and bureaucratized in large cities after 1900, paralleling the bureaucratization which marked public education by the end of the nineteenth century. Under such circumstances the parochial school actually became an agency of Americanization rather than a bulwark of immigrant culture, language, and tradition.[50] This sort of transformation of purpose occurred much later and never completely in Gary, and the Catholic parochial schools retained their ethnic identities and their cultural functions well past 1940.

Gary's immigrant Catholics were not the only ones to establish parochial schools. In addition, St. John's German Lutheran parish in the Tolleston section of Gary had a full-time parochial school with cultural functions similar to those of the Catholic parishes. This Lutheran school had over 100 pupils in 1916, but grew slowly over the next two decades, enrolling about 150 students in 1935. For several years the Trinity Evangelical Church, also German, conducted a small parochial school, but it closed in 1924 when an adequate teacher could not be found. For a time in the 1920s and 1930s, a Jewish secular school was conducted by the local chapter of the Workman's Circle of America, a Jewish Socialist fraternal order. Its curriculum emphasized the Yiddish language and Jewish culture and literature.[51]

Thus, there is considerable evidence that certain ethnic groups, mostly Roman Catholic, rejected public education as destructive of their cultural and religious traditions, values, and languages. For such immigrants, Americanization was negative rather than positive. The parochial school became a cultural defense for immigrant parents, an institutional means to blunt the Americanization of their children and to sustain and nourish the ethnic heritage. Yet the total number of immigrant children who took the parochial school alternative was relatively small—about 14 percent in 1924. The percentage of children in Gary parochial schools held firm throughout the 1920s and 1930s; in 1935 some 15 percent of Gary children attended parochial schools. These figures are lower than those for other cities with large immigrant populations. In Chicago the proportion of parochial school children ranged upward from 20 percent after 1910—24.8 percent in 1920 and 30 percent in 1940. In St. Louis 20 percent of the city's children attended Catholic schools in 1920. And in the cities of the northeast—New York, Philadelphia, and Boston, especially—Sanders has noted that Catholic parochial schools "enrolled anywhere from 20 percent to 40 percent of all school-children."

Gary differed from these larger cities in another way, as well.

Although a few Gary students (about fifty in 1935) attended Catholic Central High School in nearby Hammond, Indiana, no ethnic group thought it important enough to build a parochial high school in the steel city during this period. In the 1950s the Catholic Andrean High School was established, but it too was outside of Gary, located south of the city in the suburb of Merrillville.[52]

Although Gary was often described as a Catholic town, the Orthodox denominations constituted a larger proportion of the city's residents than that of any other major city in the United States. This demographic reality helps to explain the relatively small proportion of children in Catholic parochial schools—there simply were more immigrants who belonged to the several different Orthodox faiths. These Orthodox denominations, including separate congregations of Greeks, Serbians, Romanians, Russians, Bulgarians, Ukrainians, and Ruthenians, developed a different church-school pattern. Each of these Orthodox parishes established schools, but not as substitutes for public elementary education. Instead, they were ethnic "folk" schools which students attended for an hour or more each day after public school classes had ended. These afternoon schools should not be confused with the Protestant church schools established under William Wirt's released-time religious instruction program.

The curriculum in the ethnic after-school schools uniformly emphasized immigrant language and tradition. The folk school of the Serbian Orthodox St. Sava parish typically provided instruction in Serbian history, music, literature, and language. Greek children concentrated on learning the old country language and culture in the folk school of the St. Constantine Greek Orthodox Church; by 1933 the school had three teachers and 180 students. Similarly, St. Mary's Russian Orthodox Church conducted an afternoon folk school emphasizing the Russian language, as well as the literary, musical, and cultural heritage of the old country. In most of these Orthodox parishes a Sunday school provided still more language and culture teaching, although the emphasis was more heavily religious than in the daily folk schools. As late as the 1960s the Orthodox folk schools maintained language instruction in Gary's ethnic communities.[53] In addition, Jews from Gary's two temples, Temple Beth-El and Temple Israel, established the Hebrew Educational Alliance in 1913 for after-school instruction in Hebrew and in Jewish history and culture.[54] Joshua A. Fishman, in his comprehensive study of *Language Loyalty in the United States,* has noted the pervasiveness of such ethnic folk schools among Orthodox and Jewish immigrants throughout the nation.[55] This pattern of ethnic education in Gary, therefore, conformed to the larger national experience.

For Gary's Orthodox and Jewish immigrants, then, the ethnic folk schools offered another alternative to total reliance on the public schools. As Fishman has written, the ethnic folk school was "the product of the encounter between ethnic immigrants and urban, industrial American mass culture." In a new and unsettling world, the immigrants found in the folk school a means of maintaining their language and passing the old culture and heritage on to their children. In these ethnic group schools, Fishman argues, "ethnicity became self-conscious. It was something to be 'studied,' 'valued,' 'appreciated,' and 'believed in.'" Thus, these ethnic folk schools muted the Americanizing impact of the public schools and made them acceptable, at least through the elementary years and until the legal age for withdrawal.[56]

3

Both the traditionalists and the revisionists in educational history have asserted the importance of the public schools, although they see them as serving quite different functions. It is possible to conclude, however, on the basis of the immigrant educational experience in Gary that the immigrants had a large degree of control and self-determination when it came to educational institutions. They had a variety of educational choices open to them. The law required schooling until age fourteen, later age sixteen, but immigrant parents could decide between public and parochial school alternatives, or they could choose public schools supplemented by the ethnic folk schools and the Sunday schools. They decided how much schooling their children should have, taking what they wanted from the public schools. When the children dropped out of school in the high school years, it was because the parents wanted them to do so. Similarly, immigrant adults decided when and for what reasons they would attend night school—whether for the building of English or vocational skills, for recreation or culture, or for civics and citizenship. Moreover, we know that ethnic family life generally was strong, and that every ethnic group built a whole network of community institutions—churches, political and social groups, athletic clubs, benevolent societies, musical and dramatic organizations, ethnic Boy Scout troops, and so on. These ethnic institutions counteracted the impact of culture-destroying Americanization while serving community and educative functions. Perhaps the school as a mind-shaping and character-building institution has not been as influential as we once thought. Perhaps the public school was not as powerful as we have been led to believe.

In sum, what went on in the Gary schools in some ways fits the conceptual framework established by the revisionist historians. Clearly, the nativist establishment in Gary built a school system designed to Americanize and socialize and manipulate. The schools sought to erase the old immigrant culture and turn the children of the newcomers into capitalist competitors and consumers—to fit them, in short, into their proper niche in the corporate-industrial state. But as we have suggested, this process was only part of the story. Too often we think of schooling as something that is being done to children by the teachers and the schools. To move beyond the radical critique of American education, we need to see the process of socialization in the schools as one which cuts in two directions. We must, of course, be aware of what education meant to the socializers and the Americanizers, but we must not ignore the hopes and aspirations and desires of those who were being socialized and Americanized. The actual behavior of the immigrants over several decades suggests that they were not entirely passive participants in the schooling process.

If immigrants had a considerable degree of choice and opportunity in education, another group of educational consumers in Gary demonstrated a somewhat different pattern of schooling. Like the immigrants, Gary's blacks were subjected to the socializing and manipulating forces of the public schools. Gary's white elites—the business community, the professionals, and the educators—perceived both groups as requiring public schooling in order to fit them to the industrial-technological society and to make them orderly, responsible, law-abiding, and patriotic. The immigrants worked out several alternative means of schooling to moderate the impact of the WASP culture. For the blacks this was more difficult. From the beginning they were segregated in separate classes in white schools or compelled to attend all-black institutions. Nevertheless, within the confines of this white-imposed structure, blacks sought to shape and control their segregated schools. As the next chapter will demonstrate, schooling was a matter of lively concern and debate in Gary's black community.

5

BLACKS AND THE GARY SCHOOLS

The great migration of southern blacks to northern industrial cities during and after World War 1 created massive problems of adjustment, both for the migrants themselves and for the larger society. The dominant white society, particularly its political, social, and economic leaders, established the essential parameters of black life. In housing, for example, previous patterns of segregation solidified, and large black ghettos emerged in every major northern city. Similarly, discriminatory employment practices faced the primarily rural black newcomers. Moreover, competition for jobs and housing between blacks and whites often led to intense racial conflict and violence, such as that which flared in East St. Louis in 1917 and in Chicago in 1919. As the human flow from the South intensified, the public schools became an additional arena of racial strife and competition. The enrollment of increasing numbers of black children, often in formerly all-white schools, stimulated fear and tension among whites and led many cities to adopt or continue formal and informal school segregation policies. This pattern prevailed in Gary, one of the northern cities most heavily affected by the great migration. But segregation in the Gary schools was not a product of a large black enrollment. Rather, it was introduced in the earliest years of the school system by Superintendent William Wirt and the school board.[1]

The segregation of black children in inferior all-black schools or in separate classes in mixed schools was common practice in northern cities by 1900. Stress on educational opportunity and achievement for blacks was widespread in the nineteenth century, particularly during Reconstruction, but this had little bearing on actual practice. As David B.

Tyack has summarized the situation, "Across the nation many of the whites who controlled systems of public education excluded, segregated, or cheated black pupils. Negroes learned that the educational system that was to homogenize other Americans was not meant for them." Black parents and leaders often fought segregation, although some occasionally supported it because of the opportunities thereby opened for black teachers and administrators. Whether challenged or not, however, separate schooling was widely accepted by all shades of the political spectrum before and during the Progressive Era. Indeed, the great majority of white educational reformers became apologists for separate and inferior black schooling because they accepted industrial capitalism's demands for manual workers.[2]

Early and continued segregation in the Gary schools was, then, in line with established policy in northern cities. The details of this situation, its establishment by Wirt and the white hierarchy, as well as the resistance in the black community, however, offer tantalizing insights into how the Gary schools operated. While the rhetoric of progressive educators such as Wirt stressed the importance of a meaningful education for all, what was considered meaningful for blacks differed somewhat from that offered their white neighbors.

The city's black population did not increase significantly until the outbreak of World War 1 in Europe. Some 383 blacks, mostly railroad and construction workers and their families, had arrived in Gary by 1910. The turmoil of war, however, gradually disrupted European migration, forcing the steel company to turn from immigrants to the neglected reservoir of southern black labor. This pattern became especially prevalent after the United States entered the war, for almost one-fourth of the city's white millworkers entered the armed forces. In 1920 over 5,000 blacks resided in the city. The major influx occurred in the following decade, however, and by 1930 Gary's black community had reached 18,000, or 17.8 percent of the total population of just over 100,000. After an initial period in which the steel company housed Gary's black laborers in barracks, the workers and their families moved to the city's southern fringe. Because of limited housing, they lived side by side with eastern and southern European immigrants. Although they lived in the same neighborhoods, blacks and whites did not join the same organizations, churches, or social groupings. Nevertheless, there is no evidence of significant conflict between white working class immigrants and their black neighbors until the mid-1920s. And even then few reported incidents occurred. Indeed, there are many indications of harmony between the two. Discrimination and segregation resulted not from the beliefs and passions of the white immigrant workers, but rather from the calculated policies of the city's elite—its realtors, professionals, businessmen, steel company officials, and educators.[3]

In December, 1908, the school board, with Wirt's full support, agreed to establish a separate school for the city's 33 black elementary pupils (out of a total enrollment of about 900), while 2 black students of high school age remained in the white school. This was done, naturally, for the black children's benefit. As the *Gary Daily Tribune* editorialized:

> Negro children in white schools are many times subjected to insults which naturally embitter them against the whites. As the pupils grow older, however, there is less cause for this and in the high schools there is rarely any difficulty from that score. In Gary some objections have been raised against the segregation plan of the board of education, but fortunately those objections were raised by persons who had no children and who could hardly be expected to be competent judges. The negroes' salvation is in [their] own hands.

With muted protests, the black parents accepted the move. In 1913, after the opening of the Froebel School, a unit long to remain the city's largest, all the black children (about sixty) were transferred to the new building. Here, in the words of one of the two black teachers, "all the formal work of the colored children in the first five grades was done with colored teachers in separate classes." A dual pattern of segregation had now been set, either separate buildings or separate classes in an integrated building. Both types of segregated schooling would remain for many years. The students apparently quickly fell into the pattern. "A school club was formed by the colored pupils at Froebel school yesterday afternoon," the *Gary Daily Tribune* noted in September, 1914. "The social and school spirit will be encouraged and an effort made to inculcate a premium upon being a school boy or a school girl in Gary."[4]

In the fall of 1915 two classes of black students were transferred from Froebel to a small portable building on 21st Avenue, "more convenient to their homes." A delegation from the local chapter of the National Association for the Advancement of Colored People protested to the school board about such segregation, accusing the schools of "breeding race prejudice by segregation." But the school remained. Wirt agreed to permit black parents to send their children to the separate classes at Froebel School if they wished. He admitted, however, in reply to a subsequent protest from NAACP national headquarters, that the

Gary schools "have been segregated from the very beginning. It is a settled policy in this community to continue this segregation." In an editorial aside the *Crisis*, NAACP's journal, remarked facetiously, "No wonder the Gary schools are considered as models throughout the land." The portable building quickly became overcrowded, and within two years there were additional portables, well over two hundred pupils, and three teachers; the school board had to rent the basement of a neighboring church to use as an auditorium. Although the extensive facilities at the Froebel and Emerson schools impressed the thousands of visitors who toured the schools during these years, a large percentage of Gary's black pupils were forced to put up with overcrowded shacks and overworked teachers. Similar conditions, however, existed for approximately one-third of the city's eight thousand pupils in the fall of 1918.[5]

While the all-black portables rapidly expanded, the situation at Froebel School was going in the opposite direction, toward greater integration. An insufficient supply of black teachers—indeed, there seems to have been only one in 1917—led to the integration of many blacks in regular classes. This change in policy excited some of the white parents. In October, 1917, they petitioned the school board "that colored children be separated from the white, while attending said Froebel School." This separation, the petitioners argued, had been "a customary rule in the past and is still practiced in the schools of the North Side [Emerson and Jefferson schools]. Therefore, it is unfair that the subscribers of this petition, who are also taxpayers, should not enjoy the same privilege only because we reside on the South Side."[6] Two issues particularly bothered these immigrant parents: that the previous pattern of segregated schooling, which they had become accustomed to, had been changed, and that they feared different treatment from the predominately WASP, higher paid workers and managers who lived on the North Side. This fear of being victimized by the city's elite would long plague the immigrant neighborhoods.

The parents soon obtained strong support from 43 (out of a total of 54) of Froebel's teachers. J. W. Lester, the leader of the dissident teachers, later wrote that as the black enrollment increased "conflicts grew frequent and furious." Calling a special meeting, the teachers voted to ask the school board "to take steps to quell the rioting, and prevent still more dangerous developments." Lester prevailed upon the teachers to petition Principal Charles Coons instead, "as to carry the question over the head of the principal, would only reflect on him and hinder, rather than help, our cause." The petition, dated March 1,

1918, complained of "frequent disturbances, innumerable cases of insubordination, and other ill effects of mixing the white and colored children." The teachers feared that "with the rapidly increasing colored population, the friction will be proportionately aggravated. They now constitute a positive menace to the moral and physical welfare of both pupils and teachers." In support, the petition was accompanied by excerpts from nineteen anonymous letters from teachers about the problems created by black children in the school. The teachers' complaints were heavily racist. As one noted, "The promiscuous association of the white and colored pupils is a terrible thing. It should not be allowed, particularly in a school with the large number of foreign pupils. They will soon lose sight of the color line." The teachers, mostly native-born American women, had had no experience in working with black children. They could not handle the situation, which they readily admitted, although they projected onto the black children the cause of their difficulties.[7]

Principal Coons, whom Lester blamed for refusing to listen to the teachers' complaints, questioned many of the teachers' charges. A good administrator, he was not about to relinquish authority to his underlings. Instead, he forwarded the petition to Superintendent Wirt. Coons pointed out his own earlier recommendation against total segregation, but suggested that with the rising black enrollment the time might now be ripe for such a policy. The problem, he noted, was "troublesome," and especially so in a school run on the Gary plan. In the Froebel School, Coons wrote, "it is necessary for us to rotate mixed classes into cooking, sewing, art, swimming, etc. In some types of these special activities, these children do not seem to get along well together." Furthermore, he argued, many of the older black children were practically illiterate, and when placed in lower grades with smaller children caused special problems for the teachers. Coons, in conclusion, left the final decision to the school board, noting that he would "not insist that they be taken from this school." In any event, the school would continue to function as well as possible. Wirt refused to take the matter seriously. He apparently did not inform the school board of the situation, believing that Coons was well qualified to handle the matter. Froebel remained integrated, although soon enough an additional all-black school would emerge on the city's East Side.[8]

While Froebel School and the South Side parents and teachers were concerned about strife and segregation, to the general public all seemed well; at least so they read in the daily paper. "The Gary schools are doing more for the colored people, both children and adults, than is any other public school system in America," the *Gary Daily Tribune* noted in July, 1918. "The Gary schools not only care for all of those who voluntarily report for work but they send word to homes, churches, lodges and social gatherings, inviting our colored friends to take advantage of some one or more of the splendid things offered free to them on the same conditions as to the people of other races." The words were those of Assistant Superintendent G. W. Swartz, who was publicizing the summer school offerings for black children and adults. Two months later Swartz repeated his optimism. He pointed out in a letter to J. E. McCoughtry, vice president of the local NAACP, that many white as well as black children attended school in portable buildings because of the need to provide schools within walking distance of their homes.

> We are doing everything possible to take care of our colored population [he assured him] by giving the children the very best kind of program during the day, by opening the schools to them on Saturday, by giving them all the work they or their parents wish throughout the summer months, by opening up all of our buildings to the colored people in the evening, by permitting them to use our school buildings on Sunday under the same conditions as other citizens, by giving the men and women free instruction in all the industrial occupations in which they show an interest and by holding meetings for our colored citizens for the purpose of explaining the advantages the schools offer to them and urging them to attend evening classes.[9]

Swartz was sincere. What was important was to offer educational opportunities to blacks, and encourage them to take advantage of the situation. And, after all, conditions in Gary were considerably better than those in the South. Integration or segregation were not abstract issues, only matters of convenience.

While Swartz was publicly praising the fine conditions for black children in Gary, in private correspondence to Wirt he lamented the inferior facilities at the 21st Avenue School:

> Playgrounds—Children have practically nothing to use. . . . The gym floor should be provided with circles and other geometric figures for games. . . . Clocks—2 new clocks for rooms without any. Regulate the other clocks. No two show same time. A difference of nearly 1 hour was observed in the time of two rooms. This disorganizes the school and helps to keep things topsy turvy.

Lavatory—The facilities are wholly inadequate. Wash basins, more towels and two or three small mirrors should be provided.

Swartz believed "the teachers want to have a good school at 21st Ave. They rightfully feel that in some respects they are neglected." Wirt, in reply, assured Swartz of his desire to correct these problems, but he believed that "much of the difficulty at 21st Ave. School is due to the lack of understanding on the part of the local teachers as to the methods of securing supplies and their own responsibility in the matter." Wirt thus deftly shifted onto the teachers primary blame for the school's inadequate supplies. The children of the 21st Avenue School were not unique in being deprived of the magnificent facilities available at the Emerson and Froebel schools, for there were seven other such portable schools in the city. It is instructive to note, however, the inefficiency of the Gary school administration, which neglected the portables. The teachers were expected to make their needs known, but doing so did not guarantee adequate supplies. Some things they were expected to furnish themselves. For example, when the teachers desired a Victrola they were expected to purchase it with their own money, even though it was "very much needed for play and auditorium in day school, evening school and Saturday school." Whether this was common for other schools is unknown, but in the case of the 21st Avenue School it was obvious that the school board would not provide all the equipment deemed essential.[10]

The influx of black workers in 1918 prompted the Gary Land Company, a subsidiary of U.S. Steel, to build houses in a sparsely populated section on the East Side, which became the city's first all-black neighborhood. In early 1919 a portable school was erected on Virginia Street for children in the area. According to a school history written in 1932, "It was built at the request of the parents of the Ninth Subdivision, who felt that it would be safer for their children to have a school nearer their homes." The school's all-black population jumped from an initial thirty-five to ninety-four by September, in the first eight grades. While previous segregation had been essentially de jure, now it was also de facto. Many blacks were hostile to this further segregation. Even before the buildings were erected, blacks held a mass meeting "to take up the matter of segregation." But, of course, they could do nothing.[11] The school grew rapidly, and by 1923 there were 13 teachers and 600 children.

By 1920 racial patterns were firmly established in the Gary schools. The situation was far from satisfactory to many of the city's black citizens. Nevertheless, black commitment to schooling was remarkably strong. United States census statistics for school attendance in Gary demonstrate that a larger proportion of black children attended school than foreign-born children in each decennial year from 1910 through 1940. In 1910 some 95 percent of Gary's black school-age children attended school, compared to 79.5 percent for foreign-born whites (see table 2). The percentage of blacks attending school dropped somewhat to 80.7 in 1920 (73.6 percent for foreign-born whites), but increased to 91.1 percent in 1930 (84 percent for foreign-born whites) and 94.6 percent in 1940 (93.4 percent for foreign-born whites). Local school surveys told a similar story. A Gary school survey in 1922, for instance, reported only 15.9 percent of Gary's black school-age children as dropouts—a dropout rate lower than that reported for all Gary's major immigrant groups. By comparison, the dropout rate for the city's Greek children was 33.3 percent, for Poles 30.5 percent, for Lithuanians 28.3 percent, for Russians 25 percent, for Croatians 24.5 percent, for Serbians 23.5 percent, and for Italians 22.1 percent (see table 6). These school attendance statistics conform to a larger national pattern described in recently published research by Timothy L. Smith. Smith argues that the large proportions of black children attending school, especially in the urban North, reflected a faith in schooling as a means of personal advancement.[12] It is also likely, however, that discriminatory employment patterns in Gary made it difficult for black teenagers to secure regular employment, thus encouraging them to remain in school longer. In any case, despite the segregated patterns of schooling in Gary, blacks seized upon the opportunity for learning which the public schools provided.

At the same time, there were other beneficial aspects to segregated schooling. For example, the large number of black teachers—16 by 1922, 77 by 1930—served as a source of pride and leadership in the black community. David Tyack has noted that in those cities with large numbers of black teachers and administrators "there was generally a high degree of conscious segregation of black pupils in separate schools—and normally black teachers were only allowed to teach in these institutions." Thus, segregation, while deplorable, was not altogether objectionable to some. As E. D. Simpson, the city's first black teacher and first principal of the Virginia Street School, wrote to Wirt in early 1919:

> The number of Colored Teachers has had a sudden growth and judging from the increase in our population, there shall be a still larger force necessary to handle the many children in our schools. Personally, I am extremely anxious that each of these teachers shall acquit himself with credit; that he shall give to the children an Inspiration; to the patrons Service; and to the community a noble life. Particularly, do we need at all times men and women of

unquestioned moral fiber; men and women whose lives shall radiate light and enlightenment into the minds and souls of our children and grown-ups on and on throughout the years.[13]

Surely, not all black teachers would be such paragons of virtue or strong leadership, but many were very dedicated to enlightening and leading the black community, children as well as adults. And considering the experiences of the black children in the Froebel School with racist white teachers, there was considerable merit in desiring segregated facilities with an all-black staff. This view was most eloquently articulated by F. C. McFarlane, principal of Roosevelt School, in the late 1920s; much earlier, however, it had its spokesmen.

In a letter to the *Gary Daily Tribune* in January, 1921, one John H. Smith praised the black schools for providing teaching jobs for educated black women. "In fact," he continued, "there are no segregated schools in Gary, only so far as the parents of the children choose to make it. There is nothing to prohibit colored children from going to any of the schools, and there is nothing to prohibit white children from going to any of the schools. . . . It is only a matter of race pride on the part of the parents of the children of each race." This was not entirely true. Indeed, the existence of segregated schools in Gary resulted from de facto and de jure conditions, as well as voluntary choices by both white and black parents.[14]

While voluntary segregation was prominent, civil rights activists in the city continued to protest such conditions. The visit in April, 1921, of Dean William Pickens, NAACP's associate field secretary, elicited from Wirt and the Gary Land Company's H. S. Norton statements on their commitment to "the advancement of colored people in Gary." Both indicated that "the foundation has been firmly laid for eliminating any prejudice that might have existed." They were referring not to the demise of segregation, but to the attempt to provide somewhat equal facilities and opportunities for black children, such as the "colored trade school" established at the 25th Avenue School, which epitomized school segregation. The origins and development of the trade school are indicative of how far segregation had developed. The 21st Avenue School was moved to a new location on 25th Avenue in 1921, already the site of a white elementary school under the principalship of J. W. Standley. With its own black principal and faculty, the new school remained completely separate for two years. From 1923 to 1929 both schools were placed under the direction of one white principal; in 1929 the black school (now called Roosevelt Annex) again obtained its own black principal, F. C. McFarlane. In addition to the basic elementary classes, the black school also had a trade school for teenagers, with courses deemed fitting for blacks, such as pipe fitting, sheet metal, and mechanical drawing for boys and home economics for girls. "With the organization of the trade school, the Gary system continues to advance the new order of secondary education by adjusting instruction along the lines which function in the lives of the boys and girls after they leave school," adult school director Albert Fertsch proudly announced in an article on the program. This new "realism" in education was becoming very popular at this time, but it also served to channel blacks (as well as many whites) into manual vocations.[15]

While the establishment of the 25th Avenue School with its vocational program was a step forward in Wirt's thinking, many blacks still refused to accept the principle of forced segregation. In September, 1921, Wirt and the school board were informed of the "dissatisfaction of colored residents and parents with certain prejudicial practices—transfers, etc., now obtaining in the Gary schools." Specifically, the parents complained of the transfer of black students "to schools not carrying the same grades or class work to which the pupils are eligible and entitled. " They also protested the involuntary assignment of black students to vocational classes and the creation of "distinct Negro school centers."[16] However, the situation remained unchanged.

In 1923 a new protest tactic was attempted. Lewis Campbell, former secretary of the local NAACP, presented a petition to state School Superintendent Benjamin Burris protesting "alleged unsatisfactory school conditions" in Gary. The petition charged that black children fell behind in their work because they did not have enough school books or recitation time. These shortcomings were blamed on the superintendent's "gross neglect of the public schools of Gary." The state authorities referred the matter back to Wirt. At the same time the national office of the NAACP, informed by Campbell of the Gary situation, urged local branch president T. J. Wilson to oppose segregated schooling in the city.[17]

The following year the issue of segregation again surfaced publicly. Black attorney W. C. Hueston, a leading civil rights advocate, complained to Wirt about assignment of black children to the Virginia Street School. The principal of the nearby Pulaski School had asserted "that her school was for the Polish and the Virginia Street School was for Negroes." Hueston believed that most black children would voluntarily attend the Virginia Street School, but he added that "it is the pride of the Negroes here that we do not, at least in policy, have a separate school system." Besides, it was wrong to tell the Polish children "that we have a separate school for them and one for Negroes." Hueston's letter neatly summarized the major threads of black attitudes toward school segregation: it was probably favored by most blacks, but it was wrong in principle, and it instilled racism in recent white immigrants. Wirt, in response, argued that the Pulaski School was all white because of the wishes of the parents in that district. "In order to prevent serious race conditions in the schools," he continued, "it is the policy to offer, if possible, opportunities for determined individuals to escape conditions that conflict seriously with their prejudices. We have, therefore, one separate school for whites, two for colored, and fifteen for both." For Wirt the fault was, naturally, with the bigoted parents, who preferred segregation. He took no credit (or blame) for the situation. And in arguing that the remaining fifteen schools were integrated he was being even more disingenuous, for de facto residential segregation meant that only the Froebel School was in any real way integrated. Passing the buck was a common practice when dealing with segregation, and Wirt was as skilled as any at the practice.[18]

By the mid-1920s, then, segregation had been established in the Gary schools, but this did not mean that all accepted the pattern. Part of the problem was the lack of consistency, for segregation and integration existed side by side, with critics and defenders among both whites and blacks. The confusion among whites over which policy was the more important surfaced in 1927 during the Emerson School strike.[19] In the black community the dialogue among integrationists and separationists was more subtle, and yet more blatant, becoming personalized in the figures of F. C. McFarlane and H. Theodore Tatum. McFarlane, principal of Roosevelt Annex School, in the words of black teacher Jacob Reddix, his colleague and friend, "brought to Gary a well defined philosophy of black education which he believed would be beneficial to Negro children who had traditionally been legally segregated in the South and were increasingly subjected to *de facto* segregation in the North." McFarlane believed in separate black schools, where "Negro children could develop dignity, pride, and self-respect. Under the conditions existing in Gary in 1927, however, the black child inevitably developed an inferiority complex." This problem would be partially solved by the opening of the Roosevelt School in 1931.[20] McFarlane represented black pride and the acceptance of segregation as the means to achieve community development and cohesiveness.

Challenging McFarlane and his black separatist position was H. Theodore Tatum, who became principal of Virginia Street School in 1925. Tatum was a strong integrationist and a believer in working closely with the white power structure in the city. Nevertheless, in heading all-black schools, he was forced to encourage black community pride and involvement. "I accepted the thesis," Tatum wrote in his 1927 yearly report, "that it is the chief duty of a school to establish itself as a community asset through its contribution in enabling that community to realize on its investments in terms of citizenship, character, and social efficiency." A strong administrator, he "tried to promote a genuine feeling of confidence between the principal and teachers, and the teaching corps and student-body." Such a policy, he argued, encouraged "wholesome respect for authority and a whole-hearted participation in all school affairs." In addition to promoting internal school discipline and dedication, Tatum also emphasized the importance of working with parents and "worthwhile civic organizations." In June, 1928, when his school enrolled over 850 students in grades K–8, Tatum reported "measurable improvement in the character of instruction and the added facilities offered for same." He did complain of the dilapidated buildings, but assumed that "the superior wisdom of the school authorities" would soon solve the problem. And they did. A new brick building and adjoining portables were constructed near the all-white Pulaski School, and in the fall of 1928 the Virginia Street School moved the few blocks and became known as the East Pulaski School, entirely separate from its renamed white neighbor, the West Pulaski School.[21] They remained divided until 1951. School segregation had seemingly reached its epitome in Gary, with separate white and black schools adjoining one another at both the Pulaski and Roosevelt locations, with only the Froebel School still remaining integrated, although even here there was considerable social segregation. By the late 1920s the system had become well established, although this did not mean that it was acceptable to blacks or whites, as would soon become apparent.

Black protests against segregation and inferior facilities were infrequent and of little effect in northern cities in the early decades of the twentieth century. White resistance was, of course, partly to blame. But, in addition, no clear consensus existed within the black community as to what should be accomplished. Blacks were particularly torn between advocating integration in principle and accepting separation in practice. Despite warnings from the national NAACP urging vigilance regarding further segregation, the latter policy usually prevailed, even among strong integrationists such as Tatum. The black community was proud of the schooling facilities offered their children in Gary, often inadequate compared to Emerson and other white schools but a definite cut above what they had known in the South. And they strongly favored the Gary school plan. In weighing abstract issues against concrete realities, blacks consistently favored separate facilities, although they did not always admit that this was so. They were, of course, encouraged by Wirt, the school board, and the white elite in Gary, who first established segregation in 1908 and who always justified their actions by blaming white immigrants. Whether the immigrants were inclined toward segregation before they arrived or learned racism from the established leaders is currently in doubt, although there is strong evidence supporting the latter.[22]

In any case, segregated school patterns persisted. A 1962 investigation of the Gary schools by the NAACP confirmed intensified patterns of segregation in post-World War 2 years. In 1951 85 percent of Gary's schools were segregated, and 83 percent of the city's black children attended such schools. By 1961 90 percent of the schools had been segregated, with 97 percent of the black children enrolled in such schools.[23] And in the past decade discussions of integration have been rendered almost meaningless in Gary, by white flight to outlying suburbs. The Gary schools were segregated from the earliest years and have remained so to the present, through a combination of de facto and de jure conditions in the city. As the Emerson School strike of 1927 indicated, however, the development of a segregated school system was not always achieved smoothly and painlessly. The decade of the 1920s, thus, was hardly tranquil and harmonious.

6

THE 1920s
The Maturity of the System

The Gary plan, and the Gary schools in particular, reached maturity during the 1920s. While the basic structure of the system had been worked out before World War 1, the combination of changing economic and social conditions, Wirt's thinking, and local developments sharpened its outlines and extended its programs. The schools' support of the technological-corporate state became clearer, particularly their connection with monopoly capital and their impact on black and ethnic members of the working class, both children and adults, whose twin preoccupations of work and consumerism had to be skillfully manipulated. Segregation increased, although somewhat accidentally, because of the Emerson School strike of 1927. Thus, during the 1920s the Gary schools experienced no decisive break from the past, only a further elaboration of programs and policies now expanded and fully developed.

Robert Church, in his recent history of education in the United States, notes "a subtle but profound shift" in schooling following World War 1. "Before 1917 educational reform was infused with national purpose; the schools were regarded as vital social institutions. Increasingly, in the twenties and thirties, each school or school system became the creature of its local community and set out to perform functions directed at improving local conditions or solving local problems." This interpretation follows from the traditional view of the 1920s as a passive decade. Church notes "an increased provincialism about education after 1920, a definite sense that schooling was vital less for the changes it encouraged than for its role in maintaining traditional values and for guarding against social change."

Such a view, while capturing the essential conservativism of American society at the time (and before and since), effectively ignores widespread acceptance of consumerism and corporate capitalism. Small town values coexisted with a welcoming of the social, economic, and material fruits of urban development, often to the former's disadvantage. The trend had begun years before and continued, even increased, in the 1920s. As Columbia educator Edward Reisner noted in 1924, American life after 1900 was characterized by "a rapidly increasing complexity of economic and social conditions." These developments demanded "the elaboration of new social controls" by both federal and state governments. It was natural, Reisner wrote, that "public agencies for education should have received a great deal of attention in this time, since the schools must serve as the fundamental social control in a democratic society." There was, indeed, no sharp break with the past, only a quickening of the tempo over the years. Church's distinction is thus too abstract, ignoring fundamental economic and social continuities significantly more important than specific issues such as the urban-rural split. Church believes "it was a desperate fight—between an older set of values that had become increasingly rigid and sour in the face of powerful challenges to their survival and a newer set that were trying to fit themselves to a changing world and social structure but which were not as yet clearly defined," with the schools supporting the former.[1] In Gary, however, the latter predominated, and this was probably generally true. Rural values might be given lip service, but technology was welcomed, with its concomitant products, institutions, and dangers.

Publicity about the Gary plan substantially dropped off after World War 1, leading historians to assume that the system disintegrated following the critical report of the General Education Board in 1918. Nonetheless, adoption of the Gary system increased in the 1920s; by 1929 over two hundred cities in forty-one states had experimented with it in redesigning their elementary schools. To promote the plan and facilitate communication among its supporters, the National Association for the Study of the Platoon or Work-Study-Play School Organization was organized in 1925. Sparked by Alice Barrows, this new organization published *The Platoon School* magazine, conducted national and regional meetings, and publicized the platoon school plan among teachers and administrators. According to Roscoe Case in *The Platoon School in America* (1931), the system had four characteristics:

> (1) A school the organization and program of which are in keeping with child nature; (2) a comprehensive training for citizenship outside the school by training pupils in meeting problems which are comparable to life's problems while in school; (3) efficient use of the school plant; and (4) a spirit of experimentation, testing, and development in order that the present platoon-school system may

evolve farther in the direction of schools which more satisfactorily meet the needs of our complex and changing civilization.[2]

ase's idealistic view captured enthusiasm for the Gary plan during the ecade, even as its utility became increasingly suspect. Its adoption ationally was limited to elementary schools, with varying degrees of nplementation and success, while in Gary the high school was quickly ecoming a vital part of the system.

The most significant characteristic of public schooling during the ecade was growth, influencing all else. Nationally, public school enroll- ient jumped from 21,500,000 in 1920 to 25,500,000 in 1930, after /hich it leveled off for another two decades. This was less than a 25 per- ent increase, with the major growth coming in the cities. In Gary school nrollment shot up from about 9,000 in 1920 to over 19,000 in 1930; here was no growth during the 1930s. High school expansion in Gary /as the most spectacular, jumping from 800 to about 5,000; nationally, he number doubled from 2 million to 4 million. The increase in teaching taff in Gary was proportionate, rising from around 300 at the beginning f the decade to over 600 at the end, with additional principals and upervisors. New buildings were needed to accommodate the hordes at he gates—large, permanent, brick structures in the older neighborhoods; iortable, frame cubicles in the outlying areas. In 1922 there were two arge unit schools, built over a decade before, and about ten elementary chools scattered about the city. By 1931 there were six brick unit schools nd another fifteen elementary schools of frame or brick. Between 1922 nd 1931 the value of school property more than tripled, increasing from 1.8 million to $6.6 million.[3] Expansion—in enrollment, staff, buildings, nd expenditures—marked the Gary schools in the 1920s, expansion that vas welcomed and worshipped as a sign that society was healthy and rosperous, that children were indeed under control. But growth also en- ailed problems.

While Wirt increased his supervision over the mundane matters of space nd money, he also devoted much time to refining and defending the jary plan. The Rockefeller Foundation's Abraham Flexner, who had ippointed himself head of the Gary survey, wrote later in his autobiog- aphy that "the general effect of the report was disastrous to the ex- iloitation of the Gary system." Education, he said, was "far too com- ilicated a process to be advertised on the basis of inadequate supervision nd without definite accounting—mental, moral, and financial. With the iublication of the report the school world was relieved, and the Gary iystem ceased to be an object of excitement. It disappeared from dis- ussion as suddenly as it had arisen." Reviewers, generally, praised the report. Wirt, however, felt only disgust. While he could soberly report to one correspondent in early 1920 that "the General Education Report had not made any difference any [one] way or the other in my estimation," three months later he was warning another that the report "does not represent the conditions in the Gary schools in any respect at the time the Survey was made." Wirt never launched a public attack on the report, but in a lengthy manuscript entitled "Plain Facts About the Rockefeller Foundation Survey of the Gary Schools," written in 1918, he expressed his stifled rage:

> Eight or ten years ago it was the common practice with many professional educators to label the Gary School Plan as a joke. Judging from the survey report it is now the practice among some professional educators to admit the value of the Gary School Plan but to label the people responsible for its development as jokes.
>
> As Superintendent of the public schools at Gary, Indiana, I am not very much concerned with the effect of this report upon my own reputation. It has been blasted so many times that a blast more or less does not make very much difference. But as to the effect upon the many teachers and principals in the Gary Public Schools who have labored zealously in this experiment I am concerned. Therefore I wish to point out briefly the many errors, misrepresentations and false conclusions in the report.[4]

The report, coming hard on the heels of the defeat of the Gary plan in New York City, coupled with the outbreak of war, briefly dampened national enthusiasm for becoming Garyized. Wirt, accepting the obvious, turned his back on the national scene, following the national trend. On January 31, 1919, the *Gary Daily Tribune* announced that Wirt would speak at the First Presbyterian Church on education. The article continued:

> Although Mr. Wirt has spoken in every other leading city in the United States this is the first time during his residence in Gary that he has ever honored the city with a talk on education, his life work, and the institution which under his wonderful direction has come to be one of the most talked-about things in the history of the country. . . . During the past year he has been able to spend more time in Gary, than at any other one time, and his presence here has helped much in all activities.[5]

While this was not absolutely true—he had given a few speeches some years before—it is indicative of both Wirt's new sensitivity to the local situation and the city's need to have him stay home.

Wirt feared the GEB survey might have cooled local support; he was also anxious to get money for expansion. While he sought to rally support from all sections of the city, he concentrated upon one in particular—businessmen. "Although this age was not the first to proclaim the interdependence of business and education, it cherished the idea with loving care and proclaimed it as a perfect marriage," historian Edward Krug has written. Wirt was strongly pro-business. He was a banker and entrepreneur, and had always associated with the business and professional classes. His subordinates had the same inclinations. In late January, 1919, "Gary schoolmasters" organized a banquet for the city's businessmen. "This affair is being planned for the purpose of creating a better acquaintance and friendship between the businessmen and the instructors in the city schools," the *Daily Tribune* explained. Over the next several weeks Wirt spoke at the Presbyterian church and Temple Israel, two bastions of the business community. "These talks bring the parents and schools into closer harmony," the *Daily Tribune* noted, "and establish a bond between them, which is of invaluable good to the community."[6]

The school system's public relations campaign was far reaching. The school board announced:

> There has been some criticism to the effect that Gary schools and their heads want to run everything, want to monopolize everything and say what shall and what shall not be done. This is a mistake. It is quite contrary to what we have set out to do. The school system wants to be one of the co-operating agencies working for the betterment of the community and it will do everything possible in its power to help carry out any plans which will be confided to it.

Simultaneously the City Council announced it would investigate the schools, and the Civic Service Club staged a public meeting, with speakers from the schools, "to tell the things that Gary people want to know about the schools and have been unable to find out."[7] Both the educators and their local supporters wished to bridge the gap that existed between the public and the schools and that caused such disastrous results for the Gary plan in New York City.

The high points of this campaign came in the early years of the decade. First, in late 1921 the Gary Commercial Club, closely linked with the U.S. Steel Corporation and representing corporate leadership in the city, began an investigation of the schools, seemingly designed more as a publicity stunt than a critical appraisal. The daily paper, however, urged that the study be a serious one, "not be made willy-nilly to back up the present discipline and status of the work there but to ascertain facts." The committee should, the editors urged,

> test out the schools to see whether the pupils are acquiring character and mental power. It should ascertain whether the teachers are up to date and thorough. The Gary schools were once criticized in a survey made by the Rockefeller foundation and there were some strictures made upon the discipline. These matters, we think, have been largely corrected but the committee should keep a sharp eye out for such delinquencies. . . . Gary schools must be abreast of the age.

So, the GEB survey was taken seriously, and now it was time to see whether the schools were doing their proper job—"to fit pupils for the right kind of life." The survey was completed after six months of testimony and observation. The schools were given a clean bill of health. While some criticisms surfaced, they appeared to be "brought about by general unfamiliarity of the people with the working of the present system. . . . We believe [the report concluded] the school authorities here are endeavoring to conduct the schools along the line of meeting the requirements of an industrial city like Gary."[8] The Commercial Club thus affirmed its support of Wirt and the system, a vital matter in this industrial community.

Shortly after the report, in May, 1922, a massive school celebration was held in the heart of the business district. "Over 8,000 pupils, directed by 251 teachers, gave 637 programs during educational week," Gary's daily newspaper reported. In shop windows lining the main street students

> performed their tasks before hundreds of people without the slightest loss of poise. In some windows one found a group of students doing mechanical drawing, in another a history lesson, in another demonstrating as living pictures the stories in the classics read in the English classes. Exhibits of the class work were to be found, too, and in all, the week was an effort upon the part of the school officials and teachers to bring the work, study, play system and its accomplishments before the eyes of the Gary people who have thus far had no opportunity of viewing it first hand.

An official report was one thing; actually seeing the children engaged in a variety of stimulating and useful activities was quite another. Two years later Principal Charles Coons of Froebel School praised the current education week as a great success: "The city was captured; the strongholds of commercialism were overthrown and the whole city capitulated to this onslaught of the Educational forces of the city." There was, certainly, a merger of capitalism and education in the Steel City. Visiting the city in June, 1922, Judge Elbert H. Gary, chairman of the board of U.S. Steel, was welcomed by 6,000 Gary school children who waved flags and cheered the city's founder. At the Froebel School, where more than 3,000 children of all nationalities grouped in front of the building, "a beautiful flag was raised and 3,000 children's voices recited the creed in unison. At Virginia [Street School] park 500 colored school children cheered the visitor and sang the songs so dear to their race and color. Judge Gary was visibly impressed."[9]

The close identification of patriotism, schooling, and support of the corporate-technological state was continually encouraged by Wirt and the city's educators. During "boys' week" in May, 1923, when ten thousand Gary school children and civic club members marched in the Loyalty Day parade, they made visible a bond the superintendent rejoiced in witnessing. "Fifty different nationalities and races were included in the parade," the *Gary Post-Tribune* remarked, "but all were Americans. . . . Many of the marchers were youngsters not so far removed from the radical teachings of their ancestors, but they have been in America long enough to realize and appreciate the teachings of American schools and the meaning of American liberty." As part of the festivities, schoolboys were taken on tours of local factories, for "the heads of these industrial institutions realize the great need and advantage of assisting boys when they are young in order that when grown, they may be better able to be fitted to be either employees or employers." The purpose of these tours, as the paper noted, was "to demonstrate to the boys the necessity for being not only well educated but also for being trained for the work he expects to follow throughout his life." There was no comparable week set aside for girls, of course. But boys, because of their work potential, were singled out for praise and attention. The schools' role in the city's economic life was nowhere better illustrated than in a *Post-Tribune* editorial in 1925: "Probably the most important single industry in Gary is that of educating the children of this community. The manager of this great industry is William A. Wirt." To Robert and Helen Lynd, the schools of Middletown (Muncie) were like factories, "a thoroughly regimented world." In

Gary, on the other hand, the schools operated differently, with considerably more fluidity and heterogeneity, but the end product was the same—integrating schooling with the corporate order.[10]

The corporate model envisioned harmony between managers, workers, and clients in schools as in industry and society generally. Cooperation was essential for maximum efficiency and productivity. But in Gary the schools were not unified to Wirt's satisfaction. The teachers were a fly in the soup. The postwar depression and inflation hit hard in Gary, postponing construction of new schools until 1922 and heightening teacher dissatisfaction over salaries. Leading the fight for higher salaries was the teachers' union. First organized in 1914 and active in inaugurating the American Federation of Teachers in 1916, the Gary teachers' union was in healthy shape for a contest with Wirt and the school board over salaries. Although unionism was on the defensive after 1919, following the defeat of the steel strike in Gary and of general strike activity throughout the country, in January, 1920, the teachers' union demanded first a $20 a month and then a $40 a month increase for each teacher. Strongly supported by the local press, the teachers met opposition from a school board grumbling about too little money. This stalling swelled the union's membership. "Teachers all over this country are realizing that, to keep up with the trend of the times, they must be organized, and Gary teachers are rapidly falling into line. From present indications the local federation will be 100 per cent strong," announced one member. The teachers finally settled for a $25 raise. Soon thereafter the union lost most of its members, and by 1923 it was defunct. The Gary union's demise echoed the national trend, for the AFT was experiencing hard times in the 1920s with the disappearance of many locals, the chartering of few new ones, and the cancelation of its publication *American Teacher* in 1921.[11]

While the teachers appeared to be making some gains, Wirt, jealous of his prerogatives and always working to maintain control over the teachers, introduced a new rating system. Although initially accepted, it became a festering wound that led sixteen years later to the union's renaissance and triumph over the superintendent. The new system established four ratings—A,B,C,D—each determined by principals and supervisors and each attached to a salary scale. The catch was that only 25 percent of the teachers could have the top rating, 40 percent the B, 30 percent the C, with the remaining 5 percent getting the D and seeming dismissal. Since the same teachers usually got the A rating every year, and therefore the highest salaries, there was little chance for the remaining 75 percent to receive much of a raise. Moreover, the new system created an artificial hierarchy among the teachers. Principal

Coons immediately sensed the problem, warning Wirt in 1922 that "you are headed for a lot of trouble when you arbitrarily limit the number of teachers who can get into the upper group to 25%." But the superintendent, oblivious to criticism, ignored the issue. He was satisfied, the teachers seemed compliant, so why worry. Harmony had prevailed.[12]

With the new rating system in effect, and the union disbanded, Wirt believed now the schools could concentrate on dealing with children. To get the teachers in the right frame of mind, they were approached by the city's business leaders. The Commercial Club's survey brought business leaders and teachers together in a common effort to defend the system. Similarly, at a general teachers' meeting in late 1923 the crowd was treated to two speeches, one by the president of the local Rotary Club, and the other by a representative of International Harvester Company. The former "spoke on the ideals of service" while the latter "gave a talk on investments." The age of business had definitely arrived. But teacher discontent, sparked by the rating system, smoldered below the surface throughout the decade.[13]

The teachers' short-lived mutiny did not interrupt their support of the Gary system, which they never questioned. They agreed with Wirt that the schools' influence in and control over the community should be broadened. They seconded his belief, stated in 1927, that "the following are four fundamental requirements for success in life: good health, intelligence, reliability and industry. . . . If the children come to the school without these desirable characteristics, the school must then provide activities that will develop them." This was no new doctrine, only a reformulation of what he had been saying for many years. But it took on heightened meaning during the 1920s because of the extension of the schools' activities, particularly in reaching out to previously untapped segments of the city's population. This expansion was necessary because of the growing specialization of jobs, in industry and elsewhere, which necessitated enhanced career selection and training in high school, continuation school, and night school. Although Wirt still clung to his belief in free market competition, unable to comprehend fully the meaning of monopoly capital and the rise of the corporate state, he nonetheless accepted the increased economic (as well as other) functions of schooling. For example, night school enrollment rose significantly, reaching fifteen thousand in 1928. The Gary schools recognized that, because of rapid progress and change, education had become "necessary lifelong adjustment," adult education director Albert Fertsch announced to the National Education Association in 1928. Consequently, Fertsch asserted, the Gary schools provided "for the cultivation and stimulation of intellectual interests, not for a few years only, but as a permanent, necessary and inspirational aspect of citizenship."[14]

One temporary difficulty was in differentiating—this was a key term—between children and adults in the continuation or part-time schools. The problem was that while compulsory attendance was initially until age fourteen, in 1916 the state passed a law ordering all children between fourteen and sixteen, who were working, to attend school part-time during the day. In 1922 the law was modified, increasing the upper age from sixteen to seventeen, and stipulating that they had to pass the eighth grade and obtain a work permit from their school. While previously there had been a rather clear distinction between day school and night school students, now a third category was added, a separate day school for employed children. In 1919, when the continuation school was established in a former restaurant on the city's main street, it was estimated that there were perhaps nine hundred children who would spend two hours a week taking academic courses (trade mathematics, English, citizenship, or trade science), and another three hours enrolled in shop courses in the high schools. The next year all the classes were offered at the high schools, although separated from the regular curriculum and under the supervision of the director of adult education.[15]

If children who worked were furnished separate day facilities, it followed that adults needed the same opportunity. Men who worked at night had to be provided for. Moreover, women also desired day courses in commercial work (shorthand, typing, and bookkeeping), millinery, dressmaking, and home decoration, as well as in business English and English for the foreign-speaking. "Gary grown-ups who are seeking further educational opportunities are apparently neglecting a chance which is offered them to obtain free schooling in a number of useful subjects," the local paper editorialized when the school opened in 1920 in the restaurant formerly used by the continuation school. "The man or woman trained in business methods is in such great demand at present that it is well worth the time put in to get such instruction," added Gary's labor paper, the *Central Labor Union News.* By 1923 there were one thousand adults attending daytime commercial classes.[16]

As vocational courses were begun for adults and part-time students during the day, they were also expanded for regular high school students. Before 1920 the high schools had a rather low enrollment, composed primarily of those desiring to go on to higher education. Along with the rest of the country, however, enrollment shot up during the decade. These new, supposedly non-academically oriented students had to be provided for. Vocational and commercial programs were added to encourage them to stay in school until graduation. "A four year high school course is recommended to all who can possibly take that much time," the *Post-Tribune* stated in 1921, "and by wisely selecting the studies every graduate should be as well fitted to enter useful and remunerative employment as he is to enter college."[17] Vocational programs were relatively new and not yet popular; they soon would be.

The Gary schools were criticized by some for neglecting academic work. But defenders of the system such as Edythe Watson, writing in the *Vocational Education Magazine* in 1925, argued that "the child that completes his high school at Gary has a skilled life trade to support himself, and that is more than most of the schools can say of their graduates of high classed academic schools." Of course, vocational skills could be obtained from on-the-job training, admitted Principal Coons, but this would be purely technical in nature; by contrast, schooling offered "a general knowledge of trade . . . counteracting the tendency mechanical operations connected with modern industrial work have of deadening the mental alertness and appreciation of its workers."[18] Increased vocational counseling of both students and their parents heightened the program's efficiency. As the Gary system became more and more committed to vocationalism, it nonetheless clung tenaciously to the liberal rhetoric that emphasized the relationship between manual and mental work, that believed the comprehensive school benefited all children.

The vocational and commercial programs of the schools were something to be proud of. The Gary schools led the state in the number of pupils receiving vocational training, the *Post-Tribune* happily announced at mid-decade. The active support and cooperation of the city's business leaders enhanced the program, "where an obvious ideal of service has always been the motivating spirit. . . . The need for men who will work with their hands rather than for more to rush into the overflowing tide of youth headed for the 'white collar' jobs was recognized here 20 years ago." In terms such as "service" and "need" another side of the issue was revealed—the utility of the vocational programs in serving the diversified labor demands of local businesses and factories. The system needed trained workers, which the schools promised to furnish. It was not a question of molding children for a hostile work environment in order to placate employers and the corporate order, Wirt and his colleagues believed, but of delicately balancing the needs and interests of both. As Carleton Washburne, the famed school superintendent in Winnetka, Illinois, summarized the issue:

This education will have to be both social and individual. It must develop each child to his own fullest capacity that he may make his own particular contribution to society. It must at the same time train him to see that he can not reach his own full stature unless the society of which he is a part is also developed to its full capacity. He must learn that he is only a part of the whole and that his own good is indissolubly bound up with the good of his fellows.[19]

Wirt's rhetoric about meeting the child's needs extended beyond vocational programs and guidance to what became "individualized" instruction by mid-decade. Just what this meant is hard to say, for diverse programs, attitudes, and procedures were grouped under this rubric. "The general policy this year," Assistant Superintendent John Rossman announced in 1925, "will call for increased attention to the individual needs of the student." Such instruction differed from that in many of the private, progressive schools where, as Robert Elias has written, "the individual fulfilled himself in the degree to which no one impinged on his will." In the Steel City this thrust, always implicit when personalizing instruction, was subsumed within the dominant movement toward promoting, as the Lynds characterized the mood in Muncie, "the community values of group solidarity and patriotism." (Even in Muncie, however, many believed "that the schools should foster not only free inquiry but individual diversity, and that they best serve their communities when they discover, and equip the individual to use, his emotional and intellectual resources to the fullest extent, in however diverse ways.") Freedom through self-control versus conformity—the two are not totally incompatible, and indeed have often gone together in educational thinking and program development. Revisionist historians have recently emphasized the latter as the main thrust of public educational reform at the time. But it is too easy to dismiss the educators' views in support of individualized instruction as only misleading and designed to cover up their racism and class bias.[20]

Superintendent Wirt was an elitist who believed in the free enterprise system. He also desired to assist all children in attempting to get the schooling and training necessary to succeed according to their "potential." He assumed that children of the rich had different potential from children of the poor, of course, but there was enough overlap to make such a dichotomy less than a certainty. And the schools, by providing a stimulating environment, could possibly serve to help overcome these class differences. "The great problem of parents and educators," he wrote, "is to surround the child with an environment wherein he will be stimulated to put forth the required effort to do the necessary real, hard work involved in educating himself."[21] Not all the schools in Gary were equipped to do this, but the largest were, in Wirt's thinking, and the plan was to provide eventually all the children with suitable facilities.

Social harmony and economic interests were best served by combining a child's apparent natural abilities with training suitable to meet the needs of the marketplace. In order to facilitate this happy marriage, the Gary schools introduced ability grouping or tracking in 1924. Some children, however, would seemingly benefit more than others. Assistant Superintendent Rossman believed that some students "are naturally brighter than others and most of the teacher's time is taken up with instructing and explaining to the 'slower' children at the expense of the brighter ones." He accordingly advised teachers "to divide their classes into several small groups, each of which contains pupils of about the same intelligence. While one group is reciting the other group may be studying instead of wasting time." Students would be classified according to observations and test results. As Rossman informed the teachers at the beginning of the term, "The first few weeks should be given over to an intense campaign of learning your pupils and their individual abilities," in order to maximize "instruction on the basis of individual needs with pupils grouped in small groups within a large group." For Washburne, ability grouping was a necessary "forerunner of the widespread adoption of full individual instruction," a tentative procedure that broke the lockstep methods common in public schools. But in Gary, with its serious overcrowding in the schools and limited resources, it was a final stage in what was called individualized instruction.[22]

Supplementing ability grouping was a changed grading system. Marks were now given in letter rather than numerical form. Rossman believed the change deemphasized grades and enhanced individualized instruction. As educational writer Eugene Smith noted in *Education Moves Ahead* (1924), "It is more important to know whether a boy or girl is showing initiative, or attaining self control, or learning to live and work in harmony with others, than it is to know whether his spelling or writing was marked 76% or 82%." Rossman listed three possible goals of the new method: "1. No failures. 2. No idling on the part of any pupil. 3. Each pupil moving forward in a way that brings to him the greatest return with a reasonable amount of effort put forth." By downplaying both competition and mechanical skills development, the new marking system was seen as a substantial move forward in the struggle to improve instruction, "to teach boys and girls as individuals rather than in mass and recognize that every pupil is different and has different ideas and a different capacity."[23] Of course, like ability grouping, letter grades could also be used as a control and sorting mechanism; this was not, however, the way Rossman and his colleagues publicly defended the new system.

Additional features were added to the schools in 1926, such as special rooms for new students in order "to become adjusted to the Gary system and so that [they] may be ranked properly in the schools here." Moreover, for grades 7-12 homework was introduced "to develop habits of independent study, to promote better use of school time and to guide pupils into more extensive and intensive fields." The increased stress on individualized instruction and learning came at the height of overcrowding in the schools, when all facilities were at maximum capacity. Emphasis was thus put on hustling students through the system, not only by reducing failures, but also by encouraging promotion by subject instead of class standing. Extensive use of Saturday and summer school also helped, allowing students to catch up on work missed, or move ahead by taking more advanced classes. "That the Gary plan 'gets the pupil somewhere,' as Superintendent Wirt put it, is tellingly indicated by the fact that in a Gary public school the teachers have the children ready for the university at the age of sixteen and a half years. Elsewhere the average is 18 years," newsman James Bennett reported in the *Chicago Tribune* in 1929. Indeed, Rossman announced in 1928 that "helping boys and girls to succeed has ever been the guiding beacon to teachers and executives in Gary." Since 1923, he said, failures had been reduced from 22 per 100 students to 16—a saving of $50,000 a semester, or $100,000 a year, "but a savings incomputable to the future success and happiness of boys and girls." While there is no way of confirming these figures, there was a significant jump in high school graduates, from 121 in 1922, to 348 in 1927, to an impressive 500 in 1929. The specter of massive retardation, that is performing below grade level, was seemingly absent in Gary, where extraordinary efforts were made to speed up rather than slow down academic and behavioral development. They believed everyone profited from this system.[24]

Despite the obvious stress on individualized learning and instruction, group socialization was never abandoned. Indeed, it gained in popularity. By 1928 Wirt and Rossman were encouraging more "team work." As Wirt envisioned the Gary system, the teachers formed "a team with their pupils, with the teacher as captain," and together they worked for the welfare of the students and the system. That individualism and cooperation were not mutually exclusive—that they were in fact

two sides of the same coin, each designed to promote social harmony—
dominated educational thought at the time.[25]

The seeming paradox of encouraging individualism in a society marked
by the rapid growth of monopoly capital, which in turn stimulated emphasis on "team work," was paralleled by the effort to add post-
secondary schooling to a system bent on speeding students through
the lower grades. That is, individual progress had to be balanced
against the need to have continuous socialization for community
harmony and solidarity. Thus, as high school enrollment mounted, and
graduates increased, plans were made for starting a college in the area.
In 1922 Wirt proposed building a local facility for students in the last
two years of high school and the first two years of college. The previous year Indiana University had begun extension courses in the city,
offering credit to high school graduates, but this was not enough. More
was needed, particularly since many could not afford to move to the
main campus in Bloomington for more advanced work. The Woman's
Club, in supporting the venture, argued that students "in tender years,
might still live at home under the guidance of parents, and attend
a preparatory school." Two years later Wirt envisioned "a standardized
college in Gary offering a multitude of courses taught by the highest
class of instructors, library and laboratory facilities far in advance of
the ordinary college, and even college football and other sports that,
in the eyes of the younger generation, are the distinguishing features
of a school." A local college would enable students to "work and learn
at the same time." Just as working class students were provided with
vocational classes suited to their supposed needs, so too others, particularly from the middle class, needed more specialized academic opportunities. Funding was unavailable, however, and extension courses remained the only option until the early 1930s when Gary College was
established.[26]

The various programs of the Gary schools reflected Wirt's increasing
faith in them as society's anchor in a time of rapid social and economic
change. For example, in 1921, while the postwar depression lingered,
night school classes were expanded to include cooking, millinery, and
consumerism "to offer help to the minds and bodies of the unem-
ployed and their families." In earlier years the superintendent had urged
maximum cooperation between the schools and other child-saving organizations, such as the YMCA, Boy Scouts, and the settlement houses. By
mid-decade, however, he had reversed his position, accusing them of
unnecessarily competing with the three traditional pillars of society—
home, church, and school—in influencing children. Until "better
schools, better teachers, better parents, more aggressive church leadership

tackle the problem of youth's training, America cannot be builded upon a safe foundation," he reasoned. "All other agencies but scratch the surface, and really get nowhere." In early 1928 the Gary Woman's Club arranged for Wirt to speak to a joint meeting of the Lions, Kiwanis, Optimist, and Rotary clubs. In his talk Wirt defended modern youth, noting that "the boys and girls of this country aren't nearly as bad as they are painted." He argued that current discussions of the breakdown of character and morals among youth were nothing more than "false propaganda." He again attacked moral reformist organizations such as the Boy Scouts as "doing more harm than good." He suggested incorporating the Boy Scouts into the public schools.[27]

At a time when the schools were more successful than ever in controlling children, and were bursting at the seams, Wirt became panicky. He worried that amateurs, not experts, were influencing children; he worried that precious financial resources were being diverted from the schools; he feared that the Boy Scouts and the YMCA catered only to the elite, ignoring the rest.

> While still at college, I was convinced that only the school could secure the facilities and the time of the children necessary for the development of the wants that give value to work and the tastes that give value to leisure. With twenty-five years experience in using the school as a boys' work-agency and at the same time watching the growth and development of the numerous other boys' agencies I am now absolutely sure that this position is right.

Professionalism now totally dominated his thinking, as it did for educators throughout the country.[28]

Wirt sincerely believed that the schools, under his benevolent leadership, served the needs of all Gary's citizens, rich and poor, young and old, immigrant and native, white and black. Not all agreed with him, however. Many of the city's black citizens, in particular, had long questioned whether the schools operated to their benefit. Racism and segregation were dominant throughout the country, north and south, with serious liabilities and handicaps for those discriminated against. It was no different in Gary. The majority of Gary's black students were in separate schools, with black teachers and administrators; the rest were segregated in predominantly white schools. Moreover, the black schools were physically inferior to the few expensive unit schools, although no worse than the elementary schools which housed about one-third of the white students. While many blacks favored separate schools, others supported integration as the only means of combatting racism and securing quality schooling for their children. The issue, going back to 1908, again became public in 1927 when Wirt attempted to enroll eighteen black students in the Emerson high school, increasing the number there to twenty-four. In protest hundreds of white students went on strike, and by the end of the week the superintendent and city officials reluctantly agreed to transfer the eighteen to all-black schools. A few of the parents, backed by black leaders and the NAACP brought suit against the city to prevent the transfer. Declaring it illegal, the parents argued "that the Virginia school to which they were removed does not have the equipment for advanced pupils. It is without a gymnasium, swimming tank or modern advantages of the Emerson school in equipment and is dark and unsanitary besides not offering the scholastic merits of Emerson school." The parents lost. A few years later the Roosevelt School was opened, a superior facility with an all-black staff that cooled tempers in the black community.[29]

The black community was outraged by the white students' blatant racism and Wirt's spineless behavior. It was also, for the most part, against the principle of segregation. But the more important issue, which soon became obvious, was the securing of equal facilities, for practical and constitutional reasons. Many blacks were not, in fact, against voluntary separation, nor were they critical of Wirt and the school system. While some blacks condemned the Virginia Street School, an article in the *Sun,* Gary's black newspaper, praised it as the pride of the black community: "Gary is gradually convincing the world that it excels in its educational system as well as in steel production. Virginia school, despite its inferior facilities, is the very essence and symbol of this remarkable scholastic organization." Blacks regarded it as one of the most efficient schools in the city, and they were proud that half of its twenty-two teachers were college graduates, while the remainder held normal school diplomas. The Roosevelt School Annex, another all-black school, was similarly lauded. These schools were semi-controlled by the black community, their accomplishments were matters of great pride, and they furnished employment for black teachers who held high local status.[30]

David Tyack has recently observed that black teachers could find employment only in black schools. But at the same time, many blacks vigorously fought and protested segregation in the courts. Without direct political power, Tyack has written, blacks "turned to the courts to defend the tenuous equity that integration promised. But again and again blacks expressed in autobiographies and poems, in truancy and protests, their sense of rejection in schools dominated by a white power structure over which they had little influence." The ambiguity of the situation was striking. The Gary schools had "a world wide reputation for scholarly efficiency and the progressive use of modern educational methods," the *Sun* editorialized in January, 1928; the black teachers were "an indispensable part of this splendid system." Even the *Gary American,* the city's second black newspaper and strongly integrationist, editorialized in September, 1928, on the importance of Gary's black teachers. "Those who condemn separate schools for Negro children and who seek to criticize Negro school teachers," the paper asserted, "should ponder for a moment and they would see, if a sustained line of thought is held, that the community would be a dead and prosaic place were it not for the altruistic interests of our teachers here in our social, religious and educational welfare."[31]

Integration or segregation—the choice seemed real, but was abstract. The latter was demanded by most whites and preferred by blacks. When in 1930 some blacks protested segregation in soon-to-be-opened Roosevelt School, they were attacked by others who argued that "the establishment of a school for both white and colored students . . . would tend to destroy the 'race consciousness' of the Negro children." The following year even the *Gary American* proudly proclaimed that the dedication of the million-dollar Roosevelt School marked

> an epoch in the history of Negroes in this state. . . . This newspaper has never approved the separate public school for Negroes. . . . But if separate schools have to be established, they should be the equal of white schools in matters of equipment and efficiency of its teaching staff. In this regard the new Roosevelt high school comes up to the requirements.

Few in Gary heeded the NAACP's position, as expressed in 1929 in its letter to local branch president A. C. Bailey, that "the Association does not recognize the right of the school city to segregate Negro children no matter how excellent the accommodations for Negro children are. That is the crux of the entire Gary [Emerson] school case and is the principle for which we are fighting."[32]

The Gary schools were segregated. But black children were not necessarily treated any differently from many of the white children, particularly those of immigrant parents. All were provided with "suitable" schooling. The establishment of a "colored trade school" typified the pattern. Vocational education was necessary for black children, Albert Fertsch contended, because most did not have "adequate educational advantages" before coming to Gary. The vocational program in the "colored trade school" was based upon the "occupations in which the colored people of Gary are earning their livelihood." This was good progressive education because it highlighted what was practical, a further sign that "the Gary system continues to advance the new order of secondary education by adjusting instruction along the lines which function in the lives of the boys and girls after they leave school."[33]

The Gary schools did not, and were never designed to, change society in the 1920s. The opposite was more the case—maintaining stability and providing differentiated schooling for rich and poor, black and white, male and female, immigrant and native, thus insuring that the needs of the corporate state were met. Of course, public schools have always functioned in the interests of the dominant social, economic, and political system. Historians have recently emphasized that the innovations of these years—testing, differentiated curriculum, ability grouping, vocational guidance, and so on, while instituted under the guise of providing for children's needs and interests, in fact insured manipulation from above and hindered mobility. "Since the 1920s, evidence has accumulated that children of the poor and the working class, and those from immigrant groups, were disadvantaged by grouping, differentiation, and intelligence testing," David Cohen and Marvin Lazerson have written. "Whether educational progress was measured by curricular placement, school completion, or the tests themselves, those who were economically disadvantaged or culturally different usually came out at the bottom of the heap." On the other hand, David Tyack has argued that the new methods were not completely negative:

> As rhetoric escalated on both sides in the 1920s, scholars developed a more sophisticated understanding of "intelligence," but schools went on making discriminations between pupils through testing. . . . Some lower-class children did well on the IQ tests and were encouraged to continue their schooling into college; the tests may well have prompted social mobility for such high performers. There were, indeed, complex problems of classifying students for a differentiated school structure, and quite probably subjective judgments by teachers would have been at least as questionable as the supposedly objective intelligence tests.

Surely schools encouraged and provided for some mobility, which was necessary to insure skilled workers and managers for the economy, but it was limited.[34]

The Gary schools operated quite smoothly during the 1920s. As the number of students swelled, and the economic functions of the schools became more demanding, various programs and techniques were added to increase their value in supporting the corporate order. Relatively few—predominantly blacks and immigrants—questioned how the schools operated, for most were convinced that they and their children could do no better. The surface prosperity of the decade reinforced their acceptance of the system. Gary's citizens were manipulated by the schools, not out of fear but out of belief that they were profiting from them. And indeed many were, to some extent. As for Wirt and his colleagues, they preached individualism, while practicing mass socialization. They believed that each child could reach his or her potential, which was rather narrowly defined, while serving the community's social and economic needs. That there might be ambiguities and contradictions between individualism and cooperation, between self-aggrandizement and social order, did not concern Wirt, who, in any case, did not believe that individualism meant equality, or that teamwork meant community. The superintendent sought to insure the continued growth, prosperity, and stability of the corporate society then becoming clearly visible.

While Wirt strongly supported monopoly capital, although perhaps not truly understanding it, the Gary system was not a tool of U.S. Steel, as charged by the Chicago Federation of Labor in the mid-1920s. George Counts summarized the federation's position: "It identified the platoon system with the Gary system, and the Gary system with the United States Steel Corporation. The presumption then is obvious. The platoon plan, emanating as it does from such iniquitous sources, must itself be iniquitous. The mere mention of the name of Gary or of the Steel Corporation calls to the mind of labor one of its most powerful enemies and many bitter industrial struggles."[35] Few in Gary, apparently, agreed with such thinking. The class struggle was not evident in the Steel City following the crushing of the steel strike, as most reaffirmed their faith in the city's dominant institutions, particularly its schools.

Such unity, dependent as it was on economic prosperity, revealed its fragility following the stock market crash and subsequent depression. Economic and political interests, in particular, now took precedence over Wirt's hollow call for unity. The schools were still not criticized, but their image as a symbol of unity and harmony was shattered, never to be restored.

7

THE 1930s
The Fragility of the System

The 1930s was a dynamic era for the nation's schools, a time of questioning of basic values, of clashing political, economic, and social forces heretofore present but muted. The decade witnessed not the triumph of progressive education, as Lawrence A. Cremin and Patricia A. Graham have argued, but rather the exposure of its basic contradictions. Conflict, not consensus, dominated public life, and public schooling, at the time. The Lynds, in *Middletown in Transition* (1937), superbly captured the situation in their chapter "Training the Young," in which they identified

> a widening area of conflict in Middletown between the teacher and the educational administrator hired by the school board to "run" its schools; between school and community values; between parents who may want something other than docile conformity from the education of their children and the community bent upon achieving this solidarity; between the politico-economic pressure agencies and agencies for other types of pressures; and, above all, between the spirit of inquiring youth and the spirit of do-as-we-say-and-ask-no-questions.

Not that every community had these particular conflicts; some had more, some less, but they were widespread and denoted fundamental disagreements among diverse individuals and interest groups. Society during the previous decade had been healthy in appearance, but in fact was more like an overripe tomato ready to split apart, scattering seeds and revealing the rot within. It exploded in the decade following the Great Crash.[1]

The central issue facing public school systems in the 1930s, as with every other institution, was a severe reduction of income. This problem forced the firing of teachers and the elimination or curtailment of many programs. On the other hand, in some cities the depression seems to have spurred acceptance of programs previously unpopular. In California, for example, interest centered on making the curriculum more "practical"— that is, community- and career-oriented. School systems expanded commercial and general education courses, giving special attention to vocational training and guidance. In New York City programs were initiated to increase emphasis on "individualized and socialized education," the two polar facets of progressive education. And the influx of federal funds by mid-decade encouraged the implementation of various social, economic, and cultural programs for youth. Black children, in particular, seem to have benefited from this assistance. While many historians believe these programs were introduced for altruistic reasons, other argue that they were only an extension of the long-standing desire of educators to expand the influence of schools over children and their parents. Robert Church has summarized this argument:

> For those schoolmen who had been seeking since the beginnings of the social efficiency movement in the prewar years to bring more and more young people under the auspices of the schools, to insure a smooth transition from youth to adulthood and from dependence to productivity, the existence of hundreds of thousands of idle youths provided a golden opportunity to claim an added responsibility for the schools. Schools would hold more and more young people in "custody" for a longer period of time, thereby easing the transition into adulthood. Keeping these youths under the control of the school would protect them from alienation, radicalism, and the lure of crime until they were old enough to find jobs and become productive workers. Such moves would at once enhance the role of the school and reduce the number of people seeking jobs by shrinking the labor force to match the decreased number of jobs provided by a stagnant economy.

Schools during the depression thus experienced either contraction or expansion, and sometimes both, depending on local conditions, federal policies, and quality of leadership. But whatever the situation, they were in a state of flux.[2]

In Gary the problem was not to introduce new programs, but to maintain those already in existence which were caught in the squeeze of tightening budgets and steady school enrollment. In contrast to the 1920s, when the city's population doubled from 55,000 to over 100,000, during the 1930s it remained unchanged. The same was true for the school population, which leveled off at around 20,000, as did the number of teachers at around 550. What did change, however, was the high school enrollment and the number of high school graduates. The former increased from around 5,000 in 1930 to almost 6,000 in 1940, while the latter jumped from 500 to over 1,000 during the same period. Nationally, by the late 1930s, around 55 percent of pupils entering the ninth grade actually graduated, a significant increase over previous decades. In Gary the rate at the six predominately white high schools was 65 percent, ranging from a low of 56 percent at the heavily foreign and working class Emerson and Froebel schools, to a high of 83 percent at the middle class Horace Mann; the seventh school, the all-black Roosevelt, had the lowest average, 49 percent. While there was considerable local variation, based on class, ethnic, and racial differences, the general belief in Gary was that the work-study-play structure enhanced the holding capability of the schools. This conclusion is questionable, however, considering the national trend.[3]

While the enrollment and teaching staff remained steady, the budget shrank considerably. The crunch was not felt until 1931, when school funds dropped for the first time, necessitating drastic cuts in programs. By 1934 the school budget had been reduced by 44 percent. In order to balance the budget numerous cuts were made: teachers' salaries were reduced by around 35 percent by 1934, and were scarcely increased by the end of the decade; the school year declined from ten to nine months; locally financed school construction ceased, and drastic reductions were made in repair expenditures; night school, Saturday school and summer school programs were reduced or temporarily eliminated; and there was an overall trimming of costs. Night school enrollment fell from a high of over 17,000 in 1931 to a low of 4,000 two years later, after which it began to increase. Summer classes were resumed on a limited basis in June, 1933, and by the following February Saturday classes were again operating. The ten-month school year returned in 1936. By 1937 the system was almost fully restored, except for teacher salaries, although in 1939 cuts again became temporarily necessary.[4]

Wirt argued in 1935 that the Gary schools had weathered the depression better than those in other cities because of the greater efficiency of the platoon system. The so-called "frills," such as Saturday and summer schools, actually saved the taxpayers money, he reasoned, for they allowed children to progress "normally" instead of falling behind and thereby costing more in the long run. The previous year the Gary Principal's Association had argued that "the saving resulting from prevention of unnecessary failure through attendance in the Saturday school more than pays for the entire instructional cost in all departments." They made the same argument for retaining the summer school and the ten-month school term. Isabelle V. Jones, director of testing and measurement, warned Wirt that because of the shorter school year and reduced programs there were fewer full promotions, meaning a heightened retardation rate. Moreover, overcrowding in the classrooms prevented teachers from helping all the children.[5] Because of these concerns, restoration of programs and the ten-month year were given highest priority, while teacher salaries were considered less important. The teachers, however, thought otherwise.

Gary's teachers had accepted the ideal of unity and harmony because they believed in the corporate state and seemed to be profiting from its success. They were unwilling, however, to make continued sacrifices during the depression while others seemed to be recovering. In attempting to get a larger slice of the pie, they soon abandoned cooperation with Wirt and the school board. Before World War 1 they had organized a local of the American Federation of Teachers and in 1920 had won a small raise, after which the union disintegrated. Teacher activism was revived in 1932 by the wage cuts and the issuing of part of the monthly salary in scrip instead of cash. Members of a teachers' committee, unaffiliated with the AFT, in April expressed "willingness to cooperate with the board of education in effecting economies, including salary cuts, but they hoped the slash would be made on a graduated scale, according to the salary of the individual instructor." By early 1934 a majority of the teachers had joined the Gary Teachers' Federation, an affiliate of the National Education Association, which represented their salary grievances to the school board, but with little success.[6]

As early as 1934 the Lake County Central Labor Union had begun a campaign to organize Gary's teachers into an AFL local, but it was not until 1937 that the teachers took the step. Early in the year members of the Gary Teachers' Federation attempted to rejoin the AFT, while simultaneously a separate group of teachers was organizing independently for the same purpose. The two merged after the former received a new AFT charter and adopted the name Gary Teachers' Union, Local No. 4 (their original number).[7] The union's prime concern was to restore salaries to pre-depression levels, while also seeking implementation of a single salary schedule. Danger to academic freedom, present in other cities, was not a concern in Gary. As Flora Philley, Local No. 4's secretary, informed Wirt in November, 1937, the local "has no Committee on Academic Freedom as we have no such problem here. Our teachers enjoy full freedom to discuss with their classes any subject, however controversial, in local or national affairs. No oath has ever been required of us and no hints of 'desirable policy' are directed at us." The union was not exclusively concerned with bread and butter issues, however. On the contrary, it considered teachers' rights and political involvement to be very important. As one of the union's recruiting messages noted:

> America is moving rapidly toward a social democratic state. Teachers must decide what course they are going to steer in this new order. Gary schools are now in politics, whether we like it or not. Where and how are we going to gain the most political power? How many votes can we influence? Division is weakness. We are asking you to join the Teachers' Union to wipe out as quickly as possible this weakness.[8]

Teachers were no longer part of one big happy school family, if they had ever been. They were emerging as one strong component in a power contest that would, simultaneously, divide the superintendent from the school board, city politics from school politics, and Republicans from Democrats. Scarcity heightened conflict, as the corporate order struggled to survive.

In addition to salary increases the union was particularly anxious to obtain a single salary schedule. In late 1936 the Gary Teacher's Federation had argued that the arbitrary four-scale rating system, adopted in 1921, must be discarded. Shrewdly, it did not blame Wirt, but the system. "The wrongs and abuses that we have stressed have not proceeded from the will of the administration, they are the inescapable fruits of the old schedule," Flora Philley wrote. "Release of the well-springs of loyalty and enthusiasm that are repressed to-day, will follow the adoption of the proposed schedule and will bring us that warm understanding and fellowship in high endeavor that our mutual interests deserve."[9] Indeed, throughout the battle between the teachers and school authorities, Wirt was seldom directly blamed for the problems of the teachers. The teachers recognized Wirt's popularity in the city, although it was declining, and desired his support.

By the fall of 1937 the teachers' union was putting strong pressure on the school board. To undermine the union's strength, Wirt split the teachers into five negotiating groups: elementary teachers with less than three years training, elementary teachers with less than a B.A. degree, elementary teachers with a B.A., high school teachers, and all teachers with A or B+ rankings in 1931-32. Each group would make a separate salary recommendation to the school board. The union, however, refused to cooperate. Instead, it received a power of attorney from the first four groups to represent them before the board. The highest paid, those with A and B+ rankings, refused to recognize the union, desiring to maintain their preferred status and believing themselves to be "'career' teachers who form the nucleus of any educational system." The division among the teachers would cause conflicts for some years. In early January, 1938, all teachers received a slight pay increase, considerably less than desired, but they did get the board to adopt the single salary schedule, a major triumph. Hereafter salaries were based on training and experience, not the caprice of principals and supervisors forced to divide teachers into arbitrary salary groupings. The union, however, was not satisfied. Not only were the raises too low, it argued, but "the board had violated the principles of collective bargaining in arriving at its schedules without giving the union a chance for a final consultation."[10]

By early March, 1938, the union had gotten more militant. The board, concerned over low tax returns, was in no mood to bargain further. Even the intervention of Democratic Mayor L. B. Clayton was of no value. In a public letter to the board, the mayor argued that "there is merit in the request of the Gary Teachers' union and that a few teachers are over-paid and many are under-paid." Thus, Mayor Clayton urged the board of education to give the Gary Teachers' Union "a full and complete hearing on their petition for a readjustment of the salaries." The problem now was not just salaries, but the union's right to meet with the board in a full and open hearing. Superintendent Wirt's death on March 11 postponed the dispute for a short time. The *Gary Post-Tribune,* a Republican paper, editorialized that both the board and the teachers seemed to be taking stubborn positions: "As a matter of fact we have always felt that the interests of the board, the superintendent and the teachers were one. Certainly the record of the past 30 years would lead one to believe so." This, indeed, had seemingly been true in the past, but things were quite different by 1938.[11]

The school board put an end to the affair, temporarily, in late April by adopting a new salary schedule which included few additional raises. Moreover, the board introduced a new gimmick, the "starred maximum salary." Under this rubric "possibly inferior" teachers were not guaranteed automatic annual increments after achieving a certain salary level.

However, the board provided that automatic increases for such teachers could be resumed "if their work improves." This was a sneaky method of partially reintroducing the old merit system, and soon became one of the union's main grievances. Salary increases were slow in coming over the next few years. By early 1940 the union was very strong, with about 70 percent of the teachers as members, and what appeared to be a quasi-collective bargaining agreement with the superintendent. As Flora Philley, the local's secretary, remarked: "We have juggled our Superintendent into a position where we have collective bargaining (never using those terrible words, however) and have him boasting about the 'unity and improved morale' which he has brought about." Collective bargaining meant, in effect, that the superintendent had agreed that if he could not settle a dispute with the union, it would be guaranteed a hearing with the board. Thus, by the end of the decade the union was firmly established, grievance procedures were worked out, and teachers were no longer at the complete mercy of the superintendent and the school board, although as yet there was no binding contract. Power relationships had changed between the teachers and school authorities because of the depression and the subsequent rise of organized labor and the Democratic Party. The union would grow stronger over the years.[12]

The old paternalism was no longer accepted (if it ever really had been) because scarcity created adversary relationships that could not be papered over by threats or vague promises. The resurgence of the Democratic Party revealed the depth of discontent in the city. The election of L. B. (Barney) Clayton as mayor in 1934, the first Democrat since 1913, along with Democratic victories on the state and national levels, did not, however, lead to a drastic shift in school affairs, as many thought and feared. Indeed, nothing significant occurred for three years. In early 1937 senators from South Bend and Evansville introduced a bill in the state legislature to change the procedure for electing school board members in the state's major cities. Previously elected by the city council, now they would be appointed by the mayor. The bill also increased the size of the board from three to five members. Battle lines were quickly drawn in Gary. Mayor Clayton and his supporters favored passage, while a broad coalition, including the Kiwanis Club, current school board members, the Emerson School parents' committee, various civic leaders, and some members of the city council, vigorously opposed the "School Grab Bill."

The opposition feared the change would make school affairs a partisan football. In a hard-hitting editorial, the *Gary Post-Tribune* typified such thinking:

> For 30 years the school affairs of Gary have been conducted efficiently and satisfactorily by a board of education whose members have been elected by the city council. . . . Has there been any criticism of the type of men and women the council has chosen? No, there has not. . . . Throughout the entire 30 years Gary people have felt that the board of education has had the single interest of the schools and school children at heart. Has the board ever permitted politics to have any influence in the schools? No, it has not. . . . Is there a public demand for this change? If there is it has never been evidenced by a single statement of a private citizen or public official. Efforts have been made to stir up political feeling by bringing the name of Superintendent W. A. Wirt into the fight. This is simply political dust. The present board is controlled by Democrats who can removed Wirt if they think that act would benefit the Gary schools. This is not a fight between Wirt and anti-Wirt factions but an attack on the schools.

Mayor Clayton responded that he was considering some school reforms because "the schools had been 'soiled by politics' during Superintendent Wirt's long regime." And, he added, "many thousands of people in Gary would like to know more about the Gary schools and the way they're run. Up to now the schools have been operated somewhat like a closed corporation. The business of the schools has not been laid out on the table like that of the civil city." Resistance to the bill was seemingly widespread in Gary, with caravans of citizens traveling to Indianapolis to lobby against it, supported by a petition containing 15,000 names, but it passed anyway in early March. Not until mid-July, however, did the mayor make his two appointments to the board, currently composed of two Democrats and one Republican. Clayton appointed a foreman at U.S. Steel who was a Republican and an employee (and brother of the president) of a local bank, and whose wife was the township trustee and a loyal Democratic supporter of Mayor Clayton.[13]

The new board members, at first, did not change board policy. They supported continued resistance to the demands of the teachers' union, contrary to the mayor's position, and they backed the superintendent. However, under Wirt's successor, H. S. Jones, a new mood began to dominate relations between the board and the superintendent. The board ceased to be a rubberstamp for the superintendent's policies and wishes. For example, in 1939 the board split over the financial necessity of dropping Saturday, summer, and night school work. And in 1940, by initiating fundamental changes in the school system, the board signaled its emergence as the major power in school affairs. No longer would it languish in the superintendent's shadow. The change was certainly due more to the shift in superintendents than to the "School Grab Bill," but for the first time membership on the board became an important matter, as various power blocs and political and economic interests vied for the position.[14]

Partisan politics, to most, may have seemed missing from school affairs before 1937, but certainly political interests and values had always played an influential role in molding educational policies. That is, the city's elite, heavily Republican, had run the schools in their own economic, social, and political interests, although acting as if and surely believing that they represented the common good. That this facade of impartiality and neutrality could be maintained until the mid-1930s testified to the broad public support Wirt and the Gary system enjoyed and to the apparently apolitical nature of public schooling in general. Except in a few of the largest cities, such as New York and Chicago, sharp conflicts over the leadership and meaning of public education had been uncommon, although there were minor disagreements. But in the 1930s deep divisions were exposed within communities throughout the country.[15]

Wirt and the city's Republican leadership, believing they continued to act in the public interest, naturally blamed the Democrats and their labor allies for fomenting disunity. The superintendent, for example, argued that he was always objective, but in fact was convinced that capitalism must survive. It was the schools' duty to insure this. Indeed, it was Wirt, not Mayor Clayton, who first publicly injected politics into school matters. A lifelong Republican, Wirt early criticized Roosevelt and the New Deal. His position was sharpened in early 1933 by his membership in the Committee for the Nation, a group of influential anti-New Deal businessmen. While firmly opposing the involvement of teachers in politics, he did not follow the same advice. He believed "school teachers must let partisan politicians alone, if they expect the partisan politicians to leave them alone. Men and women who enter teaching must recognize that some one else other than teachers must save the country in partisan politics if it is to be saved." Teachers must be patient, but he wasted no time in warning the country of the dangers of the New Deal. "Until the NRA program was actually launched there was a chance to swing Roosevelt from the radical influence that surrounded him," he wrote to his old friend and colleague in the Committee for the Nation, Edward Rumely, in March, 1934:

> At the present time I do not believe that there is any such chance. Hence I have dropped out. However, I do not believe that it is too late to successfully resist the policies of President Roosevelt and his associates. To do so will be tremendously difficult and may lead to all sorts of riots and a form of Civil War. But in my judgment, there is no other way. The people in power have the mass psychology with them to an unprecedented degree and they have the police power of the government.[16]

Wirt struggled to find allies for his cause. His faith wavered in the role of the public schools to continue preaching capitalism and patriotism. He no longer had faith in the business community's support and feared the growing radicalism of educators around the country. "The fundamental difficulty from the standpoint of public education has been that the business men of this country have not been willing to be real citizens of their country," he confided to Rumely. "They have never had the time to study either social or economic problems. They have always been afraid to take a public stand on any controversial public question for fear of hurting their business." As for radical educators, commonly termed social reconstructionists, he both dreaded and exaggerated their influence, believing, for example, that they had captured the annual school superintendents' meeting in Cleveland in March, 1934. Harold Rugg, the influential Teachers College professor, he labeled "one of the foremost leaders of the so-called radical educational group." Rugg was not alone. "Unfortunately," he continued to Rumely, "during the past ten to fifteen years only the radical men in our colleges and institutions of higher education have been able to win advancement in their respective fields." Wirt protested the superintendents' support of federal funding of public schools. Such dependence on Washington would only weaken local support of and control over schools, he believed. The only way to combat the current financial crisis was to switch to the work-study-play system. On the issue of federal support, however, he did not get the backing of the Gary newspaper, which was concerned more about finances than about political theories. "We cannot permit our school system to collapse," noted one *Post-Tribune* editorial. "If federal funds are needed to carry the system, federal funds must be voted." But Wirt remained firm. "I know that the overwhelming majority of our teachers, school superintendents and college professors are sound in their attitude toward our government," he wrote in 1934. "But many of them have been so cowed by the very immensity of the socialistic campaign in the schools that they have been afraid to openly combat the sinister influences. Many others do not comprehend what the propagandists are doing. Many of us are blind. Shall we become a regimented people subject to the whims of a bureaucracy at Washington?"[17]

Wirt soon publicly challenged the radicals in and outside of Washington. His chance came in April, 1934, when his charges that radicals had infiltrated Roosevelt's administration were investigated by a special House committee. After two days of hearings the committee's Democratic majority dismissed Wirt's allegations. For the remainder of 1934 and into 1935 Wirt became a center of national attention, attacked by Democrats and those on the left, defended by those on the right who had the same suspicions. The *Gary Post-Tribune,* no foe of government spending, editorialized that there was no doubt that Roosevelt's "background is sufficient proof of his opposition to facism, socialism, or communism but it is possible even for a president not to understand the long pull meaning of the tremendous changes of the last year." The local Lions and Rotary clubs voted resolutions supporting Wirt's allegations, and throughout the community he had widespread backing. But what could be done? For Wirt, education was the answer: educate the general public about economic and political matters, and, more importantly, educate the children to protect society in the future from ignorance, which allowed radicals to gain power. "Education is involved in this 'brain trust' exposure because the education of the public has been neglected to the extent that the revolutionary plot progressed as far as it has," Wirt wrote. "Education, therefore, is to blame for the inroads of communism. Education should accept the responsibility." This, of course, put the burden on the teachers, whom Wirt charged with "the tremendous responsibility of training the plastic minds of youth." Teachers had to be fair and intellectually honest, but their job was "to teach youth the essential truths and how to apply them in their own straight thinking." Wirt always called for the objective teaching of "Truth." But what did that mean? Certainly not complete freedom of speech, although teachers apparently had academic freedom and teachers' union activists were tolerated. On the other hand, Wirt believed the public should be protected from those he considered dangerous. He refused to support the request of the League of Women Voters to allow a political science professor from the University of

Chicago, an alleged communist, to speak in one of the city's schools. Turned down by the school board, they secured instead the parish house of a local Episcopal church. Wirt believed strongly that the public should be educated, but only by those considered safe.[18]

There is no evidence that Wirt's proposal for injecting more economic matter into the curriculum was implemented in the Gary schools. But his public discussions of the political implications of the curriculum certainly sharpened the community's awareness of the connection between schooling and politics. Previously there had been a general, uninformed consensus that the curriculum was value-free. Now there was discussion over whether the schools should promote conservative or radical doctrines, sparked by the general debate sweeping the country. But in Gary it was muted, for there was no widespread movement to influence or alter the curriculum or the work-study-play system.

Indeed, by 1935, with the restoration of the Saturday, summer, and night school programs, the platoon system was almost fully restored, to the delight of Gary's citizens. For example, in April, 1934, at the height of Wirt's attack on the New Deal, the *Gary American,* the city's black paper, editorialized: "If there be misgivings in the minds of the adverse critics concerning the ability and accomplishments of Dr. Wirt, it is suggested that they examine the Gary Public School System as it has existed during these trying days of the depression and observe the high standard of intelligence acquired by the average student under the Wirt system." The teachers' union, upon Wirt's death in March, 1938, praised him as "an eminent educator" and "a great leader"; "*All children* have lost a champion whose life has been dedicated to the understanding and solution of the particular problems that limit the natural development of children in industrial centers," the union concluded. Needless to say, the *Gary Post-Tribune* was draped in black in memory of Gary's "first citizen."[19]

If there was no general criticism of Wirt or the schools, there were, nonetheless, rumblings of discontent here and there. This was particularly true within the black community, which had long fought against segregated, inferior school facilities. Gary schools were officially segregated by 1930, a situation epitomized by the opening of the all-black Roosevelt School the following year. F. C. McFarlane, the school's first principal, with an M.A. from Columbia University, was a follower of Marcus Garvey's separationist views who defended the need for all-black facilities. He remained principal of Roosevelt until 1933, a stormy tenure that brought him much criticism as well as praise. "Intelligent Negroes no longer whimper about segregation," he announced in

1930. "They have discovered that what they really want is to be free within themselves. They merely want to grow and develop along with the whites, but as a separate group. . . . They no longer seek social equality." Black parents and community leaders, as well as the *Gary American,* were quick to reject such thinking, as they had done previously, for they took great interest in their schools (perhaps more than the whites). For example, the strongly integrationist *American* accused the principal of encouraging disloyalty among his pupils. The paper held McFarlane responsible for "propaganda being gradually spread throughout the institution designed to create a spirit of animosity between the races in America, and seeking to divorce colored Americans from the principles and the ideals of Americanism." These activities could easily "sow the seed of hate and distrust." The school program was of central concern in the black community. As the paper put it, what McFarlane "does with our community life and our children . . . is our business, and we intend seeing after it."[20] The long-standing debate over segregation versus integration had previously lacked such strong political rhetoric.

In contrast to McFarlane, H. Theodore Tatum, also a Columbia M.A. and principal of East Pulaski School, smaller than Roosevelt and the city's only other all-black school, was a strong integrationist and patriot. He was continually praised, locally as well as nationally, for his administrative skills, community involvement, and American nationalism. In 1934 he said:

> All effort should tend toward the building up of the spirit of social cooperation on the part of the youth to replace that of bitterness and divisive competition which has been so evident with the adults. . . . Strive to teach the Negro youth that he is an active participant in the great game of American citizenship. Evaluate, interpret, and endeavor to instill the ideals of loyalty, patriotism, and good citizenship through all school activities.

Tatum replaced McFarlane as principal of Roosevelt. The *Gary American* was pleased with the change and praised his "quiet, unassuming manner" and his "sense and cultured leadership."[21]

While Tatum's leadership was duly recognized by Wirt, the school board, the *Gary American,* and many in the black community, there were those, presumably McFarlane supporters, who had other ideas. The Central District Citizens Club, for one, informed the school board in 1933 that it would be a "calamity" to appoint Tatum principal of

Roosevelt School. A majority of parents and students opposed the appointment, the club argued. Educational purposes would be undermined by the "mental war" between parents, students, and principal. Tempers smoldered for five years, then erupted in 1938. Believing that Tatum was trying to replace many of the older teachers with his own appointees, a group of parents began actively seeking his removal or resignation. The Roosevelt Mothers' Club filed formal charges against the principal, including "moral turpitude, improper treatment of both pupils and teachers, and a number of other perhaps less important charges." Tatum's active involvement in Republican Party affairs angered many, such as those teachers who supported Mayor Clayton because of his defense of the salary demand of the teachers' union. Even the *Gary American* repeated charges that Tatum had permitted Republican meetings in the Roosevelt auditorium, but refused the same privileges to Clayton and the Democrats. He was also accused of encouraging immorality among his students. A number of black parents asked the school board to fire him, and they also brought charges against him in the superior court. The issue died down by mid-1939, but not before Tatum was labeled "a regular martinet, ruling his school after the manner of a Hitler, rudely denying audiences to visiting parents; 'punishing' recalcitrant members of his teaching staff; expropriating authority over the affairs of the P.T.A. and permitting immoral practices among his students."[22] With continued support from the superintendent and school board, Tatum nevertheless remained principal of Roosevelt School into the 1960s, when he retired, a venerated member of the community. While Tatum won, his detractors had again demonstrated that there was great concern within the black community over school policies and personnel. The attempt to oust Tatum was a grassroots movement, a continuing sign that the city's black citizens rejected paternalism, white or black.

While Gary's black citizens seem to have been the most concerned about how the schools operated, there were others who questioned their policies and procedures. For example, there was some discussion about the role and extent of the vocational curriculum. The Gary schools had early introduced manual training courses, starting on the elementary level, and by the mid-1920s had a full-scale vocational program in progress. Indeed, one of the contemporary criticisms (continued to the present) of the Wirt system was that it was geared to turning out low- and semi-skilled workers for the steel industry. This point was challenged by those who believed the opposite, that indeed the Gary schools may have been devoting too much time and money to academic programs, thereby slighting the majority of students who were not college bound. Guy Wulfing, director of industrial education and Wirt's colleague for forty years, complained to the superintendent in the mid-1930s that "our program contains broad vocational information and situations, but it lacks the systematic handling that we have in other lines of our school work. . . . We should set up a program wherein children, supported by their parents, can look ahead with a fair degree of intelligence to some life career, and can have an intelligent foundation upon which to base their preparatory program." The same criticism of vocational training and guidance appeared in the 1940 Purdue Survey, a highly critical study of the Gary schools commissioned by the school board: "Still, the nature of the courses is 'as if the student were going to college.' There is a remarkable sameness of course work given to students who are almost sure to have widely varying futures. This pressing down on all schools approximately the same curriculum has no logical or psychological defense that would impress scarcely anyone. And still you have it." The survey questioned whether "perhaps the success of a single graduate in an eastern college has been too impressive and the vocational floundering around of many non-college graduates too easily passed over." The start of Gary College in 1932, a junior college extension of the public school system with an academic orientation, naturally gave credence to these charges. The survey's recommendation was to introduce more vocational and commercial courses in some of the high schools, particularly those in the poorer neighborhoods and Roosevelt School, while continuing college preparatory courses in the richer, white schools.[23]

While some advocated greater emphasis on vocational training for the poor, many in the black community thought otherwise. They resented the idea that their children were suited only for manual jobs. They wished to increase the number graduating from Roosevelt High School, which was less than half of those starting the ninth grade, compared to the average in the white schools of 65 percent. The Purdue Survey criticized the "many grossly ill-adapted academic courses in the Roosevelt school." But the *Gary American* responded that black schools should "cut out the so called vocations, and get right down to fundamentals in a well-rounded manner." The white establishment advocated schooling blacks for the limited jobs available to them in the present society, an attitude countered by many in the black community who took seriously the American dream of success through mobility and who envisioned a future society free of racism and segregation. They wanted to expand opportunities, not limit them.

Perhaps they were not too unrealistic, for even then Roosevelt had the third highest percentage of ninth grade students continuing their education beyond high school in the city, far ahead of the four other high schools (but this did not necessarily mean going to college, for which there are no figures for Roosevelt).[24] Many historians currently stress the role of schooling in molding all students, in whatever programs, to the economic and social needs of the corporate-technological state. In their view, the muffled debate in Gary over more or less emphasis on vocational training would seem inconsequential, mere quibbling over who would get the crumbs from the corporate banquet table. There is considerable merit in this view, but it should not detract from noticing that differences of opinion did exist and were taken seriously.

The Gary schools in the 1930s were hit by a depresison which forced the temporary curtailment of some basic programs, including the Saturday, night, and summer schools, along with drastic reductions in salaries. Most programs were retained, however, as Wirt and the school board maintained their commitment to the work-study-play system. The Gary plan had developed spasmodically over three decades, and there were now few innovations that were desired or thought possible, except for the initiation of Gary College. Action came in other areas, as political and economic interests became more open and controversial by mid-decade. The Democratic Party's rise to power and the quick growth and activity of the teachers' union helped politicize the schools, an issue first raised by Wirt in his attack on liberals and radicals in education and politics. Hereafter power politics would play a crucial role in school affairs. But it hardly touched upon the purposes of the differentiated curriculum and the overall functions of schooling. Only in the black community was there such concern.

By the eve of World War 2, public schooling in Gary was hardly the dynamic, innovative system that had existed in previous decades. It had become systematized, taken for granted, because it seemed to work and was familiar. Wirt saw no need to explain the system to Gary's citizens, as he had during the 1920s, because they supposedly understood it and he had more important things to do. But after Wirt's death in 1938 the system changed drastically, becoming more and more like school systems throughout the country. The Gary system would lose its distinctiveness because local officials and local people came to believe the schools were not meeting the changing needs of the corporate state. Certainly the Gary schools had always promoted patriotism and trained students to meet the social, behavioral, and manpower needs of technology and monopoly capital. Under Wirt's early guidance, however, they had seemingly remained aloof from local political forces. The depression shattered this facade. Hereafter schools would become the center of controversy, as politicians, teachers, and others grappled for influence over their affairs. Parents, of course, would continue to be essentially powerless, and they seldom questioned school policies (again, excepting blacks and some immigrants).

Contesting groups disagreed, somewhat, over school affairs during the 1930s, but this did not signify any basic questioning of the purposes or efficacy of schooling. Indeed, there remained an overwhelming consensus—among Republicans and Democrats, whites and blacks, rich and poor, natives and even most immigrants—that schooling was a fundamental part of modern society, particularly as it existed in Gary. What conflict existed, then, did not mean dissatisfaction with the system, only a desire for a greater share of the pie. Schools were now drawn into the public arena, where they would remain to the present.

8

URBAN SCHOOLING
AND THE REVISIONIST PERSPECTIVE

William A. Wirt arrived in Gary in the summer of 1907 eager to start
a public school system from scratch. This did not mean, however, that
he was free from personal, historical, and contemporary influences
and assumptions that would shape the type of system that emerged
in Gary. Naturally, his personal background heavily controlled his
ideas and actions, including the real and imagined history of public
schooling in the United States he shared with his contemporaries. In
Wirt's day there were common assumptions about the functions and
virtues of public schooling, and they have generally persisted to the
present. Historian Frederick M. Binder summarized those beliefs: "For
those who held comfortable positions in American society, schooling
became a more effective instrument for status maintenance. For many
struggling to overcome social and economic deprivation, education
emerged more than ever as a significant part of the good life they
sought."[1] This democratic interpretation has been extremely popular,
but in recent years contrary views have been asserted. Since we have
been influenced by revisionist interpretations in our analysis of the
Gary plan, it seems appropriate to discuss their strengths and weak-
nesses.

According to traditional interpretations, the common school revival
of the early nineteenth century, particularly in the cities, was characterized by a "seemingly boundless potential to serve the interests of
man and society." But were urban public schools initially so equali-
tarian? Hardly, according to recent interpretations. As Robert L. Church
has noted, "Common school reform was primarily an effort to reach
down into the lower portions of the population and to teach

160

children there to share the values, ideals, and controls held by the rest of society." This desire to use the schools for "social control" had many causes, particularly the breakdown of informal social controls and the sense of community that accompanied immigration, industrialization, urbanization, and the westward movement.[2]

Did the common school architects desire to facilitate the development of a new society, or preserve one they thought was unfortunately disappearing? Both. Paul H. Mattingly, for example, has argued the importance of the latter, essentially conservative, motivation. Throughout the nineteenth century, Mattingly has written, the primary goal of schooling was "the inculcation of character," which meant the development of each individual's "moral potential." Similarly, Rush Welter has written that "conservatives who occupied a variety of religious positions turned to systematic public instruction as their ancestors might have turned to an established church, to promote popular morality and obliterate threatening evils." Barbara Finkelstein has described how these goals were implemented:

> The behavior of the teachers as moral overseers, political stewards, and as parent surrogates involved them ultimately in the preservation of social order. By demanding diligence, industry, consideration for others, and achievement they reinforced the moral order of society. By demanding conformity to rules and regulations, they upheld the legal order of things. By promoting competition and by protecting private property, they reinforced economic order. By demanding respect, they reinforced the order of age and youth.[3]

Fearing the loss of personal power along with the collapse of society, conservatives considered public schooling a missionary vehicle, saving individuals as well as society.

Historians, however, have also stressed the transforming nature of schooling. Rush Welter, for instance, in addition to identifying social control motivations, discusses schoolmen who promoted "the widest possible diffusion of knowledge as the great instrument of equal rights." These educators

> transformed the traditional conservative conception of a hierarchical social order supported by institutions that were geared to its complexities, into the more generous vision of an open competitive order sustained by the universal practice of education. The effect of their changing vision was to make education the institutional embodiment of American freedom—not simply a check on popular

vagaries, nor yet a diversion of popular energies, but an act of public authority that would guarantee liberty to everyone.

Lawrence A. Cremin echoes this positive view: "By advancing liberty, the vernaculars of American education also advanced equality, at least in the sense in which the term was used during the nineteenth century. They afforded more varied and extensive opportunities for education to many who had previously enjoyed rather limited opportunities, thereby broadening access to life chances that had formerly been confined to the few." Others, however, have not been so charitable. Concerned about documenting the conscious manufacture of patriotism in the early republic, Lawrence Friedman argued that "the anarchic potentialities of the time made it necessary to inculcate youth in solid patriotic dogmas," a new endeavor that, ironically, entailed "promoting new modes of thought and behavior that could eventually cause further instability." Friedman is not kind toward those who pushed "spread-eagle patriotism," for they "promoted depersonalization and uniformity over concrete, personalized, and diversified human relationships." By this interpretation, the schools' attempt to create a national identity, always one of their major goals, becomes a self-defeating scheme of deeply conservative intentions.[4]

So far we have discussed those studies emphasizing the broad value and behavioral objectives of the common school movement. But to understand fully the topic, we must be more specific. One fruitful, and influential, approach is to trace the connection between the rise of new economic institutions and public schooling. The nineteenth century was marked by the inception of industrialization and entrepreneurial capitalism. The new capitalists needed a favorable climate of opinion and, most importantly, a secure, docile labor force. Schools could secure both, particularly the latter. As Robert L. Church has commented,

> A great deal of the motivation behind common school reform in the era after 1830 grew from this Whig desire to establish centralized, efficient agencies that would superintend the moral development of the nation in much the way that the economic institutions they advocated would superintend the development of a flourishing industrial economy. The Whigs were convinced that the two thrusts must occur simultaneously, for they were fearful . . . that economic change without the reinforcement of social control over the industrial population would spell the doom of the American experiment.

While Church is vague in analyzing the meaning of this connection,

Samuel Bowles and Herbert Gintis spell out its sinister implications in their stimulating book *Schooling in Capitalist America.* For them,

> There can be little doubt that educational reform and expansion in the nineteenth century was associated with the growing ascendancy of the capitalist mode of production. Particularly striking is the recurring pattern of capital accumulation in the dynamic advanced sectors of the economy, the resulting integration of new workers into the wage-labor system, the expansion of the proletariat and the reserve army, social unrest and the emergence of political protest movements, and the development of movements for educational expansion and reform.[5]

But even Bowles and Gintis are too general, for they are economists, not historians, and thus concerned more about contemporary connections between economics and schooling.

The means nineteenth-century industrialists used to create a tractable labor force have been traced by Paul Faler in a penetrating article on the shoemakers of Lynn, Massachusetts:

> For Lynn's inhabitants, most of them shoemakers and their families, industrialization meant inner discipline and a tightening up of the moral code through either the abolition or drastic alteration of those customs, traditions, and practices that interfered with productive labor. More than ever before, life became oriented toward work. . . . Citizens would be self-reliant, hard-working, and sober; obedient to their superiors; attentive to their labors; and self-disciplined in all their pursuits.

Organized religion played a crucial role in this effort, particularly in spreading the temperance movement, a central mechanism in controlling workers' behavior. Public schools served the same purpose, becoming a focal point "between the loose morality of the past and the more rigorous industrial morality" of the new age.[6] At this time schools were not designed to teach specific industrial skills or rigidly sort out management from labor—these responsibilities would come late in the century and after, with the introduction of manual training, the testing movement, and similar "progressive" programs. Mid-nineteenth century schooling had a broader function, as most historians now seem to agree.

Specifically, how were schools organized to accomplish their goal of instilling morality, punctuality, obedience, patriotism, and the like in children? Michael B. Katz has argued that public schooling in the nineteenth century became dominated by three characteristics: class-bias (the middle and upper classes ran the schools to benefit their own children and control the poor), racism, and bureaucratic organization. The three did not appear simultaneously throughout the country, but developed variously over time, depending on local circumstances. They appeared first in the manufacturing centers and larger cities, particularly New York and Boston. Two recent studies of schooling document the case, Carl F. Kaestle's examination of New York (1750–1850) and Stanley K. Schultz's study of Boston (1789–1860). As Boston grew rapidly, from 43,298 in 1820 to 177,840 in 1860, stability became more and more desirable, and more and more illusive, for the middle and upper classes. School administrators fought hard to contain the growing disorganization of city life. For example, they imposed administrative organization and control over the schools, abandoning the neighborhood school concept. They established graded schools for the same reason. As the school bureaucracy grew, professional administrators were hired for the sake of efficiency, replacing the amateurs on the school committee; a full-time superintendent was first appointed in 1851. By 1860 Bostonians were trapped in a dilemma: the schools were too small and grossly overcrowded, and many of the children, particularly the poor (Irish) immigrants, were clearly not getting a good academic education; yet as urban problems intensified, schools increasingly appeared the salvation of society, agencies for the preservation of democracy and order.[7]

Kaestle, in a much briefer space, tells the same story for New York City's schools. In the 1830s more children were attending private than public schools, but by 1850 a majority were enrolled in the latter; in both decades roughly 55 percent of school-age children attended school. The schools' overwhelming concern was to inculcate Christian (Protestant) morality and obedience in middle and lower class children, traits that would make them productive, law-abiding citizens. The schools also became very bureaucratic by mid-century. By 1850, Kaestle concludes, New York's school system, highly regimented as it was, "provided a symbolic gratification, a sense of getting control of the problem, and, in the middle of the century, a sense of closure, of having finished something. That something was a school system, solid and permanent." While Kaestle questions the meaning of this faith, he does not bring out the irony of the situation so important to Schultz. Both, however, stress the schoolmen's search for social order, while slighting their desire for industrial efficiency and the creation of a docile labor force. Their doubt that schools promoted mobility is seconded by other recent studies, such as Lee Soltow and Edward Stevens's analysis of "Economic Aspects of School Participation in Mid-Nineteenth-Century United States," which concludes "that the common school institution did not alter patterns of economic inequality, but, rather, tended to perpetuate them."[8]

While schools might have been taking on a modern shape in Boston, New York City, and other urban centers by the mid-nineteenth century, they were still highly unstructured, largely ineffectual institutions in most parts of the country, both urban and rural. Not until the turn of the twentieth century did schooling become a vital force in American life. Unfortunately, there are few studies of the crucial late-nineteenth century decades when the transformation took place, but enough to give us insights into the process. The common approach is to trace national trends, such as bureaucratization, without regard for local variations. Patricia A. Graham, in her interesting *Community and Class in American Education, 1865–1918,* contradicts this approach, however, by contrasting four different school systems: Johnson County, Indiana; Marquette County, Michigan; Butler County, Alabama; and New York City. She stresses the importance of local influences, particularly financial resources, although she does mention such national trends as increasing attendance and literacy, grading of classes and school consolidation, the introduction of vocational training, and racial segregation. She rejects the revisionist approach, clinging to the democratic rationale of schooling. Nonetheless, she notes the irony that

> the two groups that participated in them [i.e., schools] most actively were both outside prestige positions in American society, women, and the children of immigrants. . . . Crucial as the educational institutions were in the late nineteenth century, attendance at them did not guarantee full acceptance in the economic or social life of the nation. No one has ever believed that education alone would provide such an entrée, but at least [these] two groups of the society used it as a lever for themselves.[9]

While there were significant local variations in the late nineteenth century, important changes were occurring nationally, particularly in cities, that would bring considerable uniformity among school systems. This move toward standardization has characterized much recent writing on the subject. David B. Tyack, in particular, has used this framework to describe the rise of *The One Best System.* Drawing heavily upon the pioneering studies of historians Robert H. Wiebe, Samuel Hays, and their followers, Tyack stresses the school reformers' desire for efficiency and control. These objectives contrasted sharply with the decentralized, indeed, chaotic, conditions that still existed by the late nineteenth century in most cities: school boards were large, elective, often decentralized, with frequent conflicts between central and ward members; school responsibilities were divided among numerous city agencies; and superintendents were weak, with power in the hands of non-professionals. By the second decade of the twentieth century, all this had begun to change, although not without conflict. School boards became centralized, considerably smaller, and dominated by businessmen and other urban elites. They in turn began to delegate more and more authority to professional superintendents, who built up their own bureaucracies. Tyack has traced this transformation in New York City, Philadelphia, St. Louis, San Francisco, and Chicago. In sum, Tyack contends, structural reformers desired "to replace a rather mechanical form of public bureaucracy, which was permeated with 'illegitimate' lay influence, with a streamlined 'professional' bureaucracy in which lay control was carefully filtered through a corporate school board."[10]

But professionalization and bureaucratization were only two facets of a larger movement to make schooling more efficient and predominant in American life. School systems changed in the late nineteenth century in response to significant alterations in society. Industrialization and the rise of the corporate state greatly increased immigration, and quickened urbanization stimulated reform in a number of ways. For one thing, rapidly expanding school enrollment, particularly of recent immigrants, seemed to necessitate greater efficiency in manipulating school affairs, a program pushed by urban elites who sought to wrest control of city government from the old machines and centralize it in their own hands. In the process, school affairs soon became matters of cost accounting, chains of command, and trained experts. Once this process had begun, superintendents and their elite supporters could institute curricular and other reforms designed to expand significantly the role of schools in society. Throughout the nineteenth century schooling had been limited in scope and function. As Selwyn K. Troen has sufficiently documented for St. Louis in *The Public and the Schools,* most children attended public schools between the ages of eight and eleven, but dropped out after age twelve. This pattern began to change after 1900, with children entering earlier and staying longer, first to age fourteen, and later into high school. Children stayed in school for longer periods of time, because of both the drying up of jobs and, according to Troen, the rational perceptions of parents that schooling was necessary for the future welfare of their children.[11]

The centralization of urban school systems served to homogenize schooling by the first decade of the twentieth century. This was the goal of the structural reformers, and they apparently succeeded. In St. Louis, for example, class, religious, ethnic, and racial conflicts had previously disrupted schooling. By the eve of World War 1, such conflicts had disappeared, replaced by a broad consensus. This was logical, argues Troen, for

> the success of reform in replacing grafting politicians with a tradition of comparatively disinterested stewardship diminished even further the presence of rancor in school politics. Without the divisiveness of social antagonisms, charges of corruption, and partisan politics, the schools became relatively neutralized. Popular interest in education transcended communal fractionalism or partisan issues. . . . Major departures, even in such a radical area as compulsory education, aroused virtually no opposition.[12]

He sees no attempt or desire by the elite to manipulate the masses, only concern for their well being, which was accepted by all. Other historians, however, are more critical.

Once school administration became centralized and controlled by bureaucrats and experts, curricular and other sorts of reforms could proceed swiftly. Most recent historical research has concentrated on such reforms, examining their intent and accomplishments. Broadly taking their cue from Michael B. Katz, many historians now interpret such reforms as being influenced by class and racial bias, all within a framework of the consolidation of economic interests. This latter process, the growth of corporate capitalism and the rise of the corporate-technological state, has been seen as a particularly influential force in dictating school structures and reforms. Such a perspective is a far cry from the charitable interpretation of the first comprehensive study of early twentieth-century schooling, Lawrence A. Cremin's *The Transformation of the School.* Cremin believed progressive education was simply one aspect of the larger social and political upheaval known as the progressive movement designed to create a democratic and humane educational and social system. Progressives supposedly conceived of the school as "a fundamental lever of social and political regeneration," and they "viewed education as an adjunct to politics in realizing the promise of American life."[13]

For Cremin, schools influenced society, hopefully for the better. His views were soon attacked, particularly by those who believed the opposite —that schools were in fact shaped and directed by external forces, making them essentially pawns of those who had power. Raymond E. Callahan, for one, argued in *Education and the Cult of Efficiency* that Progressive Era schools were shaped by business influences and ideology. This framework was adopted by Edward A. Krug in *The Shaping of the American High School, 1880–1920.* The high school, Krug contended, was molded by the advocates of "social efficiency," not by those who saw education as "freedom for the child." The pattern of high school education was laid out along clearly paternalistic lines—a pattern set by educators more interested in efficient and practical as opposed to democratic and humanistic schooling, more concerned with the structure of the school than with the freedom and individuality of the students.[14]

Starting with Krug, historians began turning their attention to the mechanisms schoolmen used to enhance the social control aspects of schooling. While continuing the nationalistic and moral training of earlier years, schools began to include specific training functions in keeping with changing economic and social conditions, particularly after 1900. Marvin Lazerson, for example, has demonstrated that in Massachusetts educators "sought to integrate the schools into the industrial society" through reform of school administration, expansion of the kindergarten, and concentration on manual training and vocational guidance. Training students for industrial roles became "the surest way of preserving order in a hierarchical, bureaucratic society." Joel H. Spring takes a different tack, stressing the cooperative aspects of training for industrial efficiency and urban harmony. Summer school, playgrounds, vacation camps, boys' clubs, evening recreation programs, vocational guidance, the junior high, the homeroom, and student government—these and other new programs were introduced as means of enhancing the urban schools as "an instrument of social, economic, and political control."[15]

Most important was the diversification of the curriculum, particularly the introduction of manual and vocational courses, first on the elementary level, and increasingly after 1900 in the high schools. Both Troen and Tyack, for example, following the lead of Lazerson, Spring, and Krug, underscore the importance of transforming an essentially academic curriculum into one including shops, domestic science, agriculture, and business and clerical courses, supported by vocational guidance. "The enlargement of responsibilities both through curricular changes and the development of extracurricular programs had decisively transformed the schools," Troen writes. "In meeting the challenge of a growing urban and industrial center [St. Louis], they interjected themselves into the lives of the young by demanding a greater commitment in time and into the affairs of the community by promising assistance in solving social and economic problems."[16] For Troen, such innovations were beneficial for all students, designed to "solve" problems for them as well as for society in general.

Other historians, however, see sinister or manipulative motives behind these changes. For example, the historical essays in *Work, Technology, and Education: Dissenting Essays in the Intellectual Foundations of American Education,* edited by Walter Feinberg and Henry Rosemont, argue that schools and their supporters became almost total servants of technological change and its corporate benefactors in the twentieth century, particularly in the role of job selection and training. This was accomplished in a variety of ways. In addition to training for specific future occupational slots, Feinberg and Rosemont point out that schools served "to reinforce those images that are dominant in the society." The school was also

> the place where a child begins to learn the habits that are thought to be essential to the maintenance and the continuation of industrial society. . . . If punctuality, obedience and a generally high toleration for meaningless tasks are more commonly found in the training of children than are rationality and insight, it is because punctuality, obedience, and a toleration of boredom are the first requirement of a large number of jobs in industrial society whereas rationality and insight are not.[17]

Feinberg, a philosopher, is not so much interested in how schools have actually operated, as he is in the intellectual justifications and motives for the changes that have taken place in the twentieth century. In his book *Reason and Rhetoric: The Intellectual Foundations of 20th Century Liberal Educational Policy* he argues that

> the dominant and unyielding part of modern society was believed to be the growth of technology, [and therefore] technology was proposed to be the focal point of functional integration. The school had many roles in this process, but its major one was to teach people that the new technology was the reality around which their lives were to be organized and to teach them too to take up their place in its development. Reformers of all persuasions accepted this as the primary function of schooling.[18]

Feinberg is highly critical of this attitude, for it made man the tool of the machine, and not vice versa.

Two of the authors in the Feinberg and Rosemont volume, Samuel Bowles and Herbert Gintis, also argue that

> the school is a bureaucratic order with hierarchical authority, rule orientation, stratification by 'ability' (tracking) as well as by age (grades), role differentiation by sex (physical education, home economics, shop), and a system of external incentives (marks, promise of promotion, and threat of failure) much like pay and

status in the sphere of work. Thus schools are likely to develop in students traits corresponding to those required on the job.

Since Bowles and Gintis are economists, their emphasis is on the economic functions of schools, not their intellectual justifications. Still, in their recent *Schooling in Capitalist America: Educational Reform and the Contradictions of Economic Life,* they conclude that "the essence of Progressivism in education was the rationalization of the process of reproducing the social classes of modern industrial life. The Progressives viewed the growing corporatization of economic activity as desirable and forward-looking—indeed, the best antidote to the provincialism and elitism of U.S. culture." While Feinberg argues that schools have been devoted to preserving and extending a technological society, Bowles and Gintis put their emphasis on the omnipotence of corporate capitalism. While technology and modern capitalism are, of course, deeply integrated, they are nonetheless separate entities. Too simply, the acceptance or rejection of technology connotes a broadly held value judgment, while the growth of corporate capitalism has been more involved with power relationships and class conflict. As Bowles and Gintis note, "Analysis of the process of educational reform must consider the shifting arenas of class conflict and the mechanisms which the capitalist class has developed to mediate and deflect class conflict."[19]

The difference in the two approaches can be seen in their divergent solutions. Feinberg calls for a reconsideration of "the requirements of technology and the nature of work. . . . If technology is to serve real human needs then it must be governed by just human principles, and when this occurs there will be less need to worry about schools." Bowles and Gintis, however, demand "that an equal and liberating educational system can only emerge from a broad-based movement dedicated to the transformation of economic life. Such a movement is socialist in the sense that private ownership of essential productive resources must be abolished, and control over the production process must be placed in the hands of working people."[20] While the two views have much in common, particularly their desire for true equality and not just equality of opportunity, they represent separate conclusions as to how this can be accomplished.

Other historians have analyzed and criticized additional innovations that served corporate-technological interests, but without the ideological rigor and theoretical framework of Bowles and Gintis. In his documentary collection *Shaping the American Educational State: 1900 to the Present* Clarence J. Karier explores academic freedom, testing, sorting and tracking, IQ and its racist implications, sex and race stereotyping in the curriculum, and Americanization. Highlighting the words and deeds of the intellectual elite who have influenced the educational system, Karier demonstrates that it has been "designed to help fit people into a social system that was not necessarily their own choice. It fit people into that system by helping some barely to survive, others merely to exist, and still others to prosper. From the standpoint, then, of many of the shapers of the educational state in America, the schools were successful. They accomplished what they were designed to do." Agreeing with Feinberg and Bowles and Gintis, Karier interprets most change, whether implemented by conservatives or liberals, as aimed at sorting and controlling children, with native, upper class whites profiting at the expense of immigrants, non-whites, and the poor generally. Concerning the testing movement, Tyack agrees, for

> the notion of great and measurable differences in intellectual
> capacity became part of the conventional wisdom not only of school
> people but of the public. . . . The problem with the discriminations
> schoolmen made was not that they paid attention to differences,
> but that their technology of testing was limited in scope. They so
> often confused individual variation with gross social inequalities
> associated with poverty, oppression on the basis of color, or other
> features of the multiple subcultures of a highly plural society.[21]

Were the school reformers, with their interest in order and control, their centralized bureaucracies, their elaborate curricula and added testing and sorting paraphernalia, successful? Karier, Feinberg, and Bowles and Gintis think so, because of their power and pervasive influence. Troen agrees, but for different reasons. He concludes that by 1920 "the enlarged intersection of the schools with the lives of the young, parents, businesses, and the community engendered cooperation and hope rather than estrangement." Cremin is even more positive:

> On balance the American education system has contributed sig-
> nificantly to the advancement of liberty, equality, and fraternity,
> in that complementarity and tension that mark the relations among
> them in a free society. . . . The aspirations of American education
> have been more noble than base, and . . . its performance over the
> past two centuries has been more liberating of a greater diversity of
> human energies and potentialities than has been the case in most
> other eras and in most other places.[22]

Such praise is difficult to accept. As Michael B. Katz has concluded, "The burden of proof no longer lies with those who argue that education is and has been unequal. It lies, rather, with those who would defend the system." Tyack, going further, believes that while reformers believed in manipulation and control, they were unsuccessful in reaching their goals. For example, "Structural reform could offer, then, no sure relief from insecurity of office for the leaders, insubordination by employees, corruption and machine domination, ethnic influence and informal networks of power within the system, or any of the other forms of political behavior that the corporate model was designed to minimize." Discrimination and segregation were rampant, but Tyack adds that not all blacks and ethnic whites were passively resigned to this situation. Blacks, on the one hand, fought discrimination and segregation in the courts, while on the other they often preferred black schools with all-black teachers because of race pride and power. Many first and second generation immigrant children—for example, south Italians—protested by performing poorly and leaving early. The one best system was perhaps neither omnipotent nor omniscient. Here is the start of a new interpretation, breaking both with the essentially consensus model of Troen and his predecessors and with the repressive and manipulative model of Karier, Feinberg, Bowles and Gintis, and others.[23]

Still another view, with intriguing possibilities, attempts to mesh the consensus and control interpretations by locating two camps of reformers, conservatives and liberals. "We can divide reformers into two groups," argues Robert L. Church, "a smaller group which we may term liberals and a far larger group which we may identify as conservatives. The first group's ultimate goal was social justice; the second's, social order." While conservatives had the power, the liberals, such as John Dewey and Jane Addams, should not be ignored, for they had intellectual prominence. Church is particularly impressed by the liberals' "quest to rebuild community in the United States." Here he echoes Katz's caution that "we must be careful about the meaning we attribute to the collectivist emphasis—the frequent anti-individualistic bias—that appears in the writings of some [liberal] progressive theorists. We must be careful not to dismiss this solely as an effort to make the world comfortable for corporate capitalism. It is just as congruent with socialism, maybe even more so."[24] The problem, of course, is to try to distinguish between enforced conformity from above and a genuine belief in and an attempt to encourage community consciousness from below.

The school cannot be isolated from the society in which it functions; rather, it is an institution which mirrors that society. It socializes children according to accepted standards, values, and norms, and it reflects economic changes, ideological shifts, and political tensions. Therefore, to untangle the conflicting interpretations of modern educational reforms we must understand something of the nature of the broader progressive movement of which school reform has been a part. Recent historical scholarship has argued that progressivism—roughly, reforms instituted between 1890 and 1920—was not a monolithic movement. It involved, in fact, at least two rather distinct attempts to change society—one in the direction of structural or institutional reform, and the other in the direction of social activism.

Historians Richard Hofstadter, Gabriel Kolko, Robert H. Wiebe, Samuel P. Hays, Melvin G. Holli, and Otis L. Graham have described progressivism as a conservative-oriented movement—one which sought to reassert the dominance of elites in society and politics, one which sought to restore the freedom of the individual which was fast disappearing before the forces of immigration, industrialization, and urbanization. On the city level progressives wanted to reorganize, restructure, and streamline municipal government along efficient, businesslike lines; the city manager and the commission form of urban government fit these goals perfectly. They hoped to clean up corrupt municipal politics and eliminate vice and crime. They were suspicious of the masses, particularly the poor and the foreign-born. As Holli has written, they placed their faith in "rule by educated, upper class Americans and, later, by municipal experts rather than the lower classes. The installation in office of men of character, substance, and integrity was an attempt to impose middle class and patrician ideals upon the urban masses." They were also suspicious of the federal and state governments, trusting basically in local governments that they could control; "home rule" for the cities became their watchword. In a similar way Graham interprets progressivism as essentially conservative and backward-looking, a revolt against the changes brought on by the twentieth century. Progressives sought "to resist power not in their (i.e., private and familiar) hands, to invoke the virtue of a unified nation against awakenings of divisions, to elevate moral considerations over material ones, to indulge a nostalgia for a lost harmonious localized condition." They were small town people who never felt comfortable in the modernized world of the twentieth century. Ironically, however, many could rely upon the new business methods of order and efficiency to turn back the clock.[25] Caught between past and future, they relied on power and efficiency to secure an orderly society.

The other side of progressivism was represented by the social reformers, often settlement workers and intellectuals. They believed in "the preventive possibilities of social action." Their basic concern was to improve—economically, socially, and culturally—the conditions of the poor in the cities. Not that they did not impose their middle class American values upon these largely immigrant groups, but they also believed their first goal was to help them achieve a decent and more comfortable way of life. Such goals could be accomplished through the combined efforts of individuals working directly with the poor in their neighborhoods and the implementation of legislation and government programs, hopefully at the national level. They have been aptly characterized by Allen F. Davis in *Spearheads for Reform* as "a group of idealists who believed that they could solve some of the problems of the sprawling, crowded city by going to live in a working-class neighborhood." They were "optimists who were convinced that reform was not only necessary, but also possible, in an age when rapid industrialization and a deluge of immigrants exaggerated the social and economic differences in America and challenged the very tenets of democracy." They often shared with the structural reformers a suspicion of strong, centralized government, as Graham reminds us, yet they could accept national legislation when it was in the interests of the poor and oppressed. They were perhaps confused at times, as Don S. Kirschner argues, for "while they were moved by a tenderminded wish to liberate the downtrodden from the shackles of society, they were restrained by a tough-minded desire to protect society from the threat of the downtrodden. The result was a muddle-minded temporizing that led them in the end to accept social trimming in the guise of social reconstruction."[26]

The structural reformers were uncomfortable in the urbanized, multiethnic, class-oriented society that America was swiftly becoming. Yet they took solace from the hope that efficiency and the good management practices of business could preserve the virtues of nineteenth-century, small town America. Above all, they had supreme confidence that *they* held the key to the country's salvation. The social reformers, on the other hand, while highly critical of the by-products of urbanization, immigration, and industrialization—poverty, slums, social injustices, the destruction of a homogeneous society, the manipulation of women and children by factory owners, and the like—nonetheless somewhat reconciled themselves to the changes in society and dedicated themselves to alleviating the plight of the victims. Yet they shared many of the structural reformers' beliefs and values. "The new radicals were torn between their wish to liberate the unused energies of the submerged portions of society and their enthusiasm for social planning, which led in practice to new and subtler forms of repression," Christopher Lasch has written, "The rage for planning reflected the planners' confidence in themselves as a disinterested elite, unbound by the prejudices either of the middle class or of the proletariat. It reflected also their abiding anxiety lest the voice of reason be overwhelmed by the uproar of social conflict."[27]

Thus, while both groups of progressives were highly critical of each other's tactics and goals, they often managed to cooperate. And the one institution that they could all agree was of fundamental importance in reforming society, and that itself needed reforming, was formal education—the public schools. We now know considerably more about the development of urban public schooling than we did a scant five years ago. But while the broad outlines are available, three questions need considerably more attention: what motivated the reformers, were they omnipotent, and exactly how did the story unfold in each locality? As we have seen, it is now fashionable to concentrate on the administrative progressives, particularly in emphasizing their rationality and acceptance of bureaucracy, technology, and urbanization. But as many have noted, perhaps the emerging schoolmen and their professional bedfellows were looking backward as well as forward. It is highly questionable whether all completely accepted or even understood the meaning of an urban-dominated, corporate-technological society. Like Gary's William A. Wirt, many were small town boys who wanted to restore the simple life, even as they worked to destroy and manipulate it. There is an irony here that needs investigation. Moreover, in concentrating on the efficiency-minded centralizers, historians have ignored those social progressives who were more concerned about true child-centered schools and remaking society to benefit the masses. While they were certainly not the dominant element in school reform, as Cremin argued, they should not be ignored. And since many were women, their inclusion avoids the common male-oriented focus.[28]

In line with recognizing the social reformers' scattered contributions, we should also understand the limits of the administrative progressives' power. Blacks, immigrants, teachers, and perhaps others often had their own ideas as to how schools should function. While their strength has been limited, they have had some control over their situation, either through group action or non-involvement (that is, withdrawing children from school as early as possible, as many families have done). We believe too much has been made of the juggernaut-like force of the rise of an urbanized, corporate-technological society. American society has not been monolithic in the twentieth century, thankfully, and it seriously distorts the story to depict it as such. Indeed, what we need is more understanding of those who have escaped through the cracks, those who have survived despite the power and intentions of the bureaucrats and corporate elites, those who have resisted the system.

We have attempted to analyze modern urban schooling, as it developed in Gary, Indiana, and New York City, from some of the complex perspectives mentioned above. Recent scholarship has given us considerable insight into the dynamics of twentieth-century schooling, and we have profited immeasurably from this work. But we have tried to go beyond these interpretations to add further dimensions to the story. What we have attempted, however, is only a beginning.

TABLE 1: POPULATION OF GARY, INDIANA, 1910–40

	1910		1920		1930		1940	
	Number	%	Number	%	Number	%	Number	%
Native white	4,480	26.7	16,519	29.8	33,635	33.5	73,976	66.2
Foreign-born white	8,242	49.0	16,460	29.7	19,345	19.3	17,270	15.5
Native white, one or more foreign-born parents	3,681	21.9	17,065	30.8	26,012	25.9	—b	——
Black	383	2.3	5,299	9.6	17,922	17.8	20,394	18.2
Other races	16	.1	35	.1	3,512a	3.5	79c	.1
TOTALS	16,802	100.0	55,378	100.0	100,426	100.0	111,719	100.0

a. Mexican immigrants made up 3,486 of the total listed under "other races" in 1930.
b. Native white statistics for 1940 include native-born children with one or more foreign-born parents.
c. White population in 1940 includes Mexicans classified under "other races" in 1930.

Sources: U. S. Bureau of the Census, *Thirteenth Census of the United States, 2 Population* (Washington, D. C., 1913): 568; U. S. Bureau of the Census, *Fourteenth Census of the United States, 3 Population* (Washington, D. C., 1922): 297; U. S. Bureau of the Census, *Fifteenth Census of the United States, 1930, Population, 3, part 1* (Washington, D. C., 1932): 715; U. S. Bureau of the Census, *Sixteenth Census of the United States, 1940, Population, 2, Characteristics of the Population, part 2,* (Washington, D. C., 1943): 797.

TABLE 2: GARY SCHOOL ATTENDANCE, CHILDREN AGED 7-17, 1910-40

	1910[a]			1920			1930			1940		
	Number	In school	% in school	Number	In school	% in school	Number	In school	% in school	Number	In school	% in school
Native white	572	483	84.4	2,852	2,467	86.5	6,972	6,572	94.3	15,901[b]	15,114	95.1
Foreign-born white	317	252	79.5	960	707	73.6	718	603	84.0	286	267	93.4
Native white, one or more foreign-born parents	744	618	83.1	4,851	4,250	87.6	9,747	8,999	92.3	—	—	—
Blacks	20	19	95.0	785	634	80.7	3,027	2,759	91.1	4,027	3,810	94.6
TOTALS	1,653	1,372	83.0	9,448	8,058	85.3	20,464	18,933	92.5	20,214	19,191	94.9

a. 1910 statistics are for children aged 6 to 14.
b. Native white statistics for 1940 include native-born children with one or more foreign-born parents.

Sources: U. S. Bureau of the Census, *Thirteenth Census of the United States, 2, Population* (Washington, D. C., 1913): 568; U. S. Bureau of the Census, *Fourteenth Census of the United States, 3, Population* (Washington, D. C., 1922): 297; U. S. Bureau of the Census, *Fifteenth Census of the United States, 1930, Population, 3, part 1* (Washington, D. C., 1932): 715; U. S. Bureau of the Census, *Sixteenth Census of the United States, 1940, Population, 2, Characteristics of the Population, part 2* (Washington, D. C., 1943): 808.

TABLE 3: CHILDREN OF FOREIGN STOCK IN GARY SCHOOLS, 1910–30

Date	Total school population	Number of foreign-stock children	% of foreign-stock children
1910	1,372	870	63.4
1920	8,058	4,957	61.5
1930	18,933	9,602	50.7

Foreign stock includes foreign-born children and native-born children with one or more foreign-born parents.

Sources: Same as for table 2.

TABLE 4: NATIONALITY OF FOREIGN-STOCK CHILDREN IN GARY SCHOOLS BY PERCENTAGE, 1916

Nationality	Froebel School	Emerson School	Jefferson School
Austria-Hungary	54	22	21
Russia	25	7	15
Italy	6	2	4
Greece	1	1	4
Great Britain and Ireland		24	16
Germany	5	14	7
Scandinavia		12	11
Canada		4	7
All other countries	9	14	15

The nationality categories are somewhat inexact, since nation rather than mother tongue was used. Thus, the Poles, who formed one of Gary's largest ethnic groups, are not listed separately because most of them came from Russia or Austria. Czechs, Slovaks, Romanians, Bulgarians, Serbians, Croatians, and others from the Balkans do not get separate entries because they all came from the Austro-Hungarian empire. British, Irish, German, Scandinavian, and Canadian immigrants were consolidated into one entry for Froebel, but given separate entries for Emerson and Jefferson.

SOURCES: Abraham Flexner and Frank P. Bachman, *The Gary Schools: A General Account* (New York, 1918), p. 14.

TABLE 5: ADULT EDUCATION IN GARY, 1921–36

School year	Night school enrollment	Day school enrollment
1921–22	10,320	10,991
1922–23	12,474	12,190
1923–24	12,814	14,141
1924–25	13,423	15,808
1925–26	12,905	17,621
1926–27	15,667	19,085
1927–28	16,756	20,391
1928–29	16,763	20,954
1929–30	16,319	21,811
1930–31	17,779	22,356
1931–32	13,674	21,888
1932–33	4,138	21,253
1933–34	4,514	21,258
1934–35	6,997	21,498
1935–36	6,914	21,780

SOURCE: *Third Annual Scholastic Convocation* (Gary, June 16, 1937), pamphlet, Calumet Regional Archives, p. 8.

TABLE 6: SCHOOL ATTENDANCE OF GARY'S MAJOR ETHNIC GROUPS, 1922 and 1924

Ethnic group	Total school-age children	Public school enrollment		Parochial and private school enrollment		Not enrolled in school	
		Number	%	Number	%	Number	%
Native white							
1922	5,077	3,488	68.7	582	11.5	1,007	19.8
1924	5,857	4,285	73.2	535	9.1	1,037	17.7
Black							
1922	1,480	1,236	83.5	9	.6	235	15.9
1924	3,167	2,347	74.1	5	.1	815	25.8
Polish							
1922	1,797	449	27.8	749	41.7	549	30.5
1924	2,311	781	33.8	966	41.8	564	24.4
Austrian							
1922	1,119	679	60.7	173	15.5	267	23.8
1924	728	462	63.5	148	20.3	118	16.2
Slovak							
1922	883	427	48.4	272	30.8	184	20.8
1924	1,369	875	63.9	243	17.8	251	18.3
Hungarian							
1922	674	375	55.6	117	26.3	122	18.1
1924	677	408	60.3	152	22.4	117	17.3
Russian							
1922	600	384	64.0	66	11.0	150	25.0
1924	520	382	73.4	43	8.3	95	18.3
Italian							
1922	565	373	66.0	67	11.9	125	22.1
1924	557	454	81.5	35	6.3	68	12.2
Croatian							
1922	527	275	52.2	123	23.3	129	24.5
1924	750	452	60.3	181	24.1	117	15.6
German							
1922	455	287	63.1	92	20.2	76	16.7
1924	548	245	44.7	180	32.8	123	22.5
Lithuanian							
1922	332	192	57.8	46	13.9	94	28.3
1924	407	238	58.5	94	23.1	75	18.4
Serbian							
1922	319	230	72.1	14	4.4	75	23.5
1924	379	309	81.5	22	5.8	48	12.7
Jews							
1922	310	272	87.7	3	1.0	35	11.3
1924	362	269	74.3	5	1.4	88	24.3

TABLE 6 cont.

Ethnic group	Total school-age children	Public school enrollment		Parochial and private school enrollment		Not enrolled in school	
		Number	%	Number	%	Number	%
Swedish							
1922	265	198	74.7	24	9.1	43	16.2
1924	296	237	80.1	10	3.4	49	16.5
Irish							
1922	199	50	25.1	116	58.3	33	16.6
1924	374	243	65.0	111	29.7	20	5.3
Greek							
1922	156	99	63.5	5	3.2	52	33.3
1912	251	157	62.5	10	4.0	84	33.5
	251	157	62.5	10	4.0	84	33.5
Romanian							
1922	152	123	81.0	4	2.6	25	16.4
1924	189	154	81.5	6	3.2	29	15.3
English							
1922	135	100	74.1	11	8.1	24	17.8
1924	141	119	84.4	8	5.7	14	9.9
Czech							
1922	97	68	70.1	9	9.3	20	20.6
1924	96	78	81.2	18	18.8	0	0
Scotch							
1922	89	69	77.5	6	6.7	14	15.7
1924	92	73	79.3	0	0	19	20.7
Spanish							
1922	55	37	67.3	1	1.8	17	30.9
1924	98	51	52.0	8	8.2	39	39.8
Bulgarian							
1922	55	40	72.7	5	9.1	10	18.2
1924	86	71	82.6	3	3.5	12	13.9
Canadian							
1922	43	27	62.8	7	16.3	9	20.9
1924	88	63	71.6	5	5.7	20	22.7
Mexican							
1922	18	17	94.4	0	0	1	5.6
1924	87	58	66.7	0	0	29	33.3
All groups[a]							
1922	15,658	9,706	62.0	2,605	16.6	3,347	21.4
1924	19,618	13,009	66.3	2,797	14.3	3,812	19.4

a. This entry includes school attendance totals for the city's smaller ethnic groups not listed separately in the table.

SOURCES: Gary School Census, 1922, 1924, Calumet Regional Archives.

TABLE 7: GRADE SCHOOL AND HIGH SCHOOL ATTENDANCE IN GARY 1907–41

School year	Kindergarten through eighth grade	High school	Total
1907–08	494	18	512
1908–09	992	49	1,041
1909–10	996	98	1,094
1910–11	2,426	156	2,582
1911–12	2,999	196	3,195
1912–13	3,935	237	4,172
1913–14	4,777	273	5,050
1914–15	4,890	446	5,336
1915–16	5,126	547	5,673
1916–17	6,191	581	6,772
1917–18	7,168	630	7,798
1918–19	8,174	714	8,888
1919–20	8,682	799	9,481
1920–21	8,041	723	8,764
1921–22	8,704	939	9,643
1922–23	9,420	1,105	10,525
1923–24	10,902	1,322	12,224
1924–25	12,247	1,538	13,785
1925–26	13,022	1,852	14,874
1926–27	14,151	2,400	16,551
1927–28	14,603	2,822	17,425
1928–29	13,398	3,399	16,797
1929–30	14,436	4,100	18,536
1930–31	14,102	5,002	19,104
1931–32	14,580	4,415	18,995
1932–33	14,170	4,997	19,167
1933–34	14,157	4,834	18,991
1934–35	14,815	5,135	19,950
1935–36	14,621	5,142	19,763
1936–37	14,261	5,345	19,606
1937–38	14,245	5,563	19,808
1938–39	14,910	5,657	20,567
1939–40	14,174	5,938	20,112
1940–41	14,127	5,664	19,791

SOURCE: F. B. Knight et al., *Final Report, Purdue Survey Committee for the Gary Board of Education to the President and Board of Trustees of Purdue University* (mimeo, 1941), p. 105.

TABLE 8: NUMBER OF GARY CHILDREN NOT
ATTENDING SCHOOL BY AGES, 1922 and 1924

	1922		1924
Age	Number	Age	Number
12	16	12	54
13	12	13	53
14	29	14	41
15	68	15	66
16	234	16	218
17	360	17	393
18	448	18	361

SOURCES: Gary School Census, 1922, 1924, Calumet Regional
Archives.

A NOTE ON SOURCES

This book is based almost entirely on extensive research in primary sources. The William A. Wirt Manuscripts, located in the Lilly Library at Indiana University, Bloomington, provided an essential source. These materials, consisting of over one hundred manuscript boxes, contain Wirt's voluminous incoming correspondence and carbon copies of outgoing correspondence. This collection includes letters and memos to and from administrators and teachers in the Gary public schools, Wirt's correspondence with school administrators throughout the nation, extensive material relating to the implementation of the Gary plan in New York City, and hundreds of letters from Alice Barrows to Wirt over a twenty-year period. A second collection, the William A. Wirt Papers in the Calumet Regional Archives, Indiana University Northwest, Gary, also contains important correspondence and other material relating to the operation of the Gary public schools, as well as to the Gary plan in New York City and the national platoon school organization. Wirt's numerous writings on education and other subjects are also essential for an understanding of his views on schooling and its purposes. Among the most important of these are the following: "The Place of the Public School in a Community Program for Child Welfare," *The Child* 1 (July, 1912): 11-15; "Utilization of School Plant," *Proceedings of the National Conference of Charities and Correction* (1912): 58-62; Public Education Association of New York, *The Official Wirt Reports to the Board of Education of New York City* (New York, 1916); "Multiple Use of Child Welfare Agencies," *Addresses and Proceedings of the National Education Association* (1917): 734-38; "Creating a Child World," *The Platoon School* 1 (January, 1927): 4-7; "Making the City a Fit Place for the Rearing of Children," part 1, *The Platoon School* 3 (December, 1929): 152-58; "Making the City a Fit Place for the Rearing of Children," part 2, *The Platoon School* 4 (March, 1930): 7-13; "One Teacher or Many," *The Platoon School* 5 (March-August, 1931): 6-16; "Industrial Work in Public Schools," *The Platoon School* 6 (December, 1932): 3-16; *American Must Lose—By a "Planned Economy"* (New York, 1934); *The Great Lockout in America's Citizenship Plants* (Gary, 1937). Interviews with Wirt's sons William F. Wirt and Sherwood Wirt, and with former teachers and administrators in the Gary school system, also provided important and useful information.

Material about Alice Barrows and her long effort to promote the platoon school plan has been gathered from a number of sources. The Wirt Manuscripts, mentioned above, yielded a large number of letters from Barrows to Wirt. This material is especially strong for the period 1915 to 1918, when Barrows was involved in propagandizing for the Gary plan in New York City, but it is also very important for her years in the U.S. Office of Education and provides details about her work in making school building surveys and about the affairs of the National Association for the Study of the Platoon or Work-Study-Play School Organization and its magazine, *The Platoon School,* which Barrows edited. The Alice P. Barrows Papers at the University of Maine Library, Orono, contain Barrows letters, clippings, photographs, and, most important, her unfinished manuscript autobiography. The draft typescript covers her life to 1918 and is essential for an understanding of her ideas about education and her role in promoting the Gary plan in New York City. The records of the U.S. Office of Education (record group 12) at the National Archives also contain important information on Alice Barrows. Her field service reports, 1923–1929, which detail her activities and travels in making school building surveys, are located in the commissioner's office files, box 25, record group 12. Also, record group 12 contains an extensive reference file on the platoon plan, collected by Barrows and including correspondence, reports, and other material on the platoon plan in cities throughout the United States.

In addition, Barrows's numerous published writings—magazine and newspaper articles, official reports, and school building surveys—are essential in understanding her views on the platoon plan and on schooling in general. Among the most important of these are the following: "Report of the Vocational Guidance Survey," *Bulletin of the Public Education Association of New York* no. 9 (1912); "The Dangers and Possibilities of Vocational Guidance," *Child Labor Bulletin* 1 (June, 1912): 46–54; "Spirit of the Gary Schools," *American Teacher* 4 (June, 1915): 85–87; *A Reply to Associate Superintendent Shallow's Report on the Gary Schools* (New York, 1915); "What Is the Gary Plan?" *New York Tribune* (October 25, 1915–March 23, 1916); "The Wirt Plan of Education," *Vassar Quarterly* 1 (1916): 80–86; "The Meaning of the Wirt Plan," *New Republic* 7 (July 1, 1916): 221–23; "The Problem of Adult Education in Passaic, New Jersey," U.S. Bureau of Education bulletin no. 4 (1920); "The Work-Study-Play, or Balanced-Load Plan," *New Republic* 40 (November 12, 1924): 16–17; "Platoon School," *Encyclopedia Britannica* (Chicago, 1929), 18: 64–65; "Modern Cities and Children," *The Platoon School* 3 (June-August, 1929): 79–81; "Some Results of Dewey's Philosophy," *The Platoon School* 3 (December, 1929–February, 1930): 150–51; "Public Works for Public Schools," *School Life* 19 (January, 1934):

96–98; "Planning School Buildings," *School Life* 22 (May, 1937): 268–70; "P.W.A. and the Public Schools," *The Nation's Schools* 22 (December, 1938): 14–17; "The School Auditorium as a Theater," *School Life* 25 (January, 1940): 107, 123; "New School Buildings for Old," *American Teacher* 24 (April, 1940): 22–24. See also her school building surveys, each published as a bulletin of the U.S. Bureau of Education: Memphis, Tennessee (no. 50, 1919); Lexington, Kentucky (no. 68, 1919); Meriden, Connecticut (no. 22, 1920); Gloucester, Massachusetts (no. 23, 1920); Brunswick and Glynn County, Georgia (no. 27, 1920); Wilmington, Delaware (no. 2, 1921); Athens, Georgia (no. 25, 1921); Elizabeth City, North Carolina (no. 26, 1921); Wheeling, West Virginia (no. 28, 1921); Washington, North Carolina (no. 2, 1923); Alexandria, Virginia (no. 56, 1923); Warwick, Rhode Island (no. 33, 1930).

The Maxine Wood Papers, still retained by Miss Wood, contain useful information about Alice Barrows after the mid-1930s. This collection, including correspondence, reports, clippings, and other miscellaneous material, was helpful in reconstructing Barrows's radical activities from the 1930s on. A few Barrows letters were also found in the Mary Van Kleeck Papers, located in the Women's History Archive at Smith College, and in the Henry A. Wallace Papers at the University of Iowa. Interviews with Maxine Wood helped recapture some of the spirit and personality of Alice Barrows, and correspondence with Elsa Ueland, another Barrows friend and a former teacher in Gary, added further personal information.

A variety of primary materials provided the basis for the story of the Gary school campaign in New York City. Essential were the Barrows letters in the Wirt Manuscripts, mentioned above, which revealed the promotional activities from inside the movement. The John Purroy Mitchel Papers in the Library of Congress contained much material—correspondence, reports, pamphlets, campaign speeches, newspaper clippings—on the Gary school effort and on the Mitchel administration in general. The John Purroy Mitchel Mayoralty Papers in the New York City Municipal Archives and Records Center similarly supplied important information on Mitchel's school policies. The New York City Municipal Reference Library contains official city documents, including city council material, minutes of the board of education, and other relevant publications. The New-York Historical Society has a useful file of correspondence and related manuscripts from the Committee on Public School Inquiry (Hanus Survey, 1911–12). The Randolph Bourne Papers at Columbia University yielded information on Bourne's involvement in school reform with Barrows and others. The Morris Hillquit Papers at the State Historical Society of Wisconsin were essential in understanding the Socialist involvement in the 1917 mayoralty election and in the school strikes. The New York Public Library and the New-York Historical Society contain excellent newspaper collections

for New York City, which were utilized extensively in reconstructing the Gary school campaign and the school riots of 1917. In addition, the Indiana Room of the Gary Public Library has an extensive newspaper clipping file covering Wirt's years in New York City, 1914–17. We have also examined some Yiddish materials, including the *Jewish Daily Forward* and the monthly *Tsukunft (Future)*, which provided insight into attitudes toward schooling in the city's Jewish communities.

Further information about the functioning of the Gary schools can be found in the Guy Wulfing Papers in the Calumet Regional Archives. Wulfing was director of vocational education in Gary for many years and his papers contain much useful information about the operation of the school system. Material located at the School Service Center in Gary provided relevant information, as well, especially the records and minutes of the Gary school board and annual official reports on the Gary schools to Lake County and Indiana state superintendents of instruction. In addition, the Gary Teachers' Union, AFT Local No. 4, has preserved some of its early records, and additional Gary Teachers' Union material can be found in the American Federation of Teachers Collection, Archives of Labor History and Urban Affairs, Wayne State University, Detroit, Michigan. For the Willis Brown story, we have relied upon Wirt's correspondence in the Wirt Manuscripts, as well as upon the Ben B. Lindsey Papers in the Library of Congress and the William R. George correspondence in the George Junior Republic Papers in the Collection of Regional History and University Archives, Cornell University. The papers of the National Association for the Advancement of Colored People, located in the Library of Congress, contain a substantial amount of material on segregated schooling in Gary. Some material on the schooling of immigrants can be found in the papers of the International Institute of Gary. An essential source throughout was the daily press in Gary, which devoted considerable space to school matters and to the activities of William Wirt. We have examined complete runs of the *Gary Northern Indianian*, 1906–09, the *Gary Daily Tribune*, 1908–21, the *Gary Evening Post and Daily Tribune*, 1921–22, and the *Gary Post-Tribune*, 1922–40, as well as Gary's two black newspapers, the *Gary Sun* and the *Gary American.*

Among published accounts about the Gary schools and about the platoon school movement, the following have been most useful: William Paxton Burris, "The Public School System of Gary, Ind.," United States Bureau of Education bulletin, no. 18 (Washington, D.C., 1914); John Dewey and Evelyn Dewey, *Schools of Tomorrow* (New York, 1915); Randolph S. Bourne, *The Gary Schools* (Boston, 1916); Abraham Flexner and Frank P. Bachman, *The Gary Schools: A General Account* (New York, 1918); Charles L. Spain, *The Platoon School* (New York, 1924); Roscoe D. Case, *The Platoon School in America* (Stanford, Calif., 1931);

and F. B. Knight et al., *Final Report, Purdue Survey Committee for the Gary Board of Education to the President and Board of Trustees of Purdue University* (mimeo, 1941). Also important were the magazines *The Platoon School*, edited by Alice Barrows, and *School Life*, the official monthly journal of the U.S. Bureau of Education to which Barrows often contributed. For additional bibliography, the following guides to the literature were most helpful: James Adelbert McMillen, *The Gary System: A Bibliography* (University of Rochester Library, January 31, 1917); Velma Ruth Shaffer, *The Gary System: A Bibliography, 1916-1935* (mimeo, Columbia University School of Library Service, 1935); Alice P. Barrows, "Bibliography of the Work-Study-Play, or Platoon, Plan," U.S. Bureau of Education, *School Leaflet*, no. 10 (July, 1923); Lee Sinai, *Gary in Print: A Subject Index to Periodical Literature on Gary, 1906-1973* (Gary Public Library, 1973). Complete documentation for both primary and secondary sources may be found in the footnotes.

NOTES

ABBREVIATIONS IN NOTES

Barrows Papers	Alice P. Barrows Papers, University of Maine Library, Orono
Bourne Papers	Randolph S. Bourne Papers, Columbia University Library
George Junior Republic Papers	George Junior Republic Papers, Collection of Regional History and University Archives, Cornell University Archives, Ithaca, N.Y.
GPL	Indiana Room, Gary Public Library, Gary
LC	Library of Congress
Lindsey Papers	Ben B. Lindsey Papers, Library of Congress
Mitchel Papers	John Purroy Mitchel Papers
NAACP Papers	National Association for the Advancement of Colored People Papers, Library of Congress
NYMA	New York Municipal Archives and Records Center
Wirt MSS	William A. Wirt Manuscripts, Lilly Library, Indiana University, Bloomington
Wirt Papers	William A. Wirt Papers, Calumet Regional Archives, Indiana University Northwest, Gary
Wood Papers	Private Collection, Maxine Wood, New York City
Wulfing Papers	Guy Wulfing Papers, Calumet Regional Archives, Indiana University Northwest, Gary

INTRODUCTION

1. David B. Tyack, *The One Best System: A History of American Urban Education* (Cambridge, Mass., 1974).

2. William A. Wirt, "Gary Schools," educational report, Lake County Schools (n.p., n.d. [1913]), p. 20.

3.   John Dewey and Evelyn Dewey, *Schools of Tomorrow* (New York, 1915; reprinted 1962), p. 181. Other laudatory accounts include Randolph S. Bourne, *The Gary Schools* (Boston, 1916; reprinted, Cambridge, Mass., 1970), and William Paxton Burris, "The Public School System of Gary, Ind.," U.S. Bureau of Education bulletin no. 18 (Washington, D. C., 1914).

4.   David Gibson, "The Wirt School System," *Common Sense* (June 1912), pamphlet, n.d., GPL; Herbert F. Roberts, "Bolstering Up the Bulwarks," *Kansas Magazine*, n.d., pamphlet reprint in New York Public Library.

5.   Floyd Dell, "Were You Ever a Child? A Discussion of Education," *Liberator* 1 (November 1918): 21-22.

6.   Lawrence A. Cremin, *The Transformation of the School: Progressivism in American Education, 1876-1957* (New York, 1961), pp. 154-60.

7.   Raymond E. Callahan, *Education and the Cult of Efficiency: A Study of the Social Forces That Have Shaped the Administration of the Public Schools* (Chicago, 1962), pp. 126-47.

8.   Christopher Lasch, *The World of Nations: Reflections on American History, Politics, and Culture* (New York, 1972), p. 257. See also Joseph Featherstone, "Reconsideration: John Dewey," *New Republic* 167 (July 8, 1972): 29-30.

1. WIRT, BARROWS, AND PROGRESSIVE SCHOOLING

1.   David Gibson, "The Wirt School System," *Common Sense* (June, 1912), pamphlet, n.d., GPL.

2.   "William A. Wirt," *The Nation's Schools* 21 (May 1938): 16.

3.   William A. Wirt, "Industrial Work in Public Schools," *The Platoon School* 6 (December, 1932): 3, 4 (reprinted from the Twenty-third Biennial Report of the State Superintendent of Public Instruction [Indiana] for the school years ending July 31, 1905, and July 31, 1906 [Indianapolis, 1906]).

4.   Wirt, "Making the City a Fit Place for the Rearing of Children," *The Platoon School* 3 (December, 1929): 152-55; id., "Industrial Work," p. 9.

5.   Wirt, "Making the City a Fit Place for the Rearing of Children," part 2, *The Platoon School* 4 (March 1930): 12; id., *The Great Lockout in America's Citizenship Plants* (Gary, 1937).

6.   Wirt, "Industrial Work," pp. 12, 13; id., "Utilization of School Plant," *Proceedings of the National Conference of Charities and Correction*, (1912), p. 59. Cf. Marvin Lazerson, *Origins of the Urban School: Public Education in Massachusetts, 1870-1915* (Cambridge, Mass., 1971), chaps. 3-7.

7.   Wirt, "Industrial Work," p. 9; David B. Tyack, "Pilgrim's Progress: Toward a Social History of the School Superintendency, 1860-1960, *History of Education Quarterly*, 16 (Fall 1976): 257-300. See also William A. Bullough, *Cities and Schools in the Gilded Age: The Evolution of an Urban Institution* (Port Washington, N.Y., 1974), chap. 6.

8.   William A. Wirt to C. Oliver Holmes, November 7, 1906; Wirt to Board of Education, December 15, 1906; Wirt to Holmes, January 28, 1907; all in Wirt MSS. On Gary's early development, see Raymond A. Mohl and Neil Betten, "The Failure of Industrial City Planning: Gary, Indiana, 1906-1910," *Journal of the American Institute of Planners* 38 (July, 1972): 203-15.

9.   (Gary) *Northern Indianian*, September 13, 1907.

10.   U.S. Bureau of the Census, *Thirteenth Census of the United States* (1910) 2 *Population* (Washington, D.C., 1913): 568; *Fourteenth Census of the United States* (1920) 3 *Population* (Washington, D.C., 1922): 297; *Fifteenth Census of the United States* (1930) 3 *Population* part 1 (Washington, D.C., 1932): 715. School population figures have been compiled from newspaper sources and from the annual Report of the School Trustees to the County Superintendent, and Report of the School Trustees

to the State Superintendent, manuscripts located in School Service Center, Gary, Indiana.

11.   Randolph S. Bourne, "The Natural School," *New Republic* 2 (May 1, 1915): 326; David B. Tyack, *The One Best System: A History of American Urban Education* (Cambridge, Mass., 1974), pp. 126–76.

12.   Wirt, *The School Town of Gary*, First Annual Report of the Board of Trustees of the Town of Gary, Ind . . . for the year ending Dec. 31st, 1908 (Gary, 1909), p. 52.

13.   Wirt, *A Report on a Plan of Organization for Co-Operative and Continuation Courses*, City of New York, Dept. of Education, pamphlet (July 30, 1914), p. 2; id., "What Your Child Is Best Fitted To Do," *Bulletin of the National Association of Corporation Schools* 2 (March, 1915): 9.

14.   John Dewey and Evelyn Dewey, *Schools of Tomorrow*, (New York, 1915; reprinted 1962), p. 176; Wirt, "The Complete Use of the School Plant," Public Education Association of Philadelphia study no. 37 (Philadelphia, 1912), pp. 9–10.

15.   Wirt, untitled speech manuscript, 1926, pp. 22–23, Wirt Papers.

16.   Ibid., p. 19.

17.   Wirt, *The Great Lockout*, p. 10; id., "Making the City a Fit Place for the Rearing of Children," part 2, *The Platoon School* 4 (March, 1930): 11.

18.   Wirt to Gompers, September 28, 1916; Wirt to Chadwick, May 12, 1915, Wirt MSS.

19.   Wirt to Max Loeb, November 20, 1915, Wirt MSS. In both New York City and Chicago organized labor was against the Wirt system because they saw it as a tool of the corporations, designed to save money and use the schools to produce industrial workers. See Mary J. Herrick, *The Chicago Schools: A Social and Political History* (Beverly Hills, Calif., 1971), p. 149, and chap. 2 below.

20.   Gary to William Randolph Hearst, November 15, 1917, copy in Wirt MSS.

21.   Information on Wirt's business ventures has been obtained from the daily newspapers and assorted materials in the Wirt MSS and Wirt Papers.

22.   Wirt, "One Teacher or Many," *The Platoon School* 5 (March, 1931): 15; and see his *The Great Lockout*, for his last words on the subject.

23.   Wirt, "The School As an Agency for Propaganda" (mimeo, 1935), pp. 4–5, 35, copy in Wirt Papers.

24.   "Biography," attached to letter from Wirt to Dorothy N. Povey, May 6, 1934, Wirt MSS.

25.   Arthur B. Moehlman, "Alice Prentice Barrows," *The Nation's Schools* 30 (September 1942): 13.

26.   Alice P. Barrows, autobiography, typescript, Barrows Papers. See also Mary Van Kleeck and Alice P. Barrows, "How Girls Learn the Millinery Trade," *Survey* 24 (April 16, 1910): 105–13; Barrows, "City Civilization and Children, or the Significance of the Work-Study-Play or Platoon School Plan," speech typescript, n.d., Barrows Papers.

27.   Barrows, autobiography, pp. 79, 81, 131; People's Educational Council, minutes, May 8, 1918, typescript, Wirt MSS.

28.   Barrows, "Report of the Vocational Guidance Survey," *Bulletin of the Public Education Association of New York*, no. 9 (New York, 1912), p. 13; id., autobiography, pp. 111–14, 123–25. See also id., "The Dangers and Possibilities of Vocational Guidance," *Child Labor Bulletin* 1 (June, 1912): 46–54. On Dewey's acceptance of technology, see Walter Feinberg and Henry Rosemont, Jr., "Training for the Welfare State: The Progressive Education Movement," in Feinberg and Rosemont, eds., *Work, Technology, and Education: Dissenting Essays in the Intellectual Foundations of American Education* (Urbana, Ill., 1975), pp. 60–91.

29.   *New York Globe*, October 29, 1912, clipping file, Indiana Room, GPL; Elsa Ueland to Raymond A. Mohl, September 19, 1973, letter in authors' possession; Barrows, autobiography, pp. 131–55.

30.   Raymond A. Mohl, "Schools, Politics, and Riots: The Gary Plan in New York City, 1914-1917," *Paedagogica Historica* 15 (June, 1975): 39-72; Edwin R. Lewinson, *John Purroy Mitchel: The Boy Mayor of New York* (New York, 1965), pp. 150-63; Sol Cohen, *Progressives and Urban School Reform: The Public Education Association of New York City, 1895-1914* (New York, 1964), pp. 86-100; Diane Ravitch, *The Great School Wars: New York City, 1805-1973* (New York, 1974), pp. 189-230; Raymond A. Mohl, "Urban Education in the Twentieth Century: Alice Barrows and the Platoon School Plan," *Urban Education* 9 (October, 1974): 213-37; Randolph S. Bourne to Elizabeth Shepley Sergeant, September 23, 1915, Randolph S. Bourne Papers, Columbia University Library.

31.   Barrows to Wirt, February 8, 1915, Wirt MSS; People's Educational Council, minutes, May 8, 1918, typescript, ibid.; Barrows, "The Meaning of the Wirt Plan," *New Republic* 7 (July 1, 1916): 221-23; id., "The Wirt Plan of Education," *Vassar Quarterly* 1 (1916): 80. In 1914 Barrows married a poet named W. G. Tinckon Fernandez, but they were divorced in 1922 and Barrows resumed her maiden name. Her writings during this period were published under the name of Alice Barrows Fernandez.

32.   Barrows, "Statement in Reply to Judge Hylan's Attack on the Gary Schools," 1917, typescript, Wirt MSS; Barrows to George Foster Peabody, April 20, 1918, ibid.; id., "Wirt Plan," p. 81.

33.   People's Educational Council, minutes, 1918, Wirt MSS; *New York Call,* October 17, 1917; Barrows to Wirt, February 15, September 28, 1918, Wirt MSS; Barrows, "Importance of Continuing Propaganda for the Gary Plan at the Present Time," 1917, typescript, ibid.; F. L. Grubbs, "The International Outlook of the Peoples Council of America," *Science and Society* 37 (fall 1973): 336-42.

34.   Barrows's activities during these years can be followed in her extensive correspondence with William Wirt in the Wirt MSS; in her field service reports, 1923-29, Commissioner's Office, box 25, record group 12, U.S. Office of Education, National Archives; in her survey reports, each usually published as a U.S. Bureau of Education bulletin; and in her published articles: "The Work-Study-Play, or Balanced-Load Plan," *New Republic* 40 (November 12, 1924): 16-17; "Public Works for Public Schools," *School Life* 19 (January 1934): 96-98; "Planning School Buildings," ibid. 22 (May 1937): 268-70; "The School Auditorium as a Theater," ibid. 25 (January, 1940): 107, 123.

35.   Barrows, "First National Conference on the Work-Study-Play or Platoon Plan," U.S. Bureau of Education bulletin no. 35 (Washington, D.C., 1922); Barrows to Charles L. Spain, March 10, May 6, 19, September 18, 1925, Wirt MSS; Barrows to Wirt, March 25, May 14, 1925, ibid.

36.   Roscoe D. Case, *The Platoon School in America* (Stanford, Calif., 1931), 25-27; W. S. Deffenbaugh, "Significant Movements in City School Systems," U.S. Bureau of Education bulletin no. 16 (Washington, D.C., 1929), pp. 20-21; Charles L. Spain, *The Platoon School* (New York, 1924); Merle C. Prunty, "Platoon Schools Meet the New Deal," *The Platoon School* 8 (September 1934): 5.

37.   *New York World,* February 22, 1920, clipping file, Barrows Papers; *Passaic Daily News,* February 23, 24, March 5, 1920, ibid.; Robert W. Dunn, diary excerpts, February 25, 1920, ibid. See also Barrows's report on the Passaic Survey, "The Problem of Adult Education in Passaic, New Jersey," U.S. Bureau of Education bulletin no. 4 (Washington, D.C., 1920).

38.   Barrows, "Problem of Adult Education," pp. 16, 21, 25; [Barrows et al.], "Financial and Building Needs of Lexington, Kentucky," U.S. Bureau of Education bulletin no. 68 (Washington, D.C., 1919), p. 40; [Barrows], "A School Building Program for Gloucester, Mass.," U.S. Bureau of Education bulletin no. 23 (Washington, D.C., 1920), p. 5; Barrows, "A Brief Statement in Regard to the Platoon Schools of Cleveland, Ohio," n.d., reference file on platoon plan, box 2, record group 12,

U.S. Office of Education, National Archives; id., "Some Results of Dewey's Philosophy," *The Platoon School* 3 (December 1929–February 1930): 151.

39.   Barrows to Wirt, July 1, 1922, June 5, 1926, March 28, April 14, September 9. November 14, 1927, April 21, 1928, February 19, 1929, October 26, 1932, June 1, 1933, Wirt MSS; *Portland Oregonian*, November 4, 22, 1923.

40.   Edmund Wilson, "Miss Barrows and Doctor Wirt: An Inside Story of a Famous Episode," *Scribner's Magazine* 96 (August, 1934): 102–4; Wirt to Barrows, April 4, 1934, Maxine Wood Papers, Private Collection, New York City (copy in authors' possession); Barrows, news release, April 17, 1934, ibid.; *Investigation of Statements made by Dr. William A. Wirt,* Hearings before the Select Committee to Investigate Charges made by Dr. William A. Wirt, U.S. House of Representatives, 73rd Congress, 2nd Session (Washington, D.C., 1934); *Investigation of Certain Statements made by One Dr. William A. Wirt,* report no. 1439, U.S. House of Representatives, 73rd Congress, 2nd Session (Washington, D.C., 1934). See also John J. Healy, Jr., "William A. Wirt and the Bulwinkle Investigation of 1934" (M.A. thesis, history department, Indiana University, 1960), which is critical of the Democratic "whitewash."

41.   Maxine Wood, personal interview, East Blue Hill, Maine, August 29, 1974; Ueland to Mohl, October 20, 1973, letter in authors' possession; Wilson, p. 104.

42.   Maxine Wood, telephone interview, October 29, 1973; personal interview, August 29, 1974; Barrows, "Who Is Un-American?" 1938, speech typescript, Wood Papers.

43.   Barrows, vita sheet, 1948, Wood Papers; Maxine Wood, personal interview, August 29, 1974.

44.   Richard O. Boyer, "Eulogy at Memorial Service for Alice P. Barrows," 1954, typescript, Wood Papers; Maxine Wood, personal interview, August 29, 1974; *Interlocking Subversion in Government Departments,* Hearings before the Subcommittee to Investigate the Administration of the Internal Security Act and Other Internal Security Laws, U.S. Senate, Judiciary Committee, 83rd Congress, 1st Session, Part 12 (Washington, D.C., 1953), pp. 823–40; *New York Times,* October 3, 1954. The Maxine Wood Papers contain copies of many Barrows letters to newspapers, congressmen, presidents, and other officials protesting violations of civil liberties, the making of the hydrogen bomb, and the "Nazi-like" legislation of the McCarthy era.

2. SCHOOLS, POLITICS, AND RIOTS

1.   Burton J. Hendrick, "The Mayor of New York," *The World's Work* 32 (September 1916): 522; John Purroy Mitchel, "What We Have Done for New York," *Independent* 82 (May 10, 1915): 237–39; "Mayor Mitchel and His Work," *North American Review* 206 (August 1917): 261–70; H. S. Gilbertson, "Municipal Revolution under Mayor Mitchel," *American Review of Reviews* 56 (September, 1917): 300–303; William Hard, "The New York Mayoralty Campaign: Mayor Mitchel's Record," *New Republic* 12 (October 13, 1917): 291–94; Edwin R. Lewinson, *John Purroy Mitchel: The Boy Mayor of New York* (New York, 1965).

2.   Sol Cohen, *Progressives and Urban School Reform: The Public Education Association of New York City, 1895–1914* (New York, 1964), pp. 86–87; John Purroy Mitchel, speech at Cooper Union, October 2, 1917, transcript, box 32, Mitchel Papers, LC; anon. "The Truth about the Gary Schools," *Fusion Flashlight* 1 (October 4, 1917): 1, box 52, ibid.

3.   William G. Willcox, "Memorandum Re Industrial Education," June 30, 1914, box 7, Mitchel Papers, LC; anon. "Why New York City Adopted the Gary School," undated memorandum, box 47, ibid.; Tristram Walker Metcalfe, *What Ails the Schools* (New York, 1912), p. 31; Cohen, pp. 73–74. On the industrial education movement, see Sol Cohen, "The Industrial Education Movement," *American*

Quarterly 20 (spring 1968): 95–110; Lawrence A. Cremin, *The Transformation of the School: Progressivism in American Education, 1876–1957* (New York, 1961), pp. 21–57; Berenice M. Fisher, *Industrial Education: American Ideals and Institutions* (Madison, Wis., 1967); Arthur G. Wirth, *Education in the Technological Society* (Scranton, Pa., 1972).

4.   Howard W. Nudd, "A Small Board of Education for New York," *Bulletin of the PEA,* no. 24 (December 22, 1914); John Purroy Mitchel to Thomas W. Churchill, January 23, 1915, box 164, Mitchel Papers, NYMA; Churchill to Mitchel, April 20, 1915, box 215, ibid.; Mitchel, speech at Aldine Club luncheon, February 10, 1915, transcript, box 29, Mitchel Papers, LC; William A. Prendergast, memoir, p. 747, Oral History Archives, Columbia University.

5.   On conflict between Board of Estimate and Board of Education, see Thomas W. Churchill, "Testimony before the Legislative Committee Investigating the City's Financial Condition," December 14, 1915, transcript, box 215, Mitchel Papers, NYMA; Edward Marshall, "New York's Public Schools Are Too Cut and Dried," *New York Times Magazine,* February 2, 1913; Lewinson, pp. 150–63.

6.   Paul H. Hanus, *School Efficiency: A Constructive Study Applied to New York City* (Yonkers, N.Y., 1913); id., *Adventuring in Education* (Cambridge, Mass., 1937), pp. 175–93. See also *New York Times,* January 25, 27, 30, 31, February 1, 3, 8, 10, 18, 21, March 11, 12, 18, 21, April 8, 22, May 23, 1913; "Inflexibility the Main Fault in Our School System," *New York Times Magazine,* May 8, 1913; Diane Ravitch, *The Great School Wars: New York City, 1805–1973* (New York, 1974), pp. 182–84.

7.   Hanus, *School Efficiency,* p. viii; id., "The Real Cause of the Controversy about My Report to the Committee on School Inquiry," typescript, November 1912, Public School Inquiry Papers, New-York Historical Society; Charles P. Howland to Paul H. Hanus, November 16, 1912, ibid.; Lewinson, pp. 151–52.

8.   Hanus, *School Efficiency,* pp. 6–23, 39–45; Alice P. Barrows, "Report of the Vocational Guidance Survey," *Bulletin of the PEA,* no. 9 (1912).

9.   Hanus, *School Efficiency; New York Globe,* October 29, 1912, clipping file, GPL; Winthrop D. Lane, "Education and Work: A Twilight Zone," *Survey* 29 (November 23, 1912): 228; Abraham Flexner to Wirt, January 25, 1914, Wirt MSS.

10.   Ira S. Wile to Mitchel, January 31, 1914, box 204, Mitchel Papers, NYMA; Paul Wilson to Henry Bruère, May 25, 1914, box 191, ibid.

11.   Harriet M. Johnson to Wirt, April 15, 1914, Wirt MSS; Harriet M. Johnson, "The Schools of Gary," *Bulletin of the PEA,* no. 23 (June 5, 1914); William McAndrew to D. L. Bardwell, March 16, 1914, Wirt MSS; McAndrew to Wirt, April 7, 1914, ibid.

12.   Churchill to Wirt, May 21, June 16, 1914, Wirt MSS; Wirt to Churchill, July 30, 1914, box 7, Mitchel Papers, LC; Mitchel, *Address at the Eighty-second Commencement of the New York University* (New York, 1914), pp. 5–7; Thomas W. Churchill, "The Amazing Schools I Saw at Gary," *Delineator* 85 (September, 1914): 15; *New York Times,* October 29, November 1, 1914; *Gary Tribune,* September 1, 2, 3, 1914.

13.   Mitchel, *The Mayor to the Citizens of New York* (n.p., 1916), p. 31.

14.   Public Education Association, *The Official Wirt Reports to the Board of Education of New York City* (New York, 1916); William A. Wirt, "Report on a Proposed Reorganization for Public Schools Nos. 28, 2, 42, 6, 50, 44, 5, 53, 40, 32, 4, and 45, the Bronx, New York City," undated typescript, box 191, Mitchel Papers, NYMA; Wirt to Mitchel, September 24, 1915, box 9, Mitchel Papers, LC; Wirt to Churchill, December 23, 1914, February 27, 1915, Wirt MSS.

15.   Mitchel to Churchill, September 27, 1915, box 164, Mitchel Papers, NYMA. See also *New York Times,* September 28, 1915; *New York Globe,* September 28, 1915, clipping file, GPL.

16.   William A. Prendergast, "Why New York City Needs a New School Plan,"

American Review of Reviews 52 (November 1915): 584–88. See also William A. Prendergast to Board of Estimate and Apportionment, September 11, 1915, Wirt MSS;*New York Times,* September 17, 1915;*New York Mail,* September 16, 1915, clipping file, GPL.

17.   Bessie C. Stern to Wirt, November 1, 1915, Wirt MSS; *New York Globe,* October 15, 28, November 18, 26, December 3, 18, 1915, clipping file, GPL; Tristram Walker Metcalfe to Mitchel, November 5, 1915, box 191, Mitchel Papers, NYMA.

18.   Churchill to Mitchel, October 4, 1915, box 9, Mitchel Papers, LC; New York City, *Journal of the Board of Education of the City of New York,* October 13, 1915, 1551–53; *New York Times,* October 5, 1915; *New York Globe,* October 8, December 20, 1915; clipping file, GPL. See also *New York Globe,* October 15, 1917.

19.   Thomas W. Churchill, "Testimony," *New York Times,* February 8, 1916; "Politics against the Schools," *New Republic* 6 (February 12, 1916): 32–33.

20.   Alice P. Barrows, autobiography, pp. 156–66, Barrows Papers; Wirt to Elbert H. Gary, January 9, 1916, October 10, 1917, Wirt MSS.

21.   Barrows, autobiography, p. 160; Barrows to Wirt, January 8, 15, February 8, 12, 1915, Wirt MSS. For Bourne's writings promoting the Gary plan, see Randolph S. Bourne: "Schools in Gary," *New Republic* 2 (March 27, 1915): 198–99; "Communities for Children," ibid. 2 (April 3, 1915): 233–34; "Really Public Schools," ibid. 2 (April 10, 1915): 259–61; "Apprentices to the School," ibid. 2 (April 24, 1915): 302–3; "The Natural School," ibid. 2 (May 1, 1915): 326–28. See also Bourne's book *The Gary Schools* (Boston, 1916; reprinted, Cambridge, Mass., 1970); his articles "The Gary Public Schools," *Scribner's Magazine* 60 (September 1916): 371–80, and "Some Social Implications of the Gary School," *American Teacher* 4 (June 1915), 82–85; and his letters to newspapers: *New York Times,* June 15, December 11, 1915;*New York Globe,* October 25, 1915, April 14, 1916, clipping file, GPL.

22.   Barrows's varied activities can best be followed in her voluminous correspondence with Wirt located in the Wirt MSS, and in her unpublished autobiography. On Rhetta Childe Dorr's support, see *New York Mail,* September 16, December 15, 1915, January 17, April 3, 1916, January 25, 1917, clipping file, GPL. See also Agnes de Lima, *Modern Schools for New York City* (New York, 1916), and Howard W. Nudd, "What the Gary Plan Means for the New York City Schools," *Bulletin of the PEA,* no. 26 (December 16, 1915).

23.   Barrows to Wilson, October 17, 1916, Wirt MSS; Barrows, autobiography, pp. 165–68.

24.   Barrows to Wirt, July 22, 1915, May 24, 1916, Wirt MSS; Randolph S. Bourne to Elizabeth Shepley Sergeant, September 23, 1915, Bourne Papers. See also Barrows, *A Reply to Associate Superintendent Shallow's Report on the Gary Schools* (New York, 1915); id., "Spirit of the Gary Schools," *American Teacher* 4 (June 1915): 85–87; id., "For the Gary Plan," *School* 27 (September 26, 1915): 36; id., "The Wirt Plan of Education," *Vassar Quarterly* 1 (1916): 80–86; id., "The Meaning of the Wirt Plan," *New Republic* 7 (July 1, 1916): 221–23.

25.   William G. Willcox, "The Principle of the Gary Plan and Its Application to New York," *American City* 14 (January 1916): 6–10. See also "William G. Willcox Urges Gary Plan for Our Schools," *New York Times Magazine,* January 2, 1916, 17.

26.   McAndrew to Wirt, August 27, 1915, December 30, 1916, February 21, March 21, 1917, Wirt MSS;*New York Globe,* April 16, 1915, clipping file, GPL.

27.   Joseph L. Taylor to John H. Walsh, April 19, 1915, Wirt MSS; Taylor to Wirt, September 9, 1915, February 14, 1916, ibid.; Joseph L. Taylor, "Report on Gary (Ind.) Schools," *Educational Review* 49 (May 1915): 510–26; id., "A Report on the Gary Experiment in New York City," ibid. 51 (January 1916): 8–28; id., "The Duplicate School As an Educational Asset," *Addresses and Proceedings of the National Education Association* 55 (1917): 810–13.

28.   Alice E. B. Ritter, "Observations in the Gary Schools," March 12, 1915, typescript, Wirt MSS; Ritter to Wirt, December 15, 1915, ibid.; Angelo Patri to Wirt, June 29, 1915, ibid. See also Angelo Patri, *A Schoolmaster of the Great City* (New York, 1917).

29.   Stern to Barrows, January 15, 1916, Wirt MSS.

30.   John Martin, "The Gary Plan in New York City," *School and Society* 2 (December 25, 1915): 925–26; id., "Vocational and Occupational Education in New York City," *Nation* 102 (June 29, 1916): 696–97; *New York Times,* June 23, November 30, 1915, January 18, April 24, 1916; *New York Mail,* September 16, 1915, clipping file, GPL; Martin, "The Gary Principle Applied in New York City Schools," *Standard* 2 (November, 1915): 36.

31.   William H. Maxwell to Willcox, June 25, July 2, 12, 1917, box 234, Mitchel Papers, NYMA; New York City, Department of Education, Nineteenth Annual Report of the Superintendent of Schools for the year ending July 31, 1917 (1918), pp. 48–52; *Journal of the Board of Education,* June 27, 1917, p. 1016; *New York Globe,* March 25, 1915, April 20, 1916, clipping file, GPL.

32.   William L. Ettinger to Churchill, September 29, 1915, box 9, Mitchel Papers, LC; *New York Times,* September 24, 1915; Barrows to Wilson, December 21, 1914, box 191, Mitchel Papers, NYMA.

33.   *New York Globe,* September 25, 1915, clipping file, GPL; New York City, Department of Education, Minutes of the Board of Superintendents, June 24, 1915, October 4, 25, November 8, 1917; *Brooklyn Eagle,* March 21, 1915.

34.   *New York Times,* July 19, December 6, 1915; *Journal of the Board of Education,* November 24, 1915, p. 1790; William E. Grady, "Experimenting with Children under the Gary Plan in New York City," *Psychological Clinic* 10 (March 15, 1916): 19–26; "The Gary System in New York," *Manual Training Magazine* 17 (May, 1916): 713–15; *New York Globe,* January 20, 1916, clipping file, GPL; *Brooklyn Eagle,* January 8, 1916, ibid.

35.   New York City, Department of Education, "Survey of the Gary and Pre-vocational Schools," Seventeenth Annual Report of the City Superintendent of Schools, 1914–1915 (1916); Burdette R. Buckingham, "Survey of the Gary and Prevocational Schools of New York City," *School and Society* 3 (February 12, 1916): 245–47; *New York Times,* January 28, 1916.

36.   James F. Boydstun to Mitchel, November 10, 1915, box 191, Mitchel Papers, NYMA.

37.   *New York Globe,* October 8, 1915, clipping file, GPL.

38.   Ritter to Wirt, December 15, 1915, Wirt MSS; Barrows to Wirt, January 14, 1916, ibid.; Stern to Barrows, January 15, 1916, ibid.

39.   *Journal of the Board of Education,* January 12, 1916, p. 53; Minutes of the Board of Superintendents, November 4, 11, 1915, September 13, 20, 1917.

40.   For a sample of the religious controversy, see *New York Times,* October 4, 17, 18, 23, November 5, 10, 16, 21, 30, 1915.

41.   See, for example, Peter J. Brady to Mitchel, February 4, 9, 1916, box 10, Mitchel Papers, LC.

42.   *New York Globe,* January 15, 1916, clipping file, GPL; Joseph V. McKee, "The Gary System," *Bronx Home News,* September 27, 1915, clipping, box 47, Mitchel Papers, LC.

43.   *New York Globe,* October 8, 18, 1915, May 25, 1916, clipping file, GPL.

44.   On these various complaints, see *New York Globe,* October 23, November 9, December 2, 1915, January 15, 1916, clipping file, GPL; *Brooklyn Eagle,* January 8, 1916, ibid.; New York City, Board of Aldermen, Preliminary Report of the Committee on General Welfare (1917); Joseph V. McKee, "The Gary System," *Catholic World* 102 (January, 1916): 513.

45.   Maxwell to Willcox, July 12, 1917, box 234, Mitchel Papers, NYMA.

46.   Board of Aldermen, Committee on General Welfare, Investigation of Public Schools, 1917, transcript, NYMA, p. 605.

47. Barrows, autobiography, p. 168. A set of Barrows's articles from the *New York Tribune* can be found in clipping file, GPL.

48. Barrows to Wirt, November 17, 1915, Wirt MSS.

49. Gary School League, "Just What Is the Gary Plan?" Information Bulletin no. 1 (May, 1916); id., "Is New York to Have Real Gary or 'Mock-Gary' Schools?" bulletin no. 2 (May, 1916); id., "If You Were a Child in Yorkville," bulletin no. 5 (May, 1916); Barrows to Wirt, April 21, May 24, June 9, 1916, January 3, 1917, Wirt MSS; Alyse Gregory, *The Day is Gone* (New York, 1948), pp. 147–48.

50. Barrows to Wirt, January 3, April 18, May 28, 1917, Wirt MSS; Gary School League, reports, 1916–17, typescript, ibid.; Barrows, autobiography, pp. 174–80.

51. Barrows to Wirt, October 29, November 2, 1917, Wirt MSS; Gary School League, reports, ibid.; Barrows, autobiography, pp. 180–81.

52. Undated speech notes, 1917 mayoralty campaign, box 32, Mitchel Papers, LC; John Purroy Mitchel, "Address of Welcome," *Journal of Proceedings of the National Education Association*, fifty-fourth annual meeting (1916), p. 31.

53. Barrows, autobiography, p. 183.

54. "Why New York City Adopted the Gary School," undated memorandum, box 47, Mitchel Papers, LC; Mitchel, speech at Hettingen Hall, Long Island City, October 18, 1917, transcript, box 32, ibid. Transcripts of Mitchel's speeches can be found in box 32, Mitchel Papers, LC. See also "Gary Schools in New York," *Elementary School Journal* 18 (November, 1917): 168–71; William C. O'Donnell, Jr., "The Gary System in the Crucible of a Political Campaign," *Educational Foundations* 29 (January, 1918): 270–75.

55. *Brooklyn Eagle,* June 24, 1917, clipping, box 47, Mitchel Papers, LC; transcripts of Hylan speeches, October 5, 12, 20, November 3, 4, 1917, box 52, ibid. Hylan campaign flyer, reel 7, microfilm edition, Morris Hillquit Papers, State Historical Society of Wisconsin. See also "Gary School Plan as a City Campaign Issue," *New York Times Magazine,* October 21, 1917, pp. 5–6; "The New York City Election and the Gary Plan," *Elementary School Journal* 18 (October, 1917): 89–91.

56. Transcripts of Hillquit speeches, September 23, October 30, 1917, reel 5, Hillquit Papers; *New York Evening Post,* November 6, 1917, clipping, reel 8, ibid.; *New York World,* October 14, 1917; *New York Herald,* October 18, 1917.

57. *New York Call,* September 12, 13, October 19, 1917; *New York Tribune,* October 19, 28, 1917; "Hillquit Non-Partisan Committee of One Thousand for the Children of New York City and Their Schools," undated pamphlet, box 52, Mitchel Papers, LC.

58. Paul L. Blakely, "The Gary School in Politics," *America* (July 28, 1917), p. 408.

59. *New York Times,* October 17, 1917; *New York World,* October 17, 1917; *New York Herald,* October 17, 1917; *New York Tribune,* October 17, 1917.

60. *New York Times,* October 17, 1917; *New York World,* October 17, 1917; *New York Sun,* October 17, 1917; *New York Herald,* October 17, 1917; *New York Tribune,* October 17, 1917; *New York Globe,* October 17, 1917.

61. *New York Tribune,* October 17, 1917; *New York World,* October 17, 1917; *New York Sun,* October 17, 1917; *New York Herald,* October 18, 1917; *New York Call,* October 18, 1917.

62. *New York Times,* October 18, 1917; *New York World,* October 18, 1917; *New York Tribune,* October 18, 1917; *New York Herald,* October 18, 1917.

63. *New York Sun,* October 18, 1917; *New York Tribune,* October 18, 1917; *New York Times,* October 18, 1917.

64. *New York Sun,* October 19, 1917; *New York Times,* October 19, 1917; *New York Globe,* October 18, 1917; *New York World,* October 19, 1917; *New York Tribune,* October 19, 1917; *New York Herald,* October 19, 1917; *New York Call,* October 19, 1917; Mary Graham Bonner, "School Riots and the Gary System," *Outlook* 117 (October 31, 1917): 334–35.

65. *New York Times,* October 19, 1917; *New York Herald,* October 19, 1917; *New York Sun,* October 19, 1917; *New York Tribune,* October 19, 1917; *New York World,* October 19, 1917.
66. *New York Times,* October 20, 1917; *New York Globe,* October 19, 1917; *New York Sun,* October 20, 1917.
67. *New York Times,* October 20, 1917; *New York World,* October 20, 1917; *New York Herald,* October 20, 1917; *New York Sun,* October 20, 1917; *New York Tribune,* October 20, 1917; *Brooklyn Eagle,* October 19, 1917; "Disorder among the Children of the New York City Schools," *School and Society* 6 (October 27, 1917): 497-98.
68. *New York Sun,* October 20, 1917; *New York Times,* October 20, 1917; *New York Tribune,* October 20, 1917; *New York Herald,* October 20, 1917; *New York Call,* October 20, 1917.
69. *New York World,* October 22, 1917; *New York Sun,* October 22, 1917; *New York Tribune,* October 21, 1917.
70. *New York World,* October 21, 1917; *New York Tribune,* October 20, 21, 1917; *New York Herald,* October 20, 21, 1917; *New York Globe,* October 23, 1917; *New York Sun,* October 22, 1917; transcripts of Mitchel speeches, October 19, 20, 1917, box 32, Mitchel Papers, LC.
71. *New York Globe,* October 22, 1917; *New York Herald,* October 23, 1917; *New York Tribune,* October 23, 1917; *New York Sun,* October 23, 1917; *New York World,* October 23, 1917.
72. *New York World,* October 24, 1917; *New York Tribune,* October 24, 1917; *New York Evening Bronx,* October 23, 1917.
73. *New York Times,* October 24, 25, 26, 27, 1917; *New York World,* October 18, 21, 24, 27, 1917; *New York Globe,* October 17, 23, 31, November 2, 1917; *New York Herald,* October 19, 20, 1917. See also Hermann Hagedorn, *Mothers of New York, What of the Children?* (New York, 1917); Committee on Public Education, *Plain Facts about the Gary Schools* (New York, 1917), in box 47, Mitchel Papers, LC; Fusion Committee of 1917, *The Truth about the Gary Schools* (New York, 1917), ibid.; *The Truth about the Schools,* undated pamphlet, ibid.
74. *New York Times,* November 7, 8, 1917; Eda Amberg and William H. Allen, *Civic Lessons from Mayor Mitchel's Defeat* (New York, 1921), pp. 15-20; Melvyn Dubofsky, "Success and Failure of Socialism in New York City, 1900-1918: A Case Study," *Labor History* 9 (fall 1968): 370-71.
75. *New York Times,* December 11, 1917, December 12, 1918; *Journal of the Board of Education,* December 12, 1917, pp. 2022-23; "Mayor Hylan's Letter on the New York City Schools," *School and Society* 9 (March 22, 1919): 359-60. On the persistence of the Gary plan in some schools, see Stern to Wirt, February 17, September 24, 1920, Wirt Papers.
76. *New York Sun,* October 21, 22, 1917; *Brooklyn Daily Eagle,* October 19, 1917; *New York Globe,* October 22, 1917; *New York Herald,* October 20, 1917; *New York World,* October 22, 1917; *New York Call,* October 18, 1917; *New York Tribune,* October 20, 28, 1917; *Journal of the Board of Education,* October 24, 1917, pp. 1669-71; Bonner, p. 335.
77. Matthew J. Smith to Mitchel, October 6, 1917, box 16, Mitchel Papers, LC; *New York Tribune,* October 21, 28, 1917; *New York World,* October 21, 22, 23, 1917; *New York Sun,* October 22, 25, 1917; *New York Herald,* October 20, 1917.
78. *New York Call,* October 30, 1917; Mitchel speech at Hettingen Hall, October 18, 1917, box 32, Mitchel Papers, LC.
79. *New York Call,* October 3, 1917. On machine support for urban development, see Bruce M. Stave, "Urban Bosses and Reform," in Raymond A. Mohl and James F. Richardson, eds., *The Urban Experience* (Belmont, Calif., 1973), pp. 182-95.
80. Charles Leinenweber, "Socialists in the Streets: The New York City Socialist

Party in Working Class Neighborhoods, 1908-1918," *Science and Society* 41 (summer 1977): 152-71; *New York Call*, October 26, 1917; "Organized Labor on Education," *New Republic* 7 (May 6, 1916): 8-9; *Union Label Bulletin* 6 (May 1916): 1-2; Norbert Pfeffer to Charles Steckler, October 8, 1917, box 16, Mitchel Papers, LC. See also Zosa Szajkowski, "The Jews and New York City's Mayoralty Election of 1917," *Jewish Social Studies* 32 (October 1970): 286-306; and Irving Howe, *World of Our Fathers: The Journey of the East European Jews to America and the Life They Found and Made* (New York, 1976), pp. 278-80.

81.   *New York Tribune*, October 28, 1917; Spencer Phoenix to Samuel L. Martin, September 19, 1917, box 234, Mitchel Papers, NYMA; *New York Call*, October 20, 1917.

82.   *Jewish Daily Forward*, October 18, 1917; *New York Call*, September 13, 1917.

83.   On these points, see Sarah Crystal-Breslau, "The Gary System and the Present Campaign," *Tsukunft (Future)* 22 (November, 1917): 622-24; *Jewish Daily Forward*, October 17, 18, 19, 1917. For an interesting analysis, see Selma C. Berrol, "Education and Economic Mobility: The Jewish Experience in New York City, 1880-1920," *American Jewish Historical Quarterly* 65 (March, 1976): 257-71.

84.   H. Rogoff, "Mitchel, Hylan and the Campaign Issues," *Tsukunft* 22 (November 1917): 618.

85.   Blakely, p. 407; "The Gary System in Politics," *School and Society* 6 (October 27, 1917): 503.

86.   *Jewish Daily Forward*, October 19, 1917.

3. WILLIS BROWN

1.   Meredith Wilson, *The Music Man* (New York, 1958), p. 155.

2.   See especially Robert Wiebe, *The Search for Order, 1877-1920* (New York, 1967).

3.   Carl F. Kaestle, *The Evolution of an Urban School System: New York City, 1750-1850* (Cambridge, Mass., 1973); Stanley K. Schultz, *The Culture Factory: Boston Public Schools, 1789-1860* (New York, 1973); David J. Rothman, *The Discovery of the Asylum: Social Order and Disorder in the New Republic* (Boston, 1971); Robert S. Pickett, *House of Refuge: Origins of Juvenile Reform in New York State, 1815-1857* (Syracuse, N.Y., 1969); and Miriam Z. Langsam, *Children West: A History of the Placing-Out System of the New York Children's Aid Society, 1853-1890* (Madison, Wis., 1964).

4.   Anthony M. Platt, *The Child Savers: The Invention of Delinquency* (Chicago, 1969); Jack M. Holl, *Juvenile Reform in the Progressive Era: William R. George and the Junior Republic Movement* (Ithaca, N.Y., 1971); Robert M. Mennel, *Thorns and Thistles: Juvenile Delinquents in the United States, 1825-1940* (Hanover, N.H., 1973); Joseph M. Hawes, *Children in Urban Society: Juvenile Delinquency in Nineteenth-Century America* (New York, 1971); Steven L. Schlossman, *Love and the American Delinquent: The Theory and Practice of "Progressive" Juvenile Justice, 1825-1920* (Chicago, 1977); Sol Cohen, *Progressives and Urban School Reform: The Public Education Association of New York City, 1895-1914* (New York, 1964); James B. Lane, *Jacob A. Riis and the American City* (Port Washington, N.Y., 1974); Steven Schlossman and Stephanie Wallach, "The Crime of Precocious Sexuality: Female Juvenile Delinquency in the Progressive Era," *Harvard Educational Review* 48 (February, 1978): 65-94.

5.   Laurence A. Cremin, *The Transformation of the School: Progressivism in American Education, 1876-1957* (New York, 1961); Joel H. Spring, *Education and the Rise of the Corporate State* (Boston, 1972); Dorothy Ross, *G. Stanley Hall: The Psychologist As Prophet* (Chicago, 1972); and Stevel L. Schlossman, "G. Stanley

Hall and the Boys' Club: Conservative Applications of Recapitulation Theory," *Journal of the History of Behavioral Sciences* 9 (April, 1973): 140–47.

6.   George B. Mangold, *Child Problems* (New York, 1910), p. 1.

7.   Ibid., p. 5.

8.   Lane; Allen F. Davis, *American Heroine: The Life and Legend of Jane Addams* (New York, 1973); Charles Larsen, *The Good Fight: The Life and Times of Ben B. Lindsey* (Chicago, 1972); Holl; Joseph F. Kett, *Rites of Passage: Adolescence in America, 1790 to the Present* (New York, 1977), pp. 215–44.

9.   William A. Wirt, "Ways and Means for a Closer Union between the School and the Non-School Activities—Abstract," *National Education Association, Addresses and Proceedings,* sixty-first annual meeting, July 1–6, 1923 (Washington, 1923), 61: 446. By the mid-twenties, however, Wirt had abandoned other helping agencies, now believing *only* schools had the professional ability to control and influence properly the lives of the young.

10.   *Gary Daily Tribune,* November 18, 1908.

11.   Ibid., May 2, July 1, 1910.

12.   *Chicago Daily Tribune,* December 15, 1915; Brown to Lindsey, December 27, 1902, January 23, March 6, May 27, June 16, 1903, August 5, 30, 1904; Lindsey to Brown, September 21, 1904, Ben Lindsey Papers, LC.

13.   Lindsey to Wirt, February 14, 1914, Wirt MSS.

14.   For Lindsey's own views, see "The Boy and the Court," *Charities and the Commons* 13 (January 7, 1905): 350–57; "Love and the Criminal Law," *Journal of Education* 70 (September 2 and 16, October 2, 1909): 203–4, 258–9, 344; and "Some Experiences in the Juvenile Court of Denver," *Charities* 11 (November 7, 1903); 403–13.

15.   Lindsey to Brown, March 24, 27, 1905, Lindsey Papers; *Deseret Evening News* (Salt Lake City), July 1, 1905.

16.   Brown to Lindsey, March 23, 1906, Lindsey Papers.

17.   Brown to Lindsey, March 28, 1906, ibid.

18.   *Mill v. Brown,* 88 Pacific Reporter 609 (Utah, 1907). For additional discussion, see Schlossman, *Love and the American Delinquent.*

19.   Lindsey to George, August 6, 1907, George Junior Republic Papers, Collection of Regional History and University Archives, Cornell University Archives, Cornell University, Ithaca, N.Y.; Brown to Lindsey, August 20, 1907, May 12, 1909, Lindsey Papers.

20.   *Indianapolis Star,* September 10, 1907; *Warsaw* (Indiana) *Daily Union,* June 16, 1908; *Indianapolis News,* July 31, 1908; *Charlevoix* (Michigan) *Courier,* May 19, July 14, 21, 28, 1909.

21.   *Gary Daily Tribune,* September 21, 1910, March 22, 1911.

22.   On Eliot, see Mennel, pp. 147–48, 156.

23.   *Gary Daily Tribune,* September 27, 1910, February 9, 1912.

24.   Ibid., October 6, 19, 29, 1910.

25.   Ibid., November 3, 7, 23, December 17, 19, 1910, January 21, 1911.

26.   Ibid., February 2, 11, 1911.

27.   Ibid., March 11, 1911.

28.   Ibid., March 22, 1911; Wirt to Board of School Trustees, March 18, 1911, Wirt MSS.

29.   *Gary Daily Tribune,* March 22, 1911; *Indianapolis News,* March 30, 1911.

30.   *Gary Evening Post,* March 22, 1911. The enthusiastic newspaper support for Brown also revealed the pervasive influence of child-study ideas on innovations in juvenile reform. For instance, the *Gary Daily Tribune,* April 7, 1911, explained: "The parental school, just now starting out, it is to be hoped, will recognize that boys are not men. They are entitled to the widest latitude that brings no permanent harm to themselves or others. They are built for play. And in most cases they are all right."

31.   Lindsey to George, December 29, 1910; George to Lindsey, January 9, 1911, George Junior Republic Papers. See also Lindsey to Wirt, February 14, 1914, Wirt MSS.

32.   Buffington to Wirt, April 29, 1911; Wirt to Buffington, May 5, 1911, Wirt MSS.

33.   On the centrality of probation to progressive ideas on juvenile reform, see J. Lawrence Schultz, "The Cycle of Juvenile Court History," *Crime and Delinquency* 19 (October, 1973): 457–76, and Schlossman, *Love and the American Delinquent.*

34.   Lindsey to Wirt, February 14, 1914, Wirt MSS; *Gary Daily Tribune,* March 22, 1911.

35.   *Boyville News* 1, no. 7 (December 8, 1911); *Gary Daily Tribune,* November 24, 1911.

36.   *Gary Daily Tribune,* October 19, November 14, 18, 1911, January 11, February 9, 1912.

37.   Ibid., March 25, April 6, 1913; December 15, 1915; *Chicago Daily Tribune,* December 15, 1915; Wirt to Lindsey, March 9, 1914; Wirt to H. H. Hart, January 26, 1914, Wirt MSS.

38.   A similar development occurred in Milwaukee, as documented in Schlossman, *Love and the American Delinquent.*

39.   *Gary Daily Tribune,* July 13, September 12, 1911.

40.   Ibid., April 6, 1913; Wirt to Lindsey, March 9, 1914; Wirt to Hart, January 26, 1914, Wirt MSS.

41.   Lindsey to Wirt, February 14, 1914; Wirt to Lindsey, March 9, 1914, Wirt MSS.

42.   *Gary Daily Tribune,* December 15, 1915; *Chicago Daily Tribune,* December 15, 1915; Emmet Boyle to Wirt, June 15, 1916; Wirt to Boyle, June 19, 1916, Wirt MSS.

43.   See especially Platt, and Francis A. Allen, *The Borderland of Criminal Justice: Essays in Law and Criminology* (Chicago, 1964).

44.   *Gary Daily Tribune,* January 28, September 15, 1915; Ray to Wirt, June 22, 1910, Wirt MSS.

4. IMMIGRANTS AND THE GARY SCHOOLS

1.   U.S. Immigration Commission, *Abstract of the Report on the Children of Immigrants in Schools* (Washington, D.C., 1911), pp. 18–19, cited in Lawrence A. Cremin, *Transformation of the School: Progressivism in American Education, 1876–1957* (New York, 1961), p. 72.

2.   Wirt to Mrs. Jacob B. Smith, February 9, 1922, Wirt MSS.

3.   Ellwood P. Cubberley, *Changing Conceptions of Education* (Boston, 1909), pp. 15–16; Frank V. Thompson, *Schooling of the Immigrant* (New York, 1920), p. 1.

4.   Raymond E. Callahan, *Education and the Cult of Efficiency: A Study of the Social Forces That Have Shaped the Administration of the Public Schools* (Chicago, 1962), p. 15.

5.   Richard Watson Gilder, "The Kindergarten: An Uplifting Social Influence in the Home and the District," *Journal of Proceedings and Addresses of the National Education Association,* forty-second annual meeting (1903), p. 390.

6.   Suggestive on these developments are the following: Cremin; Marvin Lazerson, *Origins of the Urban School: Public Education in Massachusetts, 1870–1915* (Cambridge, Mass., 1971); David B. Tyack, *The One Best System: A History of American Urban Education* (Cambridge, Mass., 1974); Robert A. Carlson, "Americanization As an Early Twentieth-Century Adult Education Movement," *History of Education Quarterly* 10 (winter 1970): 440–64.

7.   Joel H. Spring, "The American High School and the Development of Social Character," in Walter Feinberg and Henry Rosemont, Jr., eds., *Work Technology, and Education: Dissenting Essays in the Intellectual Foundations of American Education* (Urbana, Ill., 1975), p. 59. On the manipulative functions of the schools, see also Samuel Bowles and Herbert Gintis, *Schooling in Capitalist America: Educational Reform and the Contradictions of Economic Life* (New York, 1976).

8.   Michael B. Katz, *Class, Bureaucracy, and Schools: The Illusion of Educational Change in America* (New York, 1971), pp. ix–x.

9.   Edna Hatfield Edmondson, "Juvenile Delinquency and Adult Crime: Certain Associations of Juvenile Delinquency and Adult Crime in Gary, Ind., with Special Reference to the Immigrant Population," *Indiana University Studies* 8 (June, 1921): 23–24; John G. Rossman, "What Gary Is Doing for Its Children," *Teachers College Record* 27 (December 1925): 283.

10.   On language difficulties in the Gary schools, see City of New York, Department of Education, *Industrial Conference Proceedings* (New York, 1914), p. 53; Abraham Flexner and Frank P. Bachman, *The Gary Schools: A General Account* (New York, 1918), p. 187; Margaret Ahearne, "Nature-Study in the Gary Schools," *Nature Study Review* (February 1915): 59–60; Frederick M. Davenport, "A Day in Educational Happy-Land," *Outlook* 116 (June 20, 1917): 290–91; "The Wirt Public Schools," *Public Health Journal* (Canada) 13 (August 1922): 342; Ueland to Mohl, October 20, 1973, in authors' possession. On special English classes for immigrant children in the 1920s, see *Gary Post-Tribune*, September 14, October 3, 1925.

11.   Rheta Childe Dorr, "Keeping the Children in School," *Hampton's Magazine* 28 (July 1911): 59; Agha Ashraf Ali, "Theories of Americanization Operative in the Gary Schools, 1907–1917" (Ph.D. dissertation, Ball State University, 1964), p. 138.

12.   *Gary Daily Tribune,* November 1, 1911, July 17, 1909, May 18, 1910.

13.   Flexner and Bachman, pp. 12–13.

14.   Ibid., pp. 10, 14.

15.   Gary School Census, 1924, Wirt Papers.

16.   *Gary Daily Tribune,* January 4, November 1, 1911; *Gary Post-Tribune,* September 6, 1939.

17.   Flexner and Bachman, pp. 52, 59–60, 114, 232–35.

18.   Charles R. Richards, *The Gary Public Schools: Industrial Work* (New York, 1919), pp. 3–4, 8–9, 14–16.

19.   Eva W. White, *The Gary Public Schools: Household Arts* (New York, 1918), p. 1; Flexner and Bachman, pp. 138–250; E. L. C. Morse, "The Origin of the Gary System," *Nation* 103 (July 27, 1916): 83.

20.   Stuart A. Courtis, *The Gary Public Schools: Measurement of Classroom Products* (New York, 1919), pp. 11, 42–43, 102, 294–95, 369–72; Flexner and Bachman, p. 119.

21.   Flexner and Bachman, p. 256; Annie Klingensmith to Wirt, April 26, 1917, Wirt MSS.

22.   *Gary Daily Tribune,* November 18, 19, 1908, February 22, March 11, 1909; Klingensmith to Wirt, April 26, 1917, Wirt MSS; Courtis, pp. 13–15.

23.   *Gary Daily Tribune,* September 10, 1918, September 18, 1920; *Gary Post-Tribune,* September 16, 1937.

24.   F. B. Knight et al., *Final Report, Purdue Survey Committee for the Gary Board of Education to the President and Board of Trustees of Purdue University* (mimeo, 1941), p. 169.

25.   *Gary Daily Tribune,* April 15, September 10, 1914; William Grant Seaman and Mary Elizabeth Abernethy, *Community Schools for Week-Day Religious Instruction: Gary, Indiana* (Gary, 1921), pp. 4–5, 8, 20–21; Wirt, "The Gary Public Schools and the Churches," *Religious Education* 11 (June, 1916): 221–26.

26.   "The Gary Schools of Religion," *Religious Education* 14 (August, 1919): 276–78; Seaman and Abernethy, pp. 13, 31; *Gary Baptist Bulletin* 2 (September 10, 1916): 2.

27.   *Gary Daily Tribune,* December 4, 9, 28, 1908, November 9, 1909, March 8, 1912.

28.   *The Gary Evening Schools* (Gary, n.d.), school pamphlet; "Evening School Activities in Gary, Indiana," *Journal of the National Education Association* 13 (December, 1924): 332–33; Albert Fertsch, "Adult Education from the Viewpoint of a City," *Proceedings of the National Education Association* (1928), pp. 267–70; Knight et al.

29.   *Gary Daily Tribune,* October 26, 1914; *Gary Post-Tribune,* May 10, 1926, November 22, 1927, January 3, 1934, July 29, 1938; John G. Rossman, *The Auditorium and Its Administration* (Gary, 1927), p. 79.

30.   *Gary Daily Tribune,* December 16, 1910, January 10, 12, 18, 1911.

31.   Estelle M. Sternberger, "Gary and the Foreigner's Opportunity," *Survey* 42 (June 28, 1919): 480–81.

32.   Gary International Institute, Committee of Management, minutes, September 11, 21, 1931, International Institute Papers, located in offices of Gary International Institute; Mattie L. McArthur, "The Immigrant and His Children," WIND radio script, May 21, 1936, ibid.

33.   Wirt to *Gary Daily Tribune,* May 11, 1918, Wirt MSS; Z. A. Chandler to Wirt, n.d. (ca. 1917), ibid.; Ada J. Dursing (Wirt's secretary) to Anna Matties (chairman of Lake County Committee on Educational War Propaganda), August 9, 1918, ibid.; Henry J. Ryan (national director of American Legion) to Wirt, January 20, 1921, ibid.; undated newspaper clipping, *Hammond Times* (ca. 1921), ibid.; Gary Klan no. 123, Knights of the Ku Klux Klan, to Wirt, March 11, 1927, ibid.; *Gary Daily Tribune,* October 3, 9, 1917. On the elimination of the German language for public schools, see Frederick C. Luebke, *Bonds of Loyalty: German Americans and World War I* (DeKalb, Ill., 1974), pp. 250–54.

34.   Sternberger, p. 280; *Reports of the U.S. Department of Labor,* "Report of the Commissioner of Naturalization, 1917" (Washington, D.C., 1918), p. 508; John B. DeVille to Wirt, November 18, 24, 1919, Wirt MSS; A. B. Dickson (general secretary of Gary YMCA) to Wirt, February 3, October 20, 1920, ibid.; Ralph Cummins (director of Gary Neighborhood House) to Wirt, September 18, 1920, ibid.; Dursing to Albert Fertsch, March 21, 1928, ibid.

35.   Morse, pp. 82–83.

36.   Colin Greer, *The Great School Legend: A Revisionist Interpretation of American Public Education* (New York, 1972), p. 92.

37.   Timothy L. Smith, "School and Community: The Quest for Equal Opportunity, 1910–1921," manuscript, p. 41, Immigration History Research Center, University of Minnesota; id., "Immigrant Social Aspirations and American Education, 1880–1930," *American Quarterly* 21 (fall 1969): 523–43; id., "Native Blacks and Foreign Whites: Varying Responses to Educational Opportunity in America, 1880–1950," *Perspectives in American History* 6 (1972): 309–35. Aspirations for schooling can also be found in some of the autobiographical immigrant literature: Mary Antin, *The Promised Land* (Boston, 1912); Leonard Covello, *The Heart Is the Teacher* (New York, 1958). See also Babette Inglehart, "The Immigrant Child and the American School: A Literary View," *Ethnicity* 3 (March, 1976): 34–52.

38.   Gary School Census, 1922, Wirt Papers; Gary School Census, 1924, ibid.

39.   David K. Cohen, "Immigrants and the Schools," *Review of Educational Research* 40 (February, 1970): 13–28; Tyack, pp. 242–55; Josef J. Barton, *Peasants and Strangers: Italians, Rumanians, and Slovaks in an American City, 1890–1950* (Cambridge, Mass., 1975), pp. 117–46; Thomas Kessner, *The Golden Door: Italian and Jewish Immigrant Mobility in New York City, 1880–1915* (New York, 1977), pp. 96–99; Stephan Thernstrom, *The Other Bostonians: Poverty and Progress in the American Metropolis, 1880–1970* (Cambridge, Mass., 1973), pp. 170–75;

Seymour Martin Lipset and Reinhard Bendix, *Social Mobility in Industrial Society* (Berkeley, Calif., 1959), pp. 255-56.

40. Carl F. Kaestle, "Conflict and Consensus Revisited: Notes toward a Reinterpretation of American Educational History," *Harvard Educational Review* 46 (August 1976): 395; Diane Ravitch, "On the History of Minority Group Education in the United States," *Teachers College Record* 78 (December, 1976): 216-19.

41. See, for example, John Bodnar, "Materialism and Morality: Slavic-American Immigrants and Education, 1890-1940," *Journal of Ethnic Studies* 3 (winter 1976): 1-19; id., "Immigration and Modernization: The Case of Slavic Peasants in Industrial America," *Journal of Social History* 10 (fall 1976): 44-71; Thomas Kessner and Betty Boyd Caroli, "New Immigrant Women at Work: Italians and Jews in New York City, 1880-1905," *Journal of Ethnic Studies* 5 (winter 1978): 19-31; Walter Feinberg, "Revisionist Scholarship and the Problem of Historical Context," *Teachers College Record* 78 (February 1977): 322. On the importance of home ownership, see Roger D. Simon, "Housing and Services in an Immigrant Neighborhood: Milwaukee's Ward 14," *Journal of Urban History* 2 (August 1976): 435-58.

42. Gary School Census, 1922, Wirt Papers.

43. Peter Roberts, *The New Immigration* (New York, 1912), p. 334; George A. Kourvetaris, *First and Second Generation Greeks in Chicago* (Athens, 1971), pp. 81-83; Kessner, pp. 95-96; Bodnar, pp. 1-19.

44. Gary School Census, 1922, 1924, Wirt Papers.

45. Knight et al., p. 105.

46. For similar efforts elsewhere, see Joseph F. Kett, *Rites of Passage: Adolescence in America, 1790 to the Present* (New York, 1977), pp. 215-44.

47. Hyman Berman, "Education for Work and Labor Solidarity: The Immigrant Miners and Radicalism on the Mesabi Range," manuscript, pp. 25-26, Immigration History Research Center, University of Minnesota; Bodnar, pp. 1-19; Michael R. Olneck and Marvin Lazerson, "The School Achievement of Immigrant Children, 1900-1930," *History of Education Quarterly* 14 (winter 1974): 453-82.

48. Gary School Census, 1924, Wirt Papers.

49. *Gary Post-Tribune*, September 12, 1924, September 6, 1927, September 5, 1931, September 6, 1932, September 18, 1933; Neil Betten and Raymond A. Mohl, "Ethnic Churches in Gary, Indiana: Religious Adjustment and Cultural Defense," *Review Journal of Philosophy and Social Science* 3 (1978); Robert D. Cross, "Origins of the Catholic Parochial Schools in America," *American Benedictine Review* 16 (June, 1965): 194-209.

50. James W. Sanders, *The Education of an Urban Minority: Catholics in Chicago, 1833-1965* (New York, 1977), pp. 105-20. See also J. A. Burns, *The Growth and Development of the Catholic School System in the United States* (New York, 1912), pp. 294-337; Thompson, pp. 151-54; Marvin Lazerson, "Understanding American Catholic Educational History," *History of Education Quarterly* 17 (fall 1977): 311-14; Howard Weisz, "Irish-American Attitudes and the Americanization of the English-Language Parochial School," *New York History* 53 (April, 1972): 157-76.

51. *Gary Daily Tribune*, September 14, 1916; *Gary Evening Post and Daily Tribune*, December 31, 1921; *Gary Post-Tribune*, September 13, 17, 1924, September 6, 1932, September 4, 1935. In addition, both Slovak Lutherans and Swedish Lutherans ran Sunday schools which were partially designed to maintain language and ethnic culture. See *Gary Daily Tribune*, March 29, 1918; *Gary Post-Tribune*, May 22, 1924.

52. Gary School Census, 1924, Wirt Papers; *Gary Post-Tribune*, September 6, 1932, September 4, 1935; Sanders, pp. xi, 12; Selwyn K. Troen, *The Public and the Schools: Shaping the St. Louis System, 1838-1920* (Columbia, Mo., 1975), p. 34.

53. Martin E. Carlson, "A Study of the Eastern Orthodox Churches in Gary, Indiana," M.A. thesis, University of Chicago, 1942; Betten and Mohl; "The Greeks in Gary, Indiana," International Institute Study, 1933, International Institute Papers;

Elizabeth N. Wilson (director, Gary International Institute) to Joshua A. Fishman, December 21, 1960, American Council for Nationalities Service Papers, shipment 2, box 8, folder 148, Immigration History Research Center, University of Minnesota.
54. *Gary Daily Tribune*, May 1, 1913; *Temple Beth-El Souvenir Album, 1908-1940* (Gary, 1940), pp. 7-9.
55. Joshua A. Fishman, *Language Loyalty in the United States* (The Hague, 1966), pp. 92-126. See also W. Lloyd Warner and Leo Srole, *The Social Systems of American Ethnic Groups* (New Haven, 1945), pp. 244-53.
56. Fishman, p. 93.

5. BLACKS AND THE GARY SCHOOLS

1. On segregated schooling, see especially Richard Kluger, *Simple Justice: The History of Brown v. Board of Education and Black America's Struggle for Equality* (New York, 1976); Meyer Weinberg, *A Chance to Learn: A History of Race and Education in the United States* (Cambridge, England, 1977); Florette Henri, *Black Migration: Movement North, 1900-1920* (Garden City, N.Y., 1975), pp. 178-86.
2. David B. Tyack, *The One Best System: A History of American Urban Education* (Cambridge, Mass., 1974), p. 110; Walter Feinberg, *Reason and Rhetoric: The Intellectual Foundations of Twentieth Century Liberal Educational Policy* (New York, 1975), pp. 108-21. For evidence of white progressives' acceptance of segregation or their inability to challenge it directly into the 1930s, see Ronald K. Goodenow, "The Progressive Education Movement and Blacks: Some Preliminary Observations on the Latent Functions of Educational Reform," paper delivered at American Educational Studies Association meeting, Denver, 1973; id., "The Progressive Educator, Race and Ethnicity in the Depression Years: An Overview," *History of Education Quarterly* 15 (winter 1975): 365-94.
3. Neil Betten and Raymond A. Mohl, "The Evolution of Racism in an Industrial City, 1906-1940: A Case Study of Gary, Indiana," *Journal of Negro History* 59 (January, 1974): 51-64; Elizabeth Balanoff, "A History of the Black Community of Gary, Indiana, 1906-1940," Ph.D. dissertation, University of Chicago, 1974.
4. *Gary Daily Tribune*, December 15, 1908; Elizabeth Lytle, "The Model Schools of Gary, Indiana," *Crisis* 13 (January, 1917): 121; *Gary Daily Tribune*, Spetember 19, 1914.
5. Lytle, p. 121; *Gary Daily Tribune*, September 29, 1916; John Foster Potts, "A History of the Growth of the Negro Population of Gary, Indiana," M.A. thesis, Cornell University, 1937, pp. 8-10.
6. Petition to the Honorable School Board, October 2, 1917, Wirt MSS.
7. J. William Lester, Sr., "Rifts in 'The World's Greatest Schools'" (Gary, 1930), pamphlet, GPL, p. 8; petition of Froebel teachers to Principal Charles S. Coons with appended letters, March 1, 1918, Wirt MSS. The complete text of these letters may be found in Ronald D. Cohen and Raymond A. Mohl, "Blacks and the Schools of Gary, Indiana, 1908-1930," *Review Journal of Philosophy and Social Science*, 1 (1976), 160-81.
8. Coons to Wirt, March 25, 1918, Wirt MSS.
9. *Gary Daily Tribune*, July 13, 1918; G. W. Swartz to J. E. McCoughtry, September 27, 1918, Wirt MSS.
10. Swartz to Wirt, October 28, 1918; Wirt to Swartz, October 30, 1918, Wirt MSS.
11. *The Sand Dune*, 1932 (yearbook of East Pulaski High School), p. 6; McCoughtry to Swartz, September 25, 1918, Wirt MSS.
12. Gary School Census, 1922, Wirt Papers; Smith, "Native Blacks and Foreign Whites: Varying Responses to Educational Opportunity in America, 1880-1950," *Perspectives in American History* 6 (1972): pp. 309-35.
13. Tyack, p. 226; E. D. Simpson to Wirt, January 20, 1919, Wirt MSS.

14.   John H. Smith to the editor, *Gary Daily Tribune*, January 17, 1921.
15.   *Gary Daily Tribune*, April 11, 1921; Jacob L. Reddix, *A Voice Crying in the Wilderness* (Jackson, Miss., 1974), pp. 107-8; Albert Fertsch, "Colored Trade School at Gary, Ind.," *School Life* 7 (November, 1921): 65. While the two schools were supposed to be separate, in 1922 there was a complaint of a white teacher who wanted to be transferred "because of the mixed classes, that is, the mingling of the different races" (Swartz to Wirt, September 20, 1922, Wirt MSS).
16.   "Program of Topics under Consideration by Peoples' Committee . . . to be brought to the attention of the Superintendent of Gary Schools and the Board of Education of Gary, Indiana," September 29, 1921, Wirt MSS.
17.   Petition to State Department of Education from Gary Citizens, and Lewis Campbell to State Department of Education, January 22, 1923, series G, container 62, NAACP Papers; *Gary Post-Tribune*, January 31, 1923; E. E. Ramsey to Wirt, April 11, 1923, Wirt MSS; James Weldon Johnson to T. J. Wilson, February 14, 1923, series G, container 62, NAACP Papers.
18.   W. C. Hueston to Wirt, September 6, 1924; Wirt to Hueston, September 11, 1924, Wirt MSS.
19.   See chapter 6 for a discussion of the 1927 Emerson School strike.
20.   Reddix, p. 109.
21.   H. Theodore Tatum, Annual Report of Virginia Street School, session 1926-27, (June 14, 1927); id., Annual Report of Virginia School, session 1927-28 (June 2, 1928), Wirt MSS.
22.   That racism was learned in Gary is the argument in Balanoff, "A History of the Black Community of Gary," and in Betten and Mohl, "The Evolution of Racism in an Industrial City." See also Michael Homel, "The Politics of Public Education in Black Chciago, 1910-1941," *Journal of Negro Education* 45 (spring 1976): 179-91.
23.   Max Wolff, "Segregation in the Schools of Gary, Indiana," *Journal of Educational Sociology* 36 (February, 1963): 253.

6. THE 1920s

1.   Robert L. Church (with Michael W. Sedlak), *Education in the United States: An Interpretive History* (New York, 1976), pp. 344, 352, 353; Edward H. Reisner, "General Historical Background, 1897-1922," in I. L. Kandel, ed., *Twenty-Five Years of American Education: Collected Essays by Former Students of Paul Monroe* (New York, 1926), p. 23.
2.   Roscoe D. Case, *The Platoon School in America*, (Stanford, Calif., 1931), p. 11.
3.   *Statistical History of the United States from Colonial Times to the Present* (Stamford, Conn., 1965), p. 207; A. H. Bell, "Development of the Gary School Plan and Matters Pertinent," undated manuscript, Wulfing Papers. Gary statistics have been compiled from various manuscript and newspaper sources. The school figures for Gary do not include night school enrollment, which was substantial—over 12,000 in 1924.
4.   Abraham Flexner, *I Remember: The Autobiography of Abraham Flexner* (New York, 1940), p. 255. The report was published in eight volumes. See the summary volume, Flexner and Bachman, *The Gary Schools;* Wirt to Bessie Stern, February 2, 1920, Wirt MSS; Wirt to L. B. Moffett, April 21, 1920, ibid.; Wirt, "Plain Facts about the Rockefeller Foundation Survey of the Gary Schools," manuscript, pp. 1-2, Wulfing Papers.
5.   *Gary Daily Tribune*, January 31, 1919.
6.   Edward A. Krug, *The Shaping of the American High School, 1920-1941* (Madison, Wis., 1972), p. 19; *Gary Daily Tribune*, January 21, February 17, 1919.

7.   *Gary Daily Tribune,* January 24, March 5, 1919. There is no information on the outcome of the city council's investigation, if it was ever held.

8.   *Gary Evening Post and Daily Tribune,* September 24, October 1, 1921, April 5, 1922.

9.   *Gary Evening Post and Daily Tribune,* May 20, June 15, 1922; Coons to John G. Rossman, June 6, 1924, Wirt MSS.

10.   *Gary Post-Tribune,* May 2, 1923, September 10, 1925; Robert S. Lynd and Helen M. Lynd, *Middletown: A Study in Contemporary American Culture* (New York, 1929), p. 188.

11.   *Gary Daily Tribune,* March 11, 1920; William E. Eaton, *The American Federation of Teachers, 1916-1961* (Carbondale, Ill., 1975), pp. 18-37.

12.   Coons to Wirt, January 16, 1922, Wirt MSS. For a brief discussion of this issue, see Flora Philley, *Teacher Help Yourself* (Gary, 1948), pp. 5-12.

13.   *Gary Post-Tribune,* November 3, 1923; interview with Ann Maloney, Gary, Ind., October 22, 1974.

14.   Wirt, "Creating a Child World," *The Platoon School* 1 (January, 1927): 5; Albert Fertsch, "Adult Education from the Viewpoint of a City," *Proceedings of the National Education Association* (1928), pp. 269-70.

15.   *Gary Post-Tribune,* January 10, 1922; *Gary Daily Tribune,* July 26, September 13, 1919.

16.   *Gary Daily Tribune,* March 2, 3, 1920; *Central Labor Union News* (Gary), March 28, 1920; *Gary Post-Tribune,* January 2, 1923.

17.   *Gary Post-Tribune,* September 6, 1921.

18.   Edythe Watson, "The Gary School System," *Vocational Education Magazine* 3 (January, 1925): 4; *Gary Post-Tribune,* March 23, 1923.

19.   *Gary Post-Tribune,* November 22, 1924, September 9, 1927; Carleton Washburne and Myron M. Stearns, *Better Schools: A Survey of Progressive Education in American Public Schools* (New York, 1928), p. 17. For a brief discussion of the popularity of vocational work in Muncie, see Lynd and Lynd, pp. 194-96.

20.   *Gary Post-Tribune,* September 8, 1925; Robert H. Elias, *"Entangling Alliances with None": An Essay on the Individual in the American Twenties* (New York, 1973), p. 54; Robert S. Lynd and Helen M. Lynd, *Middletown in Transition: A Study in Cultural Conflicts* (New York, 1937), pp. 233-34; Washburne and Stearns, pp. 259-99. On the latter point, see, for example, Joel H. Spring, *Education and the Rise of the Corporate State* (Boston, 1972); Clarence J. Karier et al., *Roots of Crisis: American Education in the Twentieth Century* (Chicago, 1973); Samuel Bowles and Herbert Gintis, *Schooling in Capitalist America: Educational Reform and the Contradictions of Economic Life* (New York, 1976); Feinberg and Rosemont, eds., *Work, Technology, and Education: Dissenting Essays in the Intellectual Foundations of American Education* (Urbana, Ill., 1975).

21.   Wirt, "Creating a Child World," p. 7.

22.   *Gary Post-Tribune,* September 2, 1924; [Rossman], "Teacher's Bulletin No. 1" (September 1, 1924): 1-2, Wirt MSS; Washburne and Stearns, p. 261; Krug, pp. 113-17; David B. Tyack, *The One Best System: A History of American Urban Education* (Cambridge, Mass., 1974), pp. 198-216.

23.   *Gary Post-Tribune,* October 8, 1925, March 12, 1926; Eugene Smith, *Education Moves Ahead: A Survey of Progressive Methods* (Boston, 1924), pp. 92-93, 97; [Rossman], "Teacher's Bulletin No. 12" (January 5, 1926): 40, 45, 46, Wirt MSS. See also Krug, pp. 142-45.

24.   *Gary Post-Tribune,* September 4, 1926, September 4, 1928; James O'Donnel Bennett, "Will to Learn Chief Goal of Gary Teachers," *Chicago Tribune,* December 9, 1929.

25.   *Gary Post-Tribune,* September 4, 1928. On cooperation and conformity in the schools, see Spring.

26.   *Gary Evening Post and Daily Tribune,* March 11, April 25, 1922; *Gary Post-Tribune,* November 7, 1924.
27.   *Gary Evening Post and Daily Tribune,* September 13, 1921; *Gary Post-Tribune,* September 1, December 15, 1927, March 16, 1928.
28.   Wirt speech, ca. 1926, manuscript, p. 12, Wirt Papers.
29.   *Gary Post-Tribune,* January 12, 1928.
30.   *Sun* (Gary), November 4, 1927.
31.   Tyack, p. 228; *Sun* (Gary), January 6, 1928; *Gary American,* September 7, 1928.
32.   *Gary American,* June 28, 1930, April 18, 1931; Walter White to A. C. Bailey, May 20, 1929, series D, container 57, NAACP Papers.
33.   Albert Fertsch, "Colored Trade School at Gary, Ind.," *School Life* 7 (November, 1921): 65.
34.   David K. Cohen and Marvin Lazerson, "Education and the Corporate Order," *Socialist Revolution* 2 (March-April, 1972): 71; Tyack, p. 216. For a more thorough study of the functions and class bias of public schooling, see Bowles and Gintis.
35.   George S. Counts, *School and Society in Chicago* (New York, 1928), p. 184.

7. THE 1930s

1.   Robert S. Lynd and Helen M. Lynd, *Middletown in Transition: A Study in Cultural Conflicts* (New York, 1937), pp. 239-40. See also Lawrence A. Cremin, *The Transformation of the School: Progressivism in American Education, 1876-1957* (New York, 1961), pp. 324-25; Patricia A. Graham, *Progressive Education: From Arcady to Academe* (New York, 1967), pp. 85-101.
2.   Irving J. Hendrick, "California's Response to the New Education in the 1930s," *California Historical Quarterly* 53 (spring 1974): 25-40; Diane Ravitch, *The Great School Wars: New York City, 1805-1973* (New York, 1974), pp. 236-38; Melvin R. Maskin, "Black Education and the New Deal: The Urban Experience," Ph.D. dissertation, New York University, 1973; Robert L. Church (with Michael W. Sedlak), *Education in the United States: An Interpretive History* (New York, 1976), p. 371. See also Edward A. Krug, *The Shaping of the American High School, 1920-1941* (Madison, Wis., 1972), pp. 201-24; Robert Greet, "The Plainfield School System in the Depression, 1930-1937," *New Jersey History* 90 (summer 1972): 69-82; Joseph Caliguire, "Union Township Schools and the Depression, 1929-1938," ibid. 93 (autumn-winter 1975): 115-27.
3.   F. B. Knight et al., *Final Report, Purdue Survey Committee for the Gary Board of Education to the President and Board of Trustees of Purdue University,* mimeo, 1941, p. 169. General enrollment statistics are drawn from the Purdue survey and the annual reports of the school board. For some national figures, see *Statistical History of the United States from Colonial Times to the Present* (Stamford, Conn., 1965), p. 214, which demonstrate that while elementary school enrollment remained steady, high school enrollment increased.
4.   *Gary Post-Tribune,* May 11, August 27, 1931, April 13, October 1, 1932, June 7, 1933, February 22, 1934, September 5, 1936, January 25, 1937, August 22, 1939.
5.   Symposium, *The Platoon School* 9 (April, 1935); 18; *Gary Post-Tribune,* April 7, June 7, 1933; Gary Principals' Association, *The Taxpayer and the Gary Public Schools,* pamphlet (Gary, 1934), p. 26; William A. Wirt et. al., *Why Does Gary Spend Money for Schools Other Than the Regular Day Schools?* pamphlet (Gary, 1935); Isabelle V. Jones to Wirt, September 10, 1935, Wirt Papers.
6.   *Gary Post-Tribune,* April 13, 1932, February 9, 22, 1934.
7.   Ibid., October 16, 1934, April 13, 14, 16, 19, 21, 1937.
8.   Flora Philley to Wirt, November 3, 1937, in folder marked "Correspondence to and from Supt. Wm. Wirt and H. S. Jones," Gary Teachers' Union MSS, Local

no. 4, Gary, Indiana; memo labeled "Gary Teachers' Union No. 4," ca. October, 1937, American Federation of Teachers Collection, Archives of Labor History and Urban Affairs, Wayne State University, Detroit Michigan. See also Flora Philley, *Teacher Help Yourself* (Gary, 1948), pp. 23–65.

9. Philley, "Arguments for Single Salary Schedule," December 8, 1936, in folder marked "Single Salary Schedule," Gary Teachers' Union MSS. See also "The Case for the Classroom Teachers as Presented by the General Salary Committee to the Gary Board of School Trustees and Superintendent Wirt, Thursday, April 29, 1937," mimeo, Wirt Papers.

10. Wirt to the teachers in the Gary Public Schools, October 1, 1937, mimeo, Wirt Papers; *Gary Post-Tribune*, December 7, 1937, January 7, 8, 13, February 23, 1938.

11. *Gary Post-Tribune*, March 3, 8, 9, 1938.

12. Ibid., April 29, 1938; Philley, *Teacher Help Yourself*, pp. 67–74, 92–93; Philley to Herbert Cole, February 24, 1940, in folder marked "Grievances," Gary Teachers' Union MSS.

13. *Gary Post-Tribune*, February 17, 18, 19, 23, 25, 26, July 15, 1937; Philley, *Teacher Help Yourself*, pp. 62–63.

14. Board of School Trustees, School City of Gary, "Minutes of School Board Meetings," 7: 469, 491, School Service Center, Gary, Indiana. See also Erwin C. Rosenau, "Notes on School Situation," ca. 1939, Erwin C. Rosenau Papers, Calumet Regional Archives, Indiana University Northwest, Gary.

15. See, for example, Wayne J. Urban, "Organized Teachers and Educational Reform during the Progressive Era: 1890–1920," *History of Education Quarterly* 16 (spring 1976): 35–52. For strong arguments that after 1900 harmony was the norm, see David B. Tyack, *The One Best System: A History of American Urban Education* (Cambridge, Mass., 1974), and Selwyn K. Troen, *The Public and the Schools: Shaping the St. Louis System, 1838–1920* (Columbia, Mo., 1975), pp. 208–26. For the rise of conflict in Middletown (Muncie) in the 1930s, as contrasted to the 1920s, see Lynd and Lynd, pp. 204–41.

16. *Gary Post-Tribune*, February 6, 1934; Wirt to Edward Rumely, March 12, 1934, Wirt Papers; Herbert M. Bratter, "The Committee for the Nation: A Case History in Monetary Propaganda," *Journal of Political Economy* 49 (August, 1941): 531–53.

17. Wirt to Rumely, March 12, 1934, Wirt Papers; Wirt, "Which Way America: Should Educators Be Alarmed?" [1934], ibid.; *Gary Post-Tribune*, March 7, 1934. For a short sketch of social reconstructionists, see Church, pp. 376–78; and for the Cleveland meeting, National Education Association, Department of Superintendents, *Official Report, Cleveland, Ohio, February 24 to March 1, 1934* (Washington, D.C., 1934).

18. *Gary Post-Tribune*, March 27, 30, April 2, 20, 1934; Wirt, "The School As an Agency for Propaganda," pp. 4–5, 34, Wirt Papers. See also John J. Healy, Jr., "William A. Wirt and the Bulwinkle Investigation of 1934," (M.A. thesis, history department, Indiana University, 1960), which takes Wirt's charges seriously.

19. *Gary American*, April 6, 1934; "A Resolution on the Passing of Superintendent William A. Wirt," March 12, 1938, in folder marked "Correspondence to and from Supt. Wm. Wirt and H. S. Jones," Gary Teachers' Union MSS; *Gary Post-Tribune*, March 12, 1938.

20. *Gary American*, October 11, 1930, June 4, 18, 1932.

21. Dennis Bethea, "The Colored Group in the Gary School System," *Crisis* 38 (August, 1931): 281; *Gary Post-Tribune*, May 8, 1934; *Gary American*, June 9, 16, 1933.

22. A. J. Butler to Mrs. James A. Patterson, June 10, 1933, Wirt MSS; *Gary American*, March 4, 11, 25, April 22, May 6, August 26, 1938, May 26, 1939.

23. Guy Wulfing to Wirt, n.d. (ca. mid-1930s), mimeo, Wulfing Papers; Wulfing to Wirt, February 5, 1936, ibid.; Knight et al., pp. 23, 62.

24. Knight et al., pp. 169, 180, 269; *Gary American*, October 6, 1939.

8. URBAN SCHOOLING

1. Frederick M. Binder, *The Age of the Common School, 1830-1865* (New York, 1974), p. 163. For the history of Gary see James B. Lane, *"City of the Century": A History of Gary Indiana* (Bloomington, Ind., 1978).
2. Ibid., p. 101; Robert L. Church (with Michael W. Sedlak), *Education in the United States: An Interpretive History* (New York, 1976), pp. 70, 79.
3. Paul H. Mattingly, *The Classless Profession: American Schoolmen in the Nineteenth Century* (New York, 1975), p. 44; Rush Welter, *The Mind of America, 1820-1860* (New York, 1975), p. 282; Barbara Finkelstein, "Pedagogy As Intrusion: Teaching Values in Popular Primary Schools in Nineteenth-Century America," *History of Childhood Quarterly* 2 (winter 1975): 368. See also Mary M. Gordon, "Patriots and Christians: A Reassessment of Nineteenth-Century School Reforms," *Journal of Social History* 2 (summer 1978), 554-73; Carl F. Kaestle, "Social Change, Discipline, and the Common School in Early Nineteenth-Century America," *Journal of Interdisciplinary History* 9 (summer 1978): 1-17.
4. Welter, p. 285; Lawrence A. Cremin, *Traditions of American Education* (New York, 1977), p. 86; Lawrence Friedman, *Inventors of the Promised Land* (New York, 1975), pp. 266, 302. Cremin is referring to the influences of family, church, and other factors in addition to schools.
5. Church, p. 70; Samuel Bowles and Herbert Gintis, *Schooling in Capitalist America: Educational Reform and the Contradictions of Economic Life* (New York, 1976), pp. 178-79. See also Alexander J. Field, "Educational Expansion in Mid-Nineteenth-Century Massachusetts: Human-Capital Formation or Structural Reinforcement?," *Harvard Educational Review* 46 (November, 1976): 521-52.
6. Paul Faler, "Cultural Aspects of the Industrial Revolution: Lynn, Massachusetts, Shoemakers and Industrial Morality, 1826-1860," *Labor History* 15 (summer 1974): 367, 387.
7. Michael B. Katz, *Class, Bureaucracy, & Schools: The Illusion of Educational Change in America* (expanded ed., New York, 1975); Carl F. Kaestle, *The Evolution of an Urban School System: New York City, 1750-1850* (Cambridge, Mass., 1973); Stanley K. Schultz, *The Culture Factory: Boston Public Schools, 1789-1860* (New York, 1973).
8. Kaestle, pp. 183-84; Lee Soltow and Edward Stevens, "Economic Aspects of School Participation in Mid-Nineteenth-Century United States," *Journal of Interdisciplinary History* 8 (autumn 1977): 243. See also Carl F. Kaestle, "'Between the Scylla of Brutal Ignorance and the Charybdis of a Literary Education': Elite Attitudes toward Mass Schooling in Early Industrial England and America," in Lawrence Stone, ed., *Schooling and Society: Studies in the History of Education* (Baltimore, 1976), pp. 177-91.
9. Patricia A. Graham, *Community and Class in American Education, 1865-1918* (New York, 1974), pp. 24-25.
10. David B. Tyack, *The One Best System: A History of American Urban Education* (Cambridge, Mass., 1974), p. 168. See also William A. Bullough, *Cities and Schools in the Gilded Age: The Evolution of an Urban Institution* (Port Washington, N.Y., 1974); William Issel, "The Politics of Public School Reform in Pennsylvania, 1880-1911," *Pennsylvania Magazine of History and Biography*, 102 (January, 1978): 59-92.
11. Selwyn K. Troen, *The Public and the Schools: Shaping the St. Louis System, 1838-1920* (Columbia, Mo., 1975); id., "The Discovery of the Adolescent by American Educational Reformers, 1900-1920: An Economic Perspective," in Stone,

pp. 239–51. See also Joseph F. Kett, *Rites of Passage: Adolescence in America, 1790 to the Present* (New York, 1977).

12. Troen, *The Public and the Schools*, pp. 224–25. For the persistence of conflict, see Diane Ravitch, *The Great School Wars: New York City, 1805–1973* (New York, 1974).

13. Lawrence A. Cremin, *The Transformation of the School: Progressivism in American Education, 1876–1957* (New York, 1961), p. 88.

14. Raymond E. Callahan, *Education and the Cult of Efficiency: A Study of the Social Forces that Have Shaped the Administration of the Public Schools* (Chicago, 1962); Edward A. Krug, *The Shaping of the American High School, 1880–1920* (Madison, Wis., 1969), p. xii; and see also Edward A. Krug, *The Shaping of the American High School, 1920–1941* (Madison, Wis., 1972).

15. Marvin Lazerson, *Origins of the Urban School: Public Education in Massachusetts, 1870–1915* (Cambridge, Mass., 1971), pp. 244–45; Joel H. Spring, *Education and the Rise of the Corporate State* (Boston, 1972), p. 149. Additional institutions, such as the juvenile court, were devised at this time to control children. See, for example, Steven L. Schlossman, *Love and the American Delinquent: The Theory and Practice of "Progressive" Juvenile Justice, 1825–1920* (Chicago, 1977). This desire for control extended even to the newborn—see Richard W. Wertz and Dorothy C. Wertz, *Lying In: A History of Childbirth in America* (New York, 1977); and to children's sexuality—see John S. Haller and Robin M. Haller, *The Physician and Sexuality in Victorian America* (Urbana, Ill., 1974). And see also, in general, Paul C. Violas, *The Training of the Urban Working Class: A History of Twentieth Century American Education* (Chicago, 1978).

16. Troen, *The Public and the Schools*, p. 207.

17. Walter Feinberg and Henry Rosemont, Jr., eds., *Work, Technology and Education: Dissenting Essays in the Intellectual Foundations of American Education* (Urbana, Ill., 1975), pp. 8–9.

18. Walter Feinberg, *Reason and Rhetoric: The Intellectual Foundations of Twentieth Century Liberal Educational Policy* (New York, 1975), pp. 248–49.

19. Feinberg and Rosemont, eds., p. 135; Bowles and Gintis, pp. 199, 235–36.

20. Feinberg, p. 284; Bowles and Gintis, p. 266.

21. Clarence J. Karier, *Shaping the American Educational State: 1900 to the Present* (New York, 1975), p. xx; Tyack, p. 216. See also Clarence Karier, Paul Violas, and Joel Spring, *Roots of Crisis: American Education in the Twentieth Century* (Chicago, 1973). On the role of play see Dom Cavallo, "Social Reform and the Movement to Organize Children's Play during the Progressive Era," *History of Childhood Quarterly* 3 (spring 1976): 509–22, and id. "The Child in American Reform: A Psychohistory of the Movement to Organize Children's Play, 1880–1920," Ph.D. dissertation, State University of New York at Stony Brook, 1976.

22. Troen, *The Public and the Schools*, p. 226; Cremin, *Traditions of American Education*, p. 127.

23. Michael B. Katz, *Class, Bureaucracy, & Schools: The Illusion of Educational Change in America* (expanded ed., New York, 1975), p. 185; Tyack, p. 176. Recent studies on the fight for integration include Meyer Weinberg, *A Chance to Learn: A History of Race and Education in the United States* (Cambridge, Eng., 1977), and Richard Kluger's excellent *Simple Justice: The History of Brown vs. Board of Education and Black America's Struggle for Equality* (New York, 1975).

24. Church, pp. 255–56, 260; Katz, expanded ed., p. 179.

25. Melvin G. Holli, *Reform in Detroit: Hazen S. Pingree and Urban Politics* (New York, 1969), pp. 162–63; Otis L. Graham, *An Encore for Reform: The Old Progressives and the New Deal* (New York, 1967), pp. 72–73.

26. Graham, pp. 167–68; Allen F. Davis, *Spearheads for Reform: The Social Settlements and the Progressive Movement, 1890–1914* (New York, 1967), p. xi; Don S. Kirschner, "The Ambiguous Legacy: Social Justice and Social Control in the Progressive Era," *Historical Reflections* 2 (summer 1975): 88. See also Holli,

pp. 157–61; Henry F. May, *The End of American Innocence* (New York, 1959), part 3, chapter 4; Christopher Lasch, *The New Radicalism in America, 1889-1963* (New York, 1965); David P. Thelen, *Robert M. LaFollette and the Insurgent Spirit* (Boston, 1976).

27.   Lasch, p. 168.

28.   Similar questions have been asked about Canadian and English schooling in the twentieth century. See, for example, Neil Sutherland, *Children in English-Canadian Society: Framing the Twentieth-Century Consensus* (Toronto, 1976); Paul H. Mattingly and Michael B. Katz, eds., *Education and Social Change: Themes from Ontario's Past* (New York, 1975), and David Wardle, *The Rise of the Schooled Society: The History of Formal Schooling in England* (London, 1974).

INDEX